Nationalism, Language, and Muslim Exceptionalism

HANEY FOUNDATION SERIES

A volume in the Haney Foundation Series,
established in 1961 with the generous support
of Dr. John Louis Haney

NATIONALISM, LANGUAGE, AND MUSLIM EXCEPTIONALISM

Tristan James Mabry

UNIVERSITY OF PENNSYLVANIA PRESS

PHILADELPHIA

Published by
University of Pennsylvania Press
Philadelphia, Pennsylvania 19104-4112

Printed in the United States of America
on acid-free paper

1   3   5   7   9   10   8   6   4   2

Library of Congress Cataloging-in-Publication Data

Mabry, Tristan James.
    Nationalism, language, and Muslim exceptionalism / Tristan James Mabry. — 1st ed.
        p. cm. — (Haney Foundation series)
    Includes bibliographical references and index.
    ISBN 978-0-8122-4691-9 (hardcover : alk. paper)
    1. Nationalism—Religious aspects—Islam—Case studies.   2. Group identity—Religious
aspects—Islam—Case studies.   3. Language and culture—Political aspects—Case
studies.   4. Islamic fundamentalism—Case studies.   5. Separatist movements—Case
studies.   6. Exceptionalism—Case studies.   I. Title.   II. Series: Haney Foundation series.
JC311.M24 2015
320.540917'67—dc23

2014030163

CONTENTS

CHAPTER 1

Introduction

The word *exceptionalism* was born of politics. In its earliest incarnation, the term was invariably prefaced by the qualifier *American* and used by leftist intellectuals to describe the apparently unique ability of the United States to avoid class warfare.[1] *Muslim exceptionalism*, on the other hand, is a much younger term that first earned currency in political science in the 1990s (Pipes 1996). Yet it bears a conceptual pedigree that easily predates Karl Marx. The idea that something sets Muslim politics and society apart from the politics and society of everyone else is the hallmark of Orientalism, a one-way conversation started by European elites in the eighteenth century (Irwin 2006). However, following the publication of Edward Said's withering magnum opus *Orientalism* (1978), much self-conscious scholarship may have eschewed the idea of Muslim exceptionalism for fear of committing academic heresy or even a "thought crime" (Kramer 2006). This is clearly no longer the case.

Even before the terrorist attacks of September 11, 2001, the general belief that all Muslim societies are built on the bedrock of a shared, immutable, and alien faith influenced "dominant attitudes in academia and, with much more devastating effects, in the media" (Filali-Ansary 1999, 18).[2] These attitudes hardened in the 1990s, when some observers noted that Muslim countries missed the "Third Wave" of democratization in the 1980s (Huntington 1991, 281). Moreover, following "the end of history," that is, the collapse of the Soviet Union (Fukuyama 1992), and the ideological bankruptcy of communism, autocratic regimes were replaced with representative governments everywhere, it seemed, except in the cradle of Islam, the Middle East (Salame 1994). In the years since 9/11, well-meaning Western proponents of interfaith tolerance—including academics, journalists, and policy makers—have tried to promote a more nuanced understanding of Islam and (to a lesser extent) the diversity of the Muslim world. Yet there remains a persistent view—on both sides of the Atlantic (Nussbaum 2012)—that the politics of all Muslims can be explained by the influence of Islam. This is evident not only in some conservative media and foreign policy circles, but also in the world of security affairs, where Muslims are perennially viewed with suspicion and alarm (Croft 2012; Kaya 2012). In short, and despite the best efforts of many civil society actors, the view that Muslims are exceptionally problematic politically is at the heart of a contentious and continuing debate (Mandaville 2013; see also, e.g., Bayat 2013; Strindberg and Warn 2011; Elshtain 2009).

Like Orientalism, the term "Muslim exceptionalism" is applied and interpreted inconsistently. One way to parse what is or is not exceptional about Muslims is to explicitly examine specific political or social variables in contrast to non-Muslims. This approach, adopted by Steven Fish, delivered a number of conclusions. In a robust comparative study, he argues Muslim societies, when compared to non-Muslim societies, are more averse to homosexuality and, to a lesser degree, averse to abortion and divorce. In addition, in societies with proportionately larger Muslim populations, both murder rates and socioeconomic inequality are lower. The caveat to the latter is that gender-based inequality is higher. Yet the most significant political finding is that democracy is "rarer" in Muslim societies (Fish 2011, 255–56). One conventional explanation for this finding, that is, that Muslims are more likely to fuse religion with political legitimacy, is empirically rejected. Instead, Fish argues there is no fundamental difference between autocrats in Muslim states and those in non-Muslim states. In other words, the same institutional impediments to democracy at work in other developing countries are essentially the same in Muslim-majority states.

Nonetheless, the view that Muslim populations are less likely to endorse democracy remains conventional even following the events of the so-called Arab Spring beginning in 2011. Cynics point to the fact that the first elections following regime change in Tunisia and Egypt returned Islamists as the victors. Considering the dynamic flow of events across the region, the question of whether or not democracy will ultimately consolidate, whether or not peaceful transfers of power to rival parties will occur routinely following future elections, is not yet known. Thus, a more substantive response to the question of whether or not Muslim societies are resistant to democracy would benefit from observations of the Arab world in years following the Arab Awakening.

Yet despite the efforts of Fish and other scholars to determine whether Muslims are somehow exceptional, there is another critical question to which the answer remains empirically unanswered: *are Muslims exceptionally resistant to ethnic nationalism?* The questions are not mutually exclusive. As a doctrine of both popular sovereignty and territorial self-determination, nationalism is essential to nation-state legitimacy. By determining the criteria for who is or is not a citizen, whether determined by where one is born or to whom,[3] a national identity enables the state to identify who is or is not a member of the *demos*. This identity is typically composed of social markers including, but not limited to, some combination of shared ancestry, religion, culture, and language. This identity defines a people, who in turn define a nation, which in turn describes the extent—and justifies the existence—of a nation-state. Nationalism is, in this sense, "the major form in which democratic consciousness expresses itself in the modern world" (O'Leary 1998, 79; Nodia 1994). Hence, if a state supports a shared culture that links the identity of otherwise diverse citizens, then "many of the problems that will *normally* appear in the effort to democratize a multinational community are simply *not* on the agenda" (Stepan 1998, 223). This is equally applicable to individual freedoms as "it is necessary to solve the national question before liberal rule can be possible" (Hall 1998, 13). In the case of American exceptionalism, for example, Samuel Huntington argued that a threat to the liberal creed that defines American national identity is nothing less than a threat to American democracy (Huntington 2004).[4]

What then should be made of a Muslim national identity? Is there anything like a Muslim demos? Is there a single nation of Islam, or are there many Muslim nations? And what of the Arabs? Is (or rather *was*) pan-Arab nationalism a doctrine shaped around religion, ethnic chauvinism, neither, or both? And what is the impact of the Arab Spring vis-à-vis nationalism: will it ultimately lead Arab states toward a stronger shared identity but separate states, or separate identities *and* separate nations? These questions draw attention to a split within the discussion(s) of Muslim exceptionalism: on one side are proponents of positions that mark Arabs as a special subset of Muslims; on the other side are observers who ascribe and/or describe characteristics that apply to any society that surrenders, as it were, to Islam.

In the case of the Arab world, the Muslim exceptionalism thesis does have some leverage due to the remarkable sociolinguistic phenomenon of diglossia, a situation whereby languages function in separate registers, one Low and one High, one illiterate and one literate, one ingrained and one acquired, one vulgar and one official. Arabic diglossia means that the Low vernaculars of Arab peoples are marginalized in the public sphere in favor of High Arabic, that is, Modern Standard Arabic, which is the sole official language of the state and its institutions, most critically those of public education. This yields a population in a state but not of a state, a population part of an amorphous

"Arab world" but not part of an ethnolinguistic nation as is typical outside of the Arab world. I call this phenomenon Arab dinationalism (see Chapter 4).

Outside of the Arab world, however, the perception that Muslims are exceptionally resistant to ethnic nationalism is challenged directly. To this end, six cases of Muslim-minority separatists—the Kurds of Iraq, the Uyghurs of China, the Sindhis of Pakistan, the Kashmiris of India, the Acehnese of Indonesia, and the Moros of the Philippines—were selected as examples of Muslim societies challenging the sovereignty of their state, though the nature of the challenge was not predetermined. To collect primary research material, the leadership of separatist parties and organizations were contacted personally and interviewed specifically regarding the raison d'être of their operation, whether Islamist, nationalist, both or neither. In regard to the relative strength of an ethnonational identity, a specific litmus test was the separatists' view of education language policy (see Chapter 3). This all required a great deal of fieldwork. Interviews with expatriate (or exiled) leaders required travel to Britain (Kurds), Sweden (Acehnese), and Germany (Uyghurs). However, most interviews were conducted on site, on the ground, in the separatist region itself. Hence, fieldwork was conducted in Iraq (Kurdistan), Pakistan (Sindh), India (Kashmir), Indonesia (Aceh), and the Philippines (Mindanao).[5] After examining and comparing all six cases, the findings of this book are as follows:

- It is clear that non-Arab Muslims are in no way resistant to ethnic nationalism.
- There is, however, variation among the cases. Some Muslim separatists are exclusively secular and ethnonational: this is so in Xinjiang, Sindh, and Iraqi Kurdistan. Others are influenced by Islamist politics: this is so in Kashmir, Aceh, and Mindanao.
- The variation between the cases is explained by the critical role of language in a population, specifically whether or not a community is linked by a language that is (1) a mother tongue, (2) written and read, (3) printed and sold. In other words, the variation is explained by the presence or absence of what is called a print culture.
- A strong print culture correlates with a strong ethnonational identity, and a strong ethnonational identity correlates with a conspicuous absence of Islamism.
- Therefore, this book argues there is an inverse relationship between Islamism and secular ethnolinguistic nationalism.

Pointedly, this suggests that Islamism is not a stronger ideological force in cases of Muslim-minority communal conflict, but rather it functions as a kind of opportunistic infection: it infects citizens who are not immunized by an ethnonational bond. Thus, the prescribed "treatment" for Islamism may, in effect, be nationalism.

Definitions

A discussion engaging such broad concepts as the *nation* or *Islam* immediately risks descending into "terminological chaos" (Connor 1994, chap. 4). Such terms are typically applied, along with any number of social and political characteristics, as classifiers of the noun *identity*, a word that is itself beset by "definitional anarchy" (Abdelal et al. 2006). This is explicable. Identity is at once ubiquitous and ephemeral, a quantity that defies operationalization. Like water—whether in the form of ice, cloud, steam, rain, etc.—an identity has different properties depending on its environment. Hence, in this book, an identity is treated as the medium through which different political markers move, whether of religion, class, gender, culture, and so on. Put another way, an identity is like a person (or people) that has no attributes, that is, a construct that cannot exist other than in the mind. A person without *any* characteristics is not a person. It is the attributes, traits, and markers that are more important than the medium, and especially so in regard to political mobilization.

In specific regard to the marker *nation*, it is important to note that this project does not engage the extensive debate among primordialists, constructivists, instrumentalists and others over national pedigrees. Defining the term *nation* is a thankless job since almost any characterization is likely to offend or dissatisfy. It may be considered a contemporary manifestation of select "premodern ethnic cores" (Smith 1991, 41; 1986), a daily plebiscite of like-minded liberal citizens (Renan [1882] 1996), a woefully misguided application of Kant's metaphysics (Kedourie [1960] 1993), an incurable pathology of modernity (Nairn 1981, 359), or an "imagined political community" (Anderson 1983, 6). Defining *Muslim* initially appears somewhat simpler: a Muslim is an adherent of Islam. *Muslim society*, on the other hand, is something else entirely. Consider the analogue of "Christian society." Do Russia and the United States share the same society if they are both populated by Christians? If there is such a thing as Muslim society, is it the same thing as a *Muslim civilization*?

Despite the mix of meanings, a working definition of Muslim society is also needed to engage the idea of Muslim exceptionalism.

Ethnicity, Nation, Nationalism

The debate over what is or is not a *nation* has continued for centuries because some definitions are exclusive; that is, my nation is organic, ancient, and authentic while your nation is synthetic, invented, and fake. If a nation is called bogus, then its erstwhile nationals have no claim to national self-determination and so cannot claim sovereignty over a nation-state. Hence, the definition of a *nation* is inextricably linked to the idea of *nationalism*. In the words of the most influential general theorist of nationalism, Ernest Gellner, "nations can be defined only in the age of nationalism" (Gellner 1983, 55). Because of this paradox, John Hall allows, "Gellner is quite right to insist that nation is far harder to define than is nationalism" (Hall 1993, 6).

Regardless of whether a nation is believed to be bona fide or counterfeit, a baseline definition links a self-defined people to a specific piece of real estate, that is, "Nationalism is primarily a political principle, which holds that the political and the national unit should be congruent" (Gellner 1983, 1). More often than not, a national unit defines itself along ethnic lines, for example, Japanese, Kazakh, German, and so forth, with exceptions made for settler states as so-called civic nations that do not explicitly restrict citizenship along bloodlines, for example, the United States or Australia. However, this begs the question of defining *ethnicity*, a term that is as contentious as *nation* for the same reasons of challenging authenticity.

"Ethnic politics," however, may address group identities based on a mix of shared family, region, religion, tradition, tongue, and so on (Posner 2005). This is an important point since ethnopolitical problems are a typical condition of deeply divided societies. This is not to say that ethnic diversity is an invitation to chaos—far from it—but when exclusive identities are expressed publicly and politically, the contract between state and society is called into question. In this regard, a "divided society" is one that is "both ethnically diverse *and* where ethnicity is a *politically salient* cleavage around which interests are organized for political purposes" (Reilly 2001, 4). Note, however, that a divided society is not necessarily segregated territorially. A divided society may be demographically integrated, as in parts of South Africa, so the political goals of ethnic politics need not include exclusive territorial sovereignty. However, when ethnopolitical demands for self-determination include a unique claim to a specific piece of territory, then the criterion for nationalism, that is, that the national unit and the political unit are congruent, is effectively met. In this case, because membership in the national unit is defined by ethnicity, the contest is effectively an ethnonational struggle. At the state level of party politics, identifying which elements of a multidimensional ethnic identity are politically salient is an "immense challenge," especially for quantitative methodologies that require "the collection of data that validly represents the multiple dimensions of ethnic diversity found in each country, and does so over time" (Laitin and Posner 2001, 17). Yet at the level of ethnonational politics, it would seem to matter less how the group defines its ethnicity—whether by blood, book, or belief—than that its members believe they share the same ethnicity, however perceived. Thus, ethnicity is far harder to define than ethnonational.

Muslims and Muslim Society

What is *Islam* and who is a *Muslim*? A concise answer is this: the word *Islam* is derived from the Arabic root for "surrender," so a *Muslim* is one who surrenders to God. What is a *Muslim society*? Theologically, there is an equally concise answer to this question: a *Muslim society* is an *ummah*, that is, a universal community of believers who declare there is no God but Allah and that Muhammad is the messenger of God. The ummah represents "the essential unity and theoretical equality of Muslims from diverse cultural and geographical settings" (Esposito 2003, 327). This de jure ideal, however, clashes immediately with any sociology that incorporates a specific culture or ethnicity into a description of a specific society. Hence, the question of whether there is a de facto global Muslim society is clearly a contentious one. This is related but distinct from the question of whether there is a Muslim *civilization*.

At this point, we must recall Samuel Huntington, who defined a civilization as the "highest cultural grouping of people and the broadest level of cultural identity people have short of that which distinguishes humans from other species" (Huntington and Ajami 1993, 24). In this view, if Islam were a cultural identity, then the ummah would qualify as a civilization. A cultural identity is "defined both by common objective elements, such as language, history, religion, customs, institutions, and by the subjective self-identification of people." So what happens if all the objective elements *except* religion are not commonly shared? Does Islam trump all? For Huntington, it did (and for his latter-day Orientalist adherents, *does*) because Islam is *exceptional*. To explain why "Islam has bloody borders," Huntington (1993, 35) cites vocal historian Bernard Lewis. It was Lewis who actually inspired the title of Huntington's famous article when he wrote—three years earlier in the *Atlantic Monthly*—that a clash *specifically* between *Islam* and the rest of the world is "no less than a clash of civilizations." The violence is explicable, according to Lewis, because "there is something in the religious culture of Islam which . . . in moments of upheaval and disruption, when the deeper passions are stirred . . . can give way to an explosive mixture of rage and hatred" (Lewis 1990, 60).

Note, however, that the views of Lewis and Huntington on Muslim civilization are coherent if and only if we accept the totality of a Muslim civilization defined as a "cultural entity" that is essentially a "religious culture." This exceptional religious culture is so overwhelmed by faith that other potential elements of ethnic identification, including the aforementioned "language, history, religion, customs, institutions, and by the subjective self-identification of people," are all but irrelevant. The power of this particular faith to smother all other attachments is often attributed to Islamic *ideas* about "the relations between government, religion, and society" (Lewis 2003, 5–6) that essentially fuse the private, the public, and the political into a single, sacred sphere.

As in the case of the imagined ummah, however, this is an ideal observed more in the breach than in practice. States with Muslim-majority populations demonstrate distinct histories, institutions, and social practices that divide the private, the public, and the political in countless ways. Accounting for the separate trajectories of Egypt, Turkey, Iran, Pakistan, and Indonesia, for example, is not possible without considering other politically salient elements— including colonial legacies, geography, and ethnonational identification—that have dramatically affected state-society relations across one-third the circumference of the Earth. In a direct response to Gellner's monolithic vision of Muslim society, Sami Zubaida retorts, "the rivals of the nation-state for solidarities and sentiments are not the universalist entities of Arabism and Islam, but more likely particularistic and factional solidarities of community and region" (Zubaida 2004, 419; 1995; 1998).

Numbering more than 1.5 billion people—or 22 percent of the planet's current population of 7 billion[6]—the collective Muslim world "is at once very large and very diverse" and clearly bears many "marks of ethnic, linguistic and cultural diversity" (Lawrence 1998, 33). To accommodate at least some of this diversity at the substate level, it is helpful to consider a range of

Muslim *populations* across multiple states and regions that are collectively grouped into the general classification Muslim *society* (which is also an effective proxy for the more general term *the Muslim world*). In other words, rather than using the term to describe an idealized ummah, "Muslim society" here means a great collective of diverse Muslim peoples. The multiplicity of Muslims is staggering, though it is fair to note that one generalization is indisputable, even as it is routinely ignored: most Muslims are Asian.

While half of all Muslim-majority *states* are in the Middle East, most Muslims are not Middle Eastern. Fewer still are Arabs: the two largest Muslim states in the region are *non*-Arab Turkey and Iran. The states with the four largest Muslim populations are in South and Southeast Asia: Indonesia alone has more Muslims than Morocco, Algeria, Egypt, Syria, Iraq, and Saudi Arabia *combined*. China has twice as many Muslims as Tunisia. Hence, any discussion of the Muslim world that fails to account for this obvious demographic dispersion is exceptionally flawed (see Table 1.1).

Muslim-Minority Separatist Conflicts

A number of large-N statistical studies have examined general patterns across states with Muslim majorities. Steven Fish, for example, shows that Muslim states are "democratic underachievers" and attributes this in part to the sorry status of women and girls in these countries (Fish 2002, 4; Pryor 2007). Jonathan Fox questions the reputation of Islam as an exceptionally contentious faith by comparing 105 ethnoreligious populations selected from the Minorities at Risk Project and finds "little evidence here to support the argument that Islam, or any religion for that matter, makes ethno-religious minorities more conflict prone" (Fox 2000, 15).[7] In a later study using the State Failure data set, Fox shows that when Muslims battle governments, "there is some evidence that Muslim groups are more violent" than Christian, Buddhist, or other groups, but cautions that "it is not conclusive and is certainly not enough to support the stereotype of the Islamic militant" (Fox 2003, 27). Another study, by Susanna Pearce (2005), of 278 territorial conflicts in the Armed Conflict Dataset of the International Peace Research Institute in Oslo (PRIO) argues unequivocally that the *intensity* of conflict is not correlated with any particular religion, including Islam. This finding correlates with later work at PRIO itself. Employing the 5-point Political Terror Scale, which is based on country reports from Amnesty International and the U.S. Department of State,

Table 1.1. The Muslim World: States with Muslim Populations Greater than Ten Million, 2012

Rank	State	Population	Muslim (%)	Muslims
1	Indonesia	248,216,193	86	213,714,142
2	Pakistan	190,291,129	95	180,776,573
3	India	1,205,073,612	13	161,479,864
4	Bangladesh	161,083,804	90	144,170,005
5	Nigeria	170,123,740	50	85,061,870
6	Turkey	79,749,461	100	79,589,962
7	Iran	78,868,711	98	77,291,337
8	Egypt	83,688,164	90	75,319,348
9	Algeria	35,406,303	99	35,052,240
10	Morocco	32,309,239	99	31,986,147
11	Ethiopia	93,815,992	34	31,803,621
12	Iraq	31,129,225	97	30,195,348
13	Afghanistan	30,419,928	99	30,115,729
14	Saudi Arabia	26,534,504	100	26,534,504
15	Sudan	25,946,220	99	25,686,758
16	Uzbekistan	28,394,180	88	24,986,878
17	Yemen	24,771,809	99	24,524,091
18	Syria	22,530,746	90	20,277,671
19	China	1,343,239,923	2	20,148,599
20	Malaysia	29,179,952	60	17,624,691
21	Russia	138,082,178	13	17,260,272
22	Tanzania	43,601,796	35	15,260,629
23	Niger	17,078,839	80	13,663,071
24	Mali	14,535,511	90	13,081,960
25	Senegal	12,969,606	94	12,191,430
26	Tunisia	10,732,900	98	10,518,242
27	Somalia	10,085,638	100	10,085,638
Subtotal				1,428,400,619
All others				146,597,203
World Muslim population				1,574,997,821

Source: Adapted from CIA World Factbook (June 2012).

Indra de Soysa and Ragnhild Nordås show that among 141 cases "countries with higher shares of Muslims suffer much lower levels of political repression," at least in contrast to states with significant numbers of Catholics (2007).

This research effectively challenges popular and professional notions that Islam (as a faith) and Muslims (as a people) are essentially undemocratic, contentious, militant, and bloodthirsty. But this research does not help answer the separate question of whether Muslims are exceptionally resistant to *nationalism*.

As for studies that examine general patterns across Muslim *societies*, there is much less on offer. Arguably, this is not for lack of interest, but for lack of data or (more problematically) for lack of reliable data. While this issue is in no way whatsoever limited to the general topic at hand, there are two specific problems here (Herrera, Kapur, and Tarontsi 2007). The first is "much of the research based on cross-national surveys aggregates micro-data into countrywide means and percentages," which effectively buries "other important aggregates such as cultural or ethnic groups." Even when disaggregated, there remains the second and specific problem of how "sub-national pluralism" is gauged, interpreted, and processed. In addition to the data sets mentioned above, the other major cross-national surveys include the World Values Survey, the International Social Survey Project, and the Comparative Survey of Electoral Systems project. These projects are eminently useful to some kinds of inquiry, but information about ethnicity is collected and coded "in an inconsistent way, and they have not given sufficient attention to ethnicity in the sample designs" (Dowley and Silver 2005, 226).

Case studies of specific states are better equipped to drill down into the socioeconomic, ethnolinguistic, and geopolitical strata underlying the structure of a select country or population, but the findings of even the most robust case study cannot effectively respond to the claim that the evidence is exceptional, and that Muslim national exceptionalism is the rule. Thus, the small-N comparative study suggests itself as the most promising method of exploration, though this raises the question, "a small number of what?" To show whether Muslims, when politically mobilized, are more likely to rally around their faith or their flag, what is the appropriate unit of analysis, the appropriate slice of time, and the appropriate scale: macro, meso, or micro? In other words, would it be better to compare the relevant words and deeds of specific leaders over time, such as Indonesia's Sukarno, Egypt's Gamal Abdel Nasser, Pakistan's Muhammad Ali Jinnah, and Turkey's Kemal Atatürk? Or would it be better to compare the voting records of different legislatures and the electoral outcomes of, say, nationalist versus Islamist platforms? Or perhaps conduct a content analysis of print and broadcast media including samples from Albania, Algeria, Kazakhstan, and Bangladesh? In fact, all of these projects could be illuminating and of potentially great merit. Nonetheless, it is reasonable to suggest that a project addressing the relevant role of nationalism versus Islam in the cohesion and mobilization of Muslim populations may also have some utility outside the academic world. To see why, it is useful to consider why falsifying this theory in the first place is wise. Could it, for example, help to solve any problems?

The short answer is yes. In general, answering this question will help to dispel some of the perennial conjecture about the path dependency of Islam in politics, such as whether Muslim societies, because of their faith and religious heritage, are ultimately incompatible with modernity, democracy, or liberty. Specifically, and even more important, answering this question is of significant strategic concern. If a number of strategically important Muslim states and societies are considered unstable, and a number of Muslim regions suffer from internecine conflict, appropriate responses—in terms of either domestic state policy or international foreign policy—would benefit tremendously from understanding the nature(s) of the problem(s). This is particularly the case when working out the dynamics of Washington and Baghdad, Yerevan and Baku, Moscow and Grozny, Beijing and Urumqi, New Delhi and Srinagar, Jakarta and Banda Aceh, Manila and Cotabato, Islamabad and Quetta, or Belgrade and Pristina. These, I believe, are problems to be solved (Schram and Caterino 2006; Monroe 2005; Shapiro 2005).

Hence, in the course of answering the question "are Muslims exceptionally resistant to nationalism?" this project seeks not only to falsify a claim, but also to assist those actors, agencies, and institutions trying to understand and engage cases of conflict in and around the Muslim world. The point of this project is *not* to prove what "caused" the conflicts in the first place. Many of these cases are burdened with extensive histories, stretching back at least decades, and in some cases centuries: the number of temporal variables alone is incalculable. For example, what is the most important factor helping to explain the rise of Abu Sayyaf in the southern Philippines: the Spanish conquest of Mindanao in the sixteenth century, the migration of Catholic settlers to the south in the twentieth, or the petrodollars of well-funded Salafis who encourage violent Muslim mobilizations in twenty-first-century conflict zones worldwide? In the case of Mindanao, it is helpful to understand that the conflict is very old but also very brittle, with fractures along cultural, religious, economic, and geographic lines.

Evidence and Cases

Because claims about the "Muslim world" apply theoretically to all Muslim societies, the cases were selected from multiple regions. In some cases, a

Table 1.2. Muslim Minorities: Cross-Regional Cases of Separatist Conflict

		Non-Muslim-majority state		Muslim-majority state	
Region	*State*	*Territory*	*Population*	*Territory*	*Population*
Central Eurasia	China	Xinjiang	Uyghur		
	Iraq			Iraqi Kurdistan	Kurd
South Asia	India	Kashmir	Kashmiri		
	Pakistan			Sindh	Sindhi
Southeast Asia	Philippines	Mindanao	Moro		
	Indonesia			Aceh	Acehnese

separatist population is a minority in more than one state, for example, Kurds in Turkey and Iraq, in which case only one group was selected to maximize diversity in the set. In addition, the majority population may or may not be Muslim-majority. There are two possible scenarios:

1. An ethnic minority population of Muslims in a state that is home to an ethnic majority who are *also* Muslim
2. An ethnic minority population of Muslims in a state that is home to an ethnic majority who are *not* Muslim

Cases representing both demographic scenarios are necessarily included in this study. Muslim minorities in non-Muslim-majority states include the Uyghurs of China, the Kashmiris of India, and the Moros of the Philippines. Muslim minorities in Muslim-majority states include the Kurds of Iraq, the Sindhis of Pakistan, and the Acehnese of Indonesia. In both scenarios, the minorities speak a different mother tongue than the majority. In either, according to proponents of ethnonationalism, the minority should mobilize as a distinct people defending and promoting a distinct ethnolinguistic culture. In contrast, and also applicable in either case, proponents of Muslim national exceptionalism expect Muslim minorities to advance an Islamist political culture that eschews any ethnic identity (see Table 1.2).

Structured Interviews

Classifying the platforms of nationalist *organizations* is unavoidably a political act. According to the People's Republic of China, for example, the East Turkistan Information Center is a terrorist organization with purported links to al-Qaeda. Yet according to the Munich-based East Turkistan Information Center it is a secular pressure group advocating an end to the repression of Uyghurs and other Muslims in Xinjiang. Note, however, that the latter piece of information was obtained not from the Terrorism Knowledge Base funded by the Department of Homeland Security or from news reports, since the ETIC itself has not been probed directly as to *the nature of its platform*. Rather, I went to Germany, where exiled ethnic Uyghurs operate the organization, met the leaders personally, and asked them a number of questions. This process—and the same set of questions—was repeated in each case.

The interviews were structured but not scripted, as some groups were more sensitive than others as to the nature of my research and their willingness to discuss openly questions about Islam, ethnicity, language, and separatism. This was followed by a number of questions related to the conflict, starting with "why are you fighting?" It is important to note here that the veracity and sincerity of statements made to an American researcher are open to question. It is safe to assume that in some cases an official from a separatist Muslim-minority party or organization may self-censor (or obscure by omission) positions likely to draw fire from the international community, including governments, intergovernmental organizations, nongovernmental organizations, and the media. Nonetheless, the point here is to present on-the-record answers to precise questions that are not otherwise available to researchers of comparative politics or international relations.

As discussed in Chapter 3, language laws and language policies, including the message and medium of state education, are a critical litmus test for ethnolinguistic mobilization. Just as separatism is necessarily territorial and therefore necessarily in conflict with one or more states, ethnolinguistic nationalism is necessarily institutional. In this book, the process of language planning—including corpus and status planning—is generally described as *language rationalization*. This term is adopted from David Laitin's exposition of Max Weber's *bureaucratic rationalization*, which interprets the evolution, and inevitable expansion of state language policy toward homogenization. Although "Weber did not systematically explore language rationalization," Laitin posits "the use of state power, through administrative regulation and public education, to standardize language within the boundaries of the state is precisely what he had in mind with his concept of rationalization" (2001, 87).

Thus, the crux of each interview addressed specific positions on languages. For example, in the case of an independent Kurdistan, what would be the official language or languages of the state? Of the schools? What would be the place of Arabic, either as an important regional language or as the sacred language of an overwhelmingly Muslim population? Over the many decades of conflict with Baghdad, did separatist leaders invoke the issue of protecting or promoting the Kurdish language? If so, why? It is important to recall here that even if some of these questions appear facile, the answers are not documented, and cannot be cited as proof positive of either indifference—as expected in the case of Muslim national exceptionalism—or essentialism, that is, ethnolinguistic identification as a zero-sum condition for the existence of the group itself.

The Plan of This Book

This book offers an original response to the broader academic literature—and persistent public perception—that there is something particular and problematic about the politics of Muslim peoples. Again, this idea takes a number of shapes, but collectively the concept is called *Muslim exceptionalism*. The two most common interpretations of the idea argue that (1) Muslims are exceptionally resistant to democracy or that (2) Muslims are exceptionally resistant to nationalism, that is, the political allegiance of Muslims is first and foremost to Islam, rather than identifying with a unique ethnicity (nationalism), and consequently to a particular nation-state (patriotism). These positions often dovetail, since a people prone to illiberal religious fundamentalism are naturally opposed to liberal democratic politics.

It is argued here that these exceptional phenomena are evident in Arab regimes that are hamstrung by the doctrine of pan-Arab nationalism that divides populations from their *patria*, and erstwhile nations from states of their own. Yet this condition applies to fewer than one in five Muslims. Aside from those in Arab states, I argue Muslim societies are subject to the same "rules" of nationalism that apply to non-Muslim nation-states. However, when Muslim-minority populations mobilize as separatists, there are two paths that may be taken: one nationalist and one Islamist. The nationalists maintain a strong ethnolinguistic identity based on a strong vernacular print culture. The Islamists, on the other hand, typically lack a strong vernacular print culture and therefore sustain only a weak ethnolinguistic identity, in which case the appeal of Islamism is stronger. Therefore, there is an inverse relationship between secular ethnolinguistic nationalism and the religious identification of Islamism.

The following chapter, "Muslim Nations," explores the parallel theories of ethnonationalism and Muslim exceptionalism in detail. Chapter 3, "National Tongues," outlines and evaluates ideas about the relationship of language, ethnicity, and national identity. Chapter 4, "Modern Standard Arabs," is an extended discussion of Arabs, Arabic, and Arab states and Arab national identity. Chapters 5 through 10 consider the six case studies under examination. This is followed by a conclusion that distills the argument and, at the same time, considers how it could inform public policy in Afghanistan.

CHAPTER 2

Muslim Nations

Islam is the blueprint of a social order.

—Ernest Gellner, *Muslim Society*

The relationship between nationalism and Islam can be discussed in a number of ways, sometimes in concert, but most often in a discordant cacophony that confuses an analysis of Islamic *thought* with an analysis of actual Muslim *societies*. Certainly the canon of Christian political thought, from Augustine to Aquinas to the liberation theology of Gustavo Gutiérrez, demonstrates that the ideas found in a single holy book can yield a multiplicity of political philosophies. In the same way, the relevant sura of the Quran and the many hadith of the Islamic tradition can yield a wide range of interpretations on the proper relationship between rulers and the ruled.[1] This discussion is normative. It is a political and moral philosophy grounded in a particular faith. Elements of religious ideas can and do influence the evolution and speciation of certain societies, though the causal arrow can point both ways. This has been evident since at least the birth of modern sociology. On one hand, Weber's *The Protestant Ethic and the Spirit of Capitalism* (1905) argued that an extant belief system was more in accord with capitalism: religion shapes society. On the other hand, Durkheim's *The Elementary Forms of the Religious Life* (1912) argued that a society worships itself by creating and observing a religion most appropriate for extant social practices: society shapes religion.

The lion's share of literature on nationalism considers a small selection of European cases. This is explicable. If nationalism is a modern phenomenon, as a preponderance of political scientists from Karl Deutsch (1912–92) forward have proposed, then most cases will come from countries with a more established record of industrialization, urbanization, modernization, and state development (Deutsch 1953). Hence, students of nationalism are more likely to come across many more references to Scotland, the Basque country or Catalonia than to the ethnopolitical tensions of Chiapas, Tatarstan, or Fiji. Within the specific context of nationalism and Islam, it should not be surprising that most research targets the Arab Middle East. This, too, is explicable. Even though it is home to fewer than one in five of the world's Muslims, the region is not only the ancestral home of the faith and the site of perennially contentious politics, but also the home of half of all Muslim-majority *states* (twenty-one of forty-four). This does not, however, explain or excuse the comparative dearth of nationalism research on Muslim populations outside the Middle East, particularly in Central, South, and Southeast Asia.

The Exceptional Ernest Gellner

Among the competing and complementary visions of nationalism and Islam, selecting a starting point is simplified somewhat by the unique contribution of Ernest Gellner: unique not only for his general theory of nationalism but also for his research on Muslim societies (Hall 2014). The latter is an area of his scholarship often overshadowed by his more universal arguments about industrialization and the development of modern national identities. But it is important to recognize that an unbroken line of thought can be traced from his earliest anthropological research in Morocco's Atlas Mountains and his general theory of nationalism all the way through his later works on Islamic fundamentalism and civil society (Gellner 1994).

The line is written in the language of High and Low Cultures, describing peasants and patricians as they struggle to keep afloat in a riptide of change. All together they are tossed by a great wave of modernization as it rips traditional social structures from their terrestrial moorings. Formerly agrarian laborers search for social support as they are transformed into modular workers in urban hives of humanity. Because those workers must communicate effectively to compete and survive, literacy and language acquire unprecedented importance among populations that may have never needed more than a basic grammar and parochial vocabulary. Thus, the Low Culture of the land is forced to fuse with the High Culture of an urban elite to yield a modern identity necessary for industrial efficiency. This new modern identity is a national identity. In defining a specific national identity, the centrality of language cannot be understated. If the uneven wave of industrialization means social mobility is suddenly determined by a shared culture, then social mobility also means at the very least a shared language. Indeed, at least since *Thought and Change*, for Gellner language "is culture" (Gellner 1964, 195; Szporluk 1998, 28).

This structural model of a literacy-based national culture, especially as distilled in *Nations and Nationalism* (Gellner 1983), found a wide and receptive audience among students of modern nationalism who typically applied this framework to industrializing Western states. This is remarkable because Gellner's point of departure was a traditionalist society, that is, Berber villages in the Atlas Mountains. With rich detail, his earlier tomes *Saints of the Atlas* (1969) and the monumental collection *Muslim Society* (1981) map the social network of rural populations connected loosely with urban centers controlled by religious elites.[2] In this case, because language and literacy required training in Classical Arabic, and thus derived from a shared faith rather than the elevated vernacular of any rustic ethnicity, Low and High Culture meant Low and High Islam. Islam, for Gellner, is therefore exceptional as it precludes the emergence of an ethnolinguistic national culture.

Of course, not every scholar of Muslim societies agrees with this model. Dale Eickelman cautions that "well over half the world's Muslims, from the southern Philippines to North Africa, live in areas where the contrast between a 'High Islamic' town and a 'Low Islamic' tribal hinterland, questionable even for pre-modern Morocco, is even less applicable" (Eickelman 1998, 259). Even so, there is one particular component of Arab cultures where the specific role of High Islam dovetails neatly with a model of High Culture in modernizing states. Simply put, in Arab states, the official language and therefore the language of state institutions, including public education, is the currently accepted incarnation of Classical Arabic, namely Modern Standard Arabic.

Sacred Languages

In the Islamic tradition, the Prophet Muhammad, through the Archangel Gabriel, heard a message from the one and only Supreme Being. And this message was delivered in his tongue, the language of the Arabs, which happened to be the tongue of God. Like Jesus, Muhammad is not known to have written anything himself: others immortalized his speech. Unlike the case with Jesus,

Muhammad's words survive not in translation but (for the faithful) *verbatim*. As opposed to the transmutations of the Christian Bible from Hebrew and Aramaic to Greek, Latin, and beyond, the Quran is a transcript. This is made more plain by the name of Islam's holy book, *Quran*, meaning "recitation," as well as a number of explicit pronouncements that describe the book as "an Arabic Quran" (Sura 12:1) expressed "in a clear, Arabic tongue" (Sura 26:195).

The High Culture of High Islam was recorded and protected by scholars who learned to read and write in what became a sacred language. Thus, the uniformity of Classical Arabic was maintained even as the empire of Islam spread far from the Arabian Peninsula. Changing the grammar of God was (and is) not taken lightly. While local populations continued to use the vernacular speech of their particular people and territory, written communication was limited to the immutable language of the one holy book. The only exception to the regular use of vernacular speech was—and is—the liturgical language of the mosque, where calls to prayer and passages from the Quran are never translated, but always called aloud in Quranic Arabic.

According to Gellner, the arrival of industrialization produces a singularly strange result in any Muslim society. While vernacular speech maintains great diversity across territories and populations, literacy is delivered by a shared religion. Because the language is sacred and because education is controlled by clerics, the price of High Culture is High Islam: religion and literacy are inextricably linked. Moreover, Gellner argues in his extended essay *Postmodernism, Reason and Religion* (1992) that this link explains the perceived popularity among Muslim populations of "religious fundamentalism": "The underlying idea is that a given faith is to be upheld firmly in its full and literal form, free of compromise, softening, re-interpretation, or diminution. It presupposes that the core of religion is doctrine, rather than ritual, and also that this doctrine can be fixed with precision and finality, which further presupposes writing" (Gellner 1992, 2). Gellner's use of the term "fundamentalism" is deliberate. As opposed to the softer term "Islamism"—defined succinctly as "the belief that Islam should guide social and political life as well as personal life" (Berman 2003, 257)—fundamentalism is absolutely literal in that Scripture really means exactly what it says (Strindberg and Warn 2011; Bruce 2007; Volpi 2011). In this way, a sacred text is less a collection of stories and metaphors than an instruction manual for living. In 1909, when Tennessee preacher George Hensley read that those who believe in Jesus "shall take up serpents" that "shall not hurt them," he and his followers handled living venomous snakes to demonstrate the sincerity of their faith.[3] (Hensley died from a snake bite in 1955.) Similarly, in fundamentalist Islam, the instruction of Sura 5:38—"cut off the hands of thieves, whether they are male or female, as punishment for what they have done"—is sometimes applied literally. Setting aside for a moment the ascendance of born-again Christians in the United States—some of whom certainly qualify as fundamentalist, particularly in their opposition to teaching evolution in public schools—Gellner argued, in 1992, that "in our age fundamentalism is at its strongest in Islam" (Gellner 1992, 4).

Latin

In an earlier age, however, the literal interpretation of Scripture was also well established in the Catholic world of pre-Reformation Europe. The Bible, too, meant what it said—*if* you could read it. Like the clerics of urban, bourgeois High Islam, who served also as public scribes, literacy in Europe was then the preserve of ecclesiastical officials, sometimes parish priests, but mostly monks. Education, too, was dominated by theology, and to question the veracity of the Bible was to invite the most severe punishment for heresy.

At the dawn of the Reformation, following many centuries of struggle between popes and every kind of secular authority—including feudal lords, kings, and emperors—political legitimacy had started to shift from the *sacerdotium* to the *regnum*, from the cross to the crown (Berman 1983). At this point, still far from the start of industrialization, the advent of printing in the early sixteenth century sparked a demand for books: at first bibles, then other works. If we were to transplant the Arabic scenario described by Gellner to this period in Europe, we would expect a print culture to develop that adopted the language of the clergy, the only institution that sustained literacy after the fall of Rome in the fifth century. Thus, Latin would become the *exclusive* language of reading, writing, and High Culture, even as Franks and Normans continued to speak their rustic mother tongues.

And, for a time, this was precisely the case. In a monograph tracing the evolution and devolution of the language, Françoise Waquet writes "of a unitary intellectual Europe in which, until a relatively recent date, learning was expressed in Latin" (2001, 1). (In this case, that "recent" date was the eighteenth century at the latest; Waquet is a historian.) However, though its use as a liturgical language meant "Latin became the property of a clerical elite" (Waquet 2001, 42), this is a far cry from claiming the language itself was supernatural. This is not to say it was supplanted easily: the evolution of competing vernaculars into print languages was a very, very slow process. Dante's *Divine Comedy*, for example, was written in his own Tuscan tongue and published in the early 1300s, *yet more than two hundred years elapsed* before Renaissance humanists in Florence actively promoted what was to become "Italian" literature in place of Latin. This tension between Latin and vernaculars climaxed in the early sixteenth century. This point is illustrated, literally, in a portrait by Agnolo Bronzino (see Figure 2.1). Painted about 1537, the image of a young scholar, Ugolino Martelli, depicts his right hand resting on the Greek text of Homer's *Iliad*, with a Latin text by Virgil resting nearby; in his left hand is a book by Martelli's role model, Pietro Bembo, in the Tuscan/Italian language. Earlier, in 1525, Bembo had published a kind of manifesto (*Prose nelli quali si ragiona della volgar lingua*) that urged regional authors to write in their own language instead of Latin (Schneider 2002, 78). In the wake of both Gutenberg and Luther, the Catholic Church ultimately reasserted the exclusivity of Latin for liturgical uses at the Council of Trent in 1546, but even then "Latin was seen as a means for defending the Church's authority and control over the faithful: nobody, not even the most determined opponents of 'vulgarization' advanced the argument that the language possesses some sort of sacred character" (Schneider 2002, 47).

Why the Church could not sustain the supremacy of Latin as the pan-national language of literacy is addressed in the final work of Adrian Hastings. His *Construction of Nationhood* (1997) argues that the dissimilar development of Islamic and Christian national languages was the result of the peculiarities of writing in a sacred medium. Unlike the Hebrew of Moses or the Arabic of Muhammad, the Christian tradition separated the message from the medium. Even the original Aramaic of Jesus and his disciples "has never been seen as sacred." Indeed, what Hastings finds most striking is the "willingness again and again to translate—into Syriac, Armenian, Coptic, Ethiopian and Latin in the early centuries, then Slavonic and finally almost numberless other languages" (Hastings 1997, 194).

Some of that willingness may have sprung from early Christians impressed by the phenomenon of glossolalia (from the Greek *glossai* meaning "tongues, languages" and *lalein* "to speak"), or the miracle of ecstatically expressing a religious experience by "speaking in tongues." As attributed to the apostle Luke in the New Testament, fifty days after Jesus's crucifixion, during the traditional Jewish festival of Pentecost, the Holy Spirit appeared as tongues of

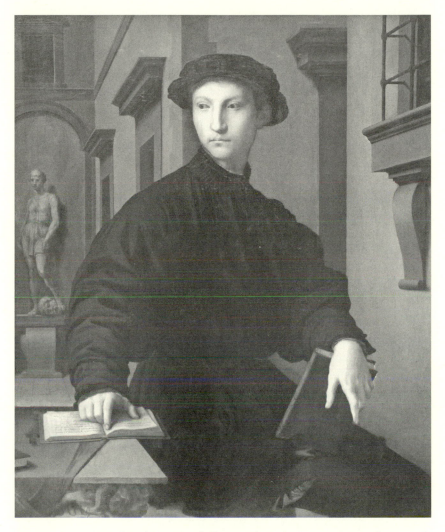

Figure 2.1. *Portrait of Ugolino Martelli*, by Agnolo Bronzino, ca. 1537. Oil on panel, 102 × 85 cm. Staatliche Museen zu Berlin.

flame that descended on a group of disciples who suddenly and fluently spoke the gospel in languages other than their own. This attracted spectators who, in the King James version of the event, "were all amazed and marveled, saying one to another, Behold, are not all these which speak Galileans? And how hear we every man in our own tongue, wherein we were born? Parthians, and

Medes, and Elamites, and the dwellers in Mesopotamia, and in Judaea, and
Cappadocia, in Pontus, and Asia, Phrygia, and Pamphylia, in Egypt, and in
the parts of Libya about Cyrene, and strangers of Rome, Jews and proselytes,
Cretes and Arabians, we do hear them speak in our tongues the wonderful
works of God."[4] In the Christian Bible, similar events were explicitly described several times.[5] Proponents of vernacular literature could be excused for
claiming scripturally authorized precedents for the policy of translating
the Christian message into as many languages as necessary. The message of the
gospel, not the medium, is what matters most.

While many Anglophiles are familiar with the story of William Tyndale, who was burned alive in 1536 for the offense of having *printed* an English translation of the New Testament ten years before; *written* vernacular
translations had appeared in Europe many centuries before. As early as the
eighth century, for example, the Venerable Bede "is said to have translated
the gospel of John into Anglo-Saxon, which may be the earliest written
translation in English of any portion of the Bible" (Bratcher 1993, 758). But
printed books would not be mass produced and sold on the open market
until the sixteenth century. Between Bede and Tyndale, the efforts of local
clergy independently practicing translation (this despite a "don't ask, don't
tell" relationship with the Vatican) were shared with a much broader public.
But with Tyndale, and for the first time, parishioners across the European
continent were presented with literature *printed* in a fixed version of their
own vernacular speech.

While this could not have happened on such a scale without the techno-
logical innovations of movable type and the printing press, it is important to
note that Hastings's account of these events cannot be construed in any way
as modernist. "Nation-formation and nationalism," he tells us, "have in themselves almost nothing to do with modernity" (Hastings 1997, 205). And there
is certainly nothing in his general position on nationalism to suggest that the
arrival and elevation of distinct post-Latin literary languages had anything
to do with industrialization. Rather, he offers an alternative argument that
credits printed language with the development of national identities: identities that crystallized as a result of translating the Christian message into an
array of living languages. In other words, "the clergy simply by doing their
job enhanced national consciousness through the widespread diffusion of vernacular literature. It was, I believe, this process going on all across Europe,
which, far more than anything specifically political, stabilized the main na-

tional identities, as societies separated by their literatures" (Hastings 1997, 193). All of this was eventually made possible by a willingness to translate the word of God into whatever language was needed to communicate the message.

Regardless of whether the ascendance of vernaculars was caused by the clergy or by commerce, the important point is that a de facto sacred language was ultimately replaced everywhere by mother tongues that were written as they were spoken, printed on paper, and disseminated among those who spoke the same "vulgar" language. While Benedict Anderson credits the market demand of "print capitalism" for the phenomena, his view of early modern Europe is in harmony with Hastings's: "the fall of Latin exemplified a larger process in which the sacred communities integrated by old sacred languages were gradually fragmented, pluralized, and territorialized" (Anderson 1983, 19).

However, it is important to note that in some cases the de facto sacred language of the Church, that is, Latin, was replaced by national languages that had ossified as liturgical languages. These print languages, like Latin, ultimately lost their living speech cultures, but acquired the de facto (though not doctrinal) status of a sacred language. In Greek Orthodox services, for example, the language of the priests is Koine Greek. The same may be said of Church Slavonic in several Slavic states, classical Georgian in its titular state, the Coptic language—the vestigial tongue of pharaonic peoples—in Egypt, and Ge'ez in Ethiopia. As for Latin, the fealty of the Holy See to liturgical Latin continued through the twentieth century. The Tridentine Mass, practiced in Latin for fifteen centuries, was displaced in the wake of the Second Vatican Council (1965) in favor of vernacular observances. This mirrored the broader and contemporaneous trend in the Protestant community of translating the Bible into as many languages as possible, especially those of indigenous peoples who might not yet have developed scripts of their own. Most famously, the linguist and ordained Baptist minister Reverend Eugene A. Nida (1915–2011) led the American Bible Society in translating Scripture into more than two hundred languages, including Navajo, Quecha, Hmong, and Inuktitut. While the triumph of national tongues over sacred Latin would seem to be total, it is remarkable to note that in the early years of the twenty-first century liturgical Latin received a reprieve. In 2007, more than four decades after Vatican II, Pope Benedict XVI surprised many by endorsing a wider use of Latin services: "What earlier generations held as sacred, remains sacred and great for us, too, and it cannot be, all of a sudden, entirely forbidden or even considered harmful" (Fisher 2007; O'Malley 2008).

Hebrew

In regard to the *modern* struggle between sacred and profane language policy, one of the only non-Arab parallels is the development of Hebrew in the state of Israel.[6] A sacred but socially comatose language was sustained for centuries among the Jewish Diaspora as a liturgical and scholarly medium. Indeed, for a "people of the book" it is hard to distinguish between the two. As an intrinsic component of religious education, Hebrew was a critical element of Jewish identity even though different vernacular languages, such as Yiddish, German, Polish, or Russian, were spoken at home. In the nineteenth century, the language of the Talmud and Torah was reinvented as the language of a European print culture, propelled in no small part by the ascendance of Hebrew as a component of Jewish nationalism in the final decades of the Romanov Empire (Aberbach 2008).

Following the foundation of Israel, this print language evolved further as the shared official language of a modernizing state. Thus, questions that later arose regarding the nature of that state—is it a civic state for ethnic Jews (however defined) or a theocratic state for religiously observant Jews?—could have been compounded by the adoption of an inflexible sacred language as an official language of the state, enhancing the religious elements of Judaism within state institutions. Instead, Hebrew was transformed, expanded, and allowed to develop with all the flexibility of a living language. While small groups of ultraorthodox in Israel do see the language as sacred and refuse to speak Hebrew outside a synagogue, William Safran (2005) reminds us that the early Zionists were secular—indeed socialist—and settled pragmatically on Hebrew as a compromise between the Yiddish of European Jews and the languages of Middle Eastern Jews, including Arabic and Ladino.

This decision was central to the state-building enterprise of Israel as new institutions sought to rationalize an ideological choice through language planning. Though Hebrew had survived in an ossified and ecclesiastical form, the ancient language of a desert people had waxed and waned across centuries of displacement, expulsion, and occasional integration (Myhill 2004). Its reinvention as an official language injected unprecedented vigor, but as native speakers emerged in succeeding generations, the language evolved into the mother tongue of new citizens in a new nation-state. This development may have affected more flexible attitudes in the Jewish Diaspora, particularly in the United States. Despite the reverence for Hebrew as a liturgical language, sacred Jewish texts are reaching a much broader audience, a development spurred by strong sales of a new English translation of the Talmud (Berger 2005).

Arabic

In contrast with both Christianity and the modern language policies of Israel, a much different take on translation steered the development of Islam in another direction. Hastings emphasizes the sacred nature of the Quran, a record of the word of God as spoken by God in the original Arabic that precludes even the possibility of translation. As a result, the spread of Islam necessarily meant the spread of Arabic. Vernacular speech may or may not survive among different Muslim communities, but literacy will be delivered in the language of their holy book. In consequence, "the whole cultural impact of Islam is necessarily to Arabize, to draw peoples into a single world community of language and government. And this is what it did. Even the language of Egypt disappeared before it, except as a Christian liturgical language [Coptic]. Nations are not constructed by Islam but deconstructed" (Hastings 1997, 201). This process continues in some corners of the nominally Arab world, where ethnic minority Muslims such as Berbers struggle to retain their own vernacular but adopt Arabic as "the principal language of education and formal communication" (Eickelman 1998, 267). For Gellner, this is to be expected: the ethnicity of Muslim minorities is unimportant since their Muslim identity is what matters most. After all, in his view "the modern Muslim 'nation' is often simply the sum-total of Muslims on a given territory" (Gellner 1992, 15). Minority ethnic groups like Berbers are also Muslims, so eventually Gellner's model forecasts they will be assimilated into the ummah of the larger political unit. Their vernacular languages may continue as long as their speakers find them natural, but no minority citizen would be considered literate without the ability to read and write in Arabic. It is the symmetry of this sacred language with literacy that, Gellner argues, allows Arabic to function as an erstwhile national language in a Muslim state, irrespective of the polyglot ethnicities who may live there. If the vernacular tongue happens to be some variety of Arabic already, then this is fortunate.

Thus, it should come as no surprise that "within Islam, Arab nationalism is somehow more natural or fundamental than other nationalism" (Gellner 1985, 3).

While Gellner's basic position on the exceptional resistance of Muslims to nationalism hinges on an Islamic High Culture that stifles the development of ethnic High Cultures, the specific dynamic of Arabic and Arab Muslims is addressed in the next chapter. Yet it must be noted that the sanctity of the Arabic Quran, even outside the Arab world, remains a powerful proscriptive against translation. Even in the post-Taliban Afghanistan of 2007, for example, a Quran translated into Dari, one of the country's two official languages, was labeled "un-Islamic." Following street protests and an emergency meeting of the loya jirga (parliament), the book's translator and its distributor were arrested as they tried to flee the country, with four others arrested for aiding and abetting the alleged crime (Kroeger 2007). In 2009, following a short trial, the publisher was sentenced to five years in jail; the translator was sentenced to twenty (Associated Press 2009).

The Illusion of Arabic Ubiquity

The dynamic of Arabic among non-Arab Muslims is a common source of confusion. There is a widespread perception that all Muslims somehow speak or use Arabic *outside* their religious observances. There are two reasons for this. The first is that Muslims everywhere are expected to have some knowledge of Classical Arabic so that they may recite the Quran. Typically, this is learned at a traditional Islamic school, or *madrassa*. This is not unlike the system of Hebrew schools in the United States that teach Jewish students to recite the Torah. In neither case, however, would knowledge of liturgical Arabic or liturgical Hebrew grant fluency or literacy in the modern language of an Arab state or Israel, respectively. Studying the Torah in Toronto will not enable a student to function effectively in the streets of Tel Aviv. Unlike Hebrew schools, however, madrassas in many developing countries—especially failing states like Pakistan—may not only supplement the education sponsored by the state, but actually supplant it, though in this case the language of instruction would be the official language of the state, for example, Malay in Malaysia or Urdu in Pakistan, while Arabic is taught as a subject.

Another problem contributing to the perception of Arabic ubiquity is the conflation of any language written with Arabic letters as actual Arabic. This is due to the *appearance* of other languages that employ the Arabic script to write their own vernacular, even when they belong to different language families and are entirely unrelated. For example, a *Los Angeles Times* reporter in Xinjiang, China, reporting on the Muslim Uyghur population, wrote of "Arabic signs" in Urumqi, the region's capital, and claimed that the indigenous people "speak a Turkic language and read Arabic" (Lee 2006). This is just plain wrong. Uyghurs read and write Uyghur, a Turkic language of the Altaic family and a relative of Mongolian. It is unrelated to the Semitic language Arabic, but is written using a modified form of the Arabic script. The mistake is akin to claiming that English and Italian are the same language because they both use a Latin script. This is not an isolated example. A reporter for National Public Radio, commenting on the Little Pakistan neighborhood of Midwood, Brooklyn, claimed "every other sign is in Arabic" (Rodriguez 2006). Again, this is not true. The signs in Midwood, as in other enclaves of immigrants from Pakistan, are in Urdu, an Indo-European language that is *written* using an Arabic-derived script.

To illustrate this point, consider the English word "door." Expressed in languages from entirely different families—Afro-Asiatic, Indo-European, and Altaic, for example—the word is said aloud, as one would expect, in completely different ways. Hence, the word *door* in Somali, an Afro-Asiatic language, is pronounced "afaaf"; in Italian, an Indo-European language, it is pronounced "porta"; in Turkish, an Altaic language, it is pronounced something like "kapuh." Employing the Latin alphabet to approximate these sounds phonetically is straightforward. Though some letters exist in certain languages but not in others, for example, the German ü or the Spanish ñ, the script is immediately familiar because it is the same script used to write English. As a writing system, the Arabic *script* functions in precisely the same way. Hence, the word for *door* in Persian (Farsi), an Indo-European language, is pronounced "dar," but is written using Arabic letters as در . The source of the confusion is simply that در in print looks like a word in Standard Arabic so it is assumed to be in Standard Arabic.

This is not to say most Muslims could not recognize key terms or phrases from the Quran. The flag of Iraq, for example, is emblazoned with the ubiquitous "God is Greatest" and the flag of Saudi Arabia bears the *Shahada*, that is, the declaration of Islamic faith: "There is no god but God and Muhammad is the Messenger of God." But outside the Arab world, few Muslims in a state like Bangladesh or Kazakhstan would ever endorse adopting Arabic as the functioning national or official language of their country. The sacred

Table 2.1. One Word, Two Scripts, Six Languages: *Door*

			English word: Door	
Language family	*Language*	*Script*	*Pronounced*	*Written*
Afro-Asiatic	Arabic	Arabic	*bab*	باب
	Somali	Latin	*albaabka*	*albaabka*
Altaic	Turkish	Latin	*kapuh*	*kapı*
	Uyghur	Arabic	*ishik*	ئىشىك
Indo-European	Farsi	Arabic	*dar*	در
	Italian	Latin	*porta*	*porta*

language of Arabic is observed in the practice of Islam, but the cultural language of a politically dominant ethnicity is far more likely to determine the effective language of communication and commerce across a modern state. Thus, Malay Muslims in Malaysia not only speak Malay, but also read and write Malay. Arabic is the language of religious instruction and observance, but *not* public education and *not* social mobility. The same can be said of Turks in Turkey, Kyrgyz in Kyrgyzstan, and so on (see Table 2.1).

Gellner Versus Gellner

Inexplicably, Gellner omits the importance of ethnicity or culture among Muslim populations outside the Arab world or inside the majority of Muslim states that are non-Arab. This is not simply a question of timing: the accelerated frequency of clashes involving Muslim ethnicities was demonstrated well before Gellner published *Muslim Society* in 1981, perhaps most vividly by the failure of a postcolonial state to survive on the basis of a shared religion, namely the secession of East Pakistan and the establishment of a Bengali nation-state, Bangladesh. Indeed, Brendan O'Leary notes "the break-up of Pakistan in 1971 suggests that a polyethnic or multinational state in which Islam is the sole unifying cultural bond rests on brittle foundations" (O'Leary 1998, 75).

Instead, in the last years of his life, Gellner focused on questions of civil society, which included the consideration of Islam as an alternative social order for the modern Muslim state, entirely distinct from the civic and/or ethnic nationalisms of Western liberal democracies. Islam, he argued, provided people displaced by industrialization with a tradition of literacy and laws that can function equally well as the basis for a successful state of modular citizens. These modern Muslims do not, however, develop a civil society but an ummah, a community that shares the same faith and follows its laws. Put another way, "the essence of nationalism in the West is that a High—literacy-linked—culture becomes the pervasive, membership-defining culture of the total society; the same thing has happened in Islam, but it expresses in fundamentalism rather than nationalism" (Gellner 1994, 22). Even if this assertion was true (it is not), the expectation that the economies of modern Muslim states should "function equally well" is tenuous at best (Mabry 1998).

It would be easy to dismiss an author's anomalous position between parallel theories of nationalism as a relatively minor omission, a footnote in the development of political sociology, were it not for two troubling points. The first is that Gellner's elegant map of the "modernist paradigm" has directed thinking about states, institutions, and identities across the social sciences for at least a generation (Smith 1998). His interpretation of the nature and relations of people, economies, societies, states, identities, culture, and modernity has emerged as the political sociology equivalent of what the natural sciences call a grand unification theory, a set of laws that govern everything. His model of nationalism "continues to occupy a unique place in the small world of the theorists of nationalism" (Roger 2000, 189). As a universal theory, it is not always acknowledged or even necessary at the meso or micro level of analysis, but it operates nonetheless.

The second pressing reason for repairing the rift between Gellner's general theory of nationalism and his exceptionalist view of Islam is the very real danger of misguiding contemporary thought about Muslims in general. It is the same kind of thinking that prompted Bernard Lewis, "the [George W. Bush] White House's favorite Arabist scholar" (*Economist* 2006), to warn that Europe would turn Muslim by the end of the twenty-first century and become part of the Maghreb, along with Morocco and Algeria.[7] (Despite his hyperbole, the influence of Lewis, in particular, should not be underestimated. In 2006, U.S. Vice President Dick Cheney noted that they have "met often, particularly during the last four-and-a-half years, and Bernard has always had some very good meetings with President Bush.")[8] This is but one of many "dire predictions concerning the future of (secular) European political and social systems" (Warner and Wenner 2006, 471). These alarmist forecasts disregard two important points. First, unlike the political strength of the Catholic Church in, for example, Ireland or Poland, "the decentralized institutional structure" of Islam "impedes collective action" (Warner and Wenner 2006,

458). Second, and more important, is the diversity of Muslims in Europe. It is hard to imagine, for example, an Islamist party in Germany composed of Turks, Kurds, and Persians working in concert for a common political goal.

Conclusion

As the cross-regional case studies in this book will show, Muslims and Muslim societies are not necessarily resistant to ethnolinguistic nationalism. This research refutes the latter-day Orientalism of Samuel Huntington, Bernard Lewis, and innumerable journalists by showing that Muslim minorities, especially when endowed with their own print culture, seek autonomy or independence in the same manner as ethnic minorities protecting a unique culture (Lockman 2004). This mirrors the experience of many other non-Muslim nationalist movements, such as the Quebecois in Canada, the Catalans in Spain, and the remnant Russians of the independent Baltic states.

The range of conflicts among and between Muslim societies and states suggests that modernity is forcing the same choices on followers of Islam that nascent Christian nations were forced to make over the many centuries of secularization and the many decades of industrialization in the West. Despite a "modernization deficit" in Muslim-majority countries, this is not a quick or easy process, but it is progressing (Hunter, Malik, and Center for Strategic and International Studies 2005). In other words, "as a system of belief, Islam may be no more secularizable than Roman Catholicism or Christian fundamentalism, but Muslims, and Muslim societies, are secularizable, and the process is well advanced" (Eickelman 1998, 268).[9] If so, then the process of making nations out of Muslims is advancing as well.

And yet, raising the issue of ethnic conflict among Muslim populations—even as far away from Arabia as the southern Philippines—continues to invite the often innocent but stupefying simplification that the source of the conflict is probably the intolerant politics of Islam rather than the differences of ethnic or cultural communities. It may be argued that more than a decade after the attacks of 9/11, a range of scholarship has falsified this premise, and thus the position is academically anachronistic. I do not believe this to be the case, but it must also be noted that policy makers and government analysts are not academics. For example, in a 2012 interview, a National Security Agency analyst (who must remain anonymous) expressed a belief that for any given population of Muslims, their exclusive political identification is

Islamist, while their ethnonational identification is essentially irrelevant. It is fair to say—at least in the United States—that Muslim exceptionalism remains a popular perception that continues to color policy discourse.

In his discussion of nationalism and religion, Arabic and Islam, it would seem that Gellner raised the right questions, but that a perspective limited to the anthropology of the Hejaz and the Maghreb foreshortened his answers. As a result, the majority of Muslims who neither speak Arabic nor share the same tribal affiliations or segmented social structures of ethnic Arab societies are disregarded. While Lewis and the late Huntington and Hastings are equally enthusiastic about Muslim exceptionalism, there is nonetheless good reason to exempt Gellner from the harshest criticism. In regard to the general relationships between nation and state, culture and country, Gellner got it right, even if his treatment of the Muslim world is more than a little truncated.

CHAPTER 3

National Tongues

The limits of my language are the limits of my world.
—Ludwig Wittgenstein, *Tractatus Logico-Philosophicus*

The relationship between a nation and any one of its nationals is personal. Within any national community, the definition of the nation is linked, inextricably, with the definition of the self. There is no shortage of social, political, economic, ethnic, and religious markers that may serve to mobilize the masses in a particular national contest. In many cases it is a particular marker that matters most—Protestant or Catholic in Northern Ireland, Sunni or Shiite in Arab Iraq, "color" in Apartheid South Africa, and so on. In this case, "a specific characteristic of a nation often becomes the rallying point in a national struggle and, in such event, is described as indivisible from the nation itself" (Connor 1994, 105). However, when language is a clear component of a national definition—Japanese language for the Japanese, Icelandic for Icelanders, Turkish for the Turks, etc.—then a clear understanding of exactly what *our* language is or is not becomes very important.

What is not yet clear is this: "what is or is not a bona fide language?" This chapter addresses this question, then proceeds to define and describe the evolution of text, which, as is argued in successive chapters, is indeed a necessary condition for a strong ethnonational identity, and therefore is critical to contain alternate political identities, including but not limited to Islamic fundamentalism.

Linguistics: Language, Dialect, Vernacular, Diglossia

Aside from a notable lacuna in the American academy, the centrality of language in politics and sociology, especially in regard to conflict, is indisputable (Laitin 1998, 24). Its definition is not. Though it would be reasonable to expect precise definitions of "language" and "dialect" from linguistics, this optimism is unfounded.

The Concise Oxford Dictionary of Linguistics offers only that a language is defined "in different ways according to different theories" (Matthews 1997). These include the classic view of Ferdinand de Saussure, a Swiss linguist, who saw language as a "system underlying the speech of a community," as well as Noam Chomsky's "generative grammar," that is, a view of language as an innate set of logical rules that generates sentences. It is easier, however, to come at the problem from below by first considering a definition of "dialect" as "any distinct variety of a language, especially one spoken in a specific part of a country or other geographical area." Nonetheless, even this definition is qualified with a two-ton caveat:

> The criterion for distinguishing "dialects" from "languages" is taken, in principle, to be that of mutual intelligibility. For example, speakers of Dutch cannot understand English unless they have learned it, and vice versa; therefore Dutch and English are different languages. But a speaker from Amsterdam can understand one from Antwerp: therefore they speak different dialects of the same language. But (*a*) this is a matter of degree, and (*b*) ordinary usage often contradicts it. For example, Italian "dialects" ("dialetti") are so called though many from the north and south are not mutually intelligible. By contrast Danish and Norwegian are called "languages" though speakers understand each other reasonably well. (Matthews 1997)

Alert readers will notice, of course, one glaring difference between Danish or Norwegian and the *dialetti* of Sicily and Piedmont: the former are official languages of sovereign nation-states; the latter are not.[1]

This definition of dialect/language, which is really more of a discussion, comfortably employs the term *speakers*. This begs the question of whether a language *not* spoken is either a dead language or, more plainly, not a language in the first place. A spoken language is, again according to Oxford, a *vernacular*, a *mother tongue*, that is "native to a given community, as opposed to a learned or other second language: e.g. the native languages of Catholic Europe in the Middle Ages and later, in opposition to Latin. Thence generally of languages that are not standardized, of non-standard varieties of those that are, of forms used locally or characteristic of non-dominant groups or classes." Tellingly, just as in the case of "dialect," the term "vernacular" is also qualified with a pair of sociopolitical qualifiers: (1) "standardized" and (2) "non-dominant groups or classes." After considering only three linguistic terms—language, dialect, and vernacular—questions of power and politics are immediate and inevitable.

So what should be made of languages that are not vernaculars? The example of Latin in premodern Europe is already cited historically, but as linguistics evolved through the 1950s and especially the 1960s, the same questions of perspective that muddied the dialect/language distinction actually clarified a special situation called diglossia. In this scenario, distinct varieties of a language are employed separately but consistently according to social context, with one variety elevated to a higher status than the other. The higher status language is written and used in public affairs; the lower status language is not written and is used in private affairs. As a model attributed to Charles Ferguson and his landmark article (1959), diglossia marked a paradigm shift in linguistics. He divided language into High and Low varieties and cited Arabic as the archetype. A High variety is marked by its use in socially formal contexts, by greater prestige, by a literary heritage, by *the need to study* its standardized form, and by its stability over time.[2] (The example of Arabic and the clear parallels of High and Low language varieties to Gellner's High and Low Cultures are addressed at length in the next chapter.) Joshua Fishman later expanded on Ferguson by showing that bilingualism could function in much the same way as diglossia, though in this case speakers within the same community switch not between High and Low varieties of the same language but between different languages. He cited bilingual Jews who spoke both Yiddish and German as archetypical (Fishman 1967). But as for selecting which variety (or language) is higher than another, it is important to note that *intelligibility* is not a prerequisite but prestige is. In selecting a High variety, the quality that "outranks intelligibility as a criterion for the choice" is *status* (Fasold 1984, 3).

Objections may be raised on the point of what is or is not considered "mutually intelligible." Intelligibility may be hindered by any number of differences, including (1) unfamiliar usage of otherwise familiar words (a toilet in Canada is a *washroom*; this is a shibboleth for identifying Americans who ask for the *bathroom*), (2) different accents in the pronunciation of the same words (in Glasgow, *tea* is *tay*), (3) altered words for the same things (such as endings for gender, tense, or even spelling, for example, *curb* and *kerb* can both mean the edge of a sidewalk or pavement), (4) different words for the same things (*truck* versus *lorry*), (5) different things described by the same words (a *tortilla* in Spain is an omelet but a *tortilla* in Mexico is thin, round bread), and more distantly (6) an entirely different syntax, such as the English *white house* rendered in Spanish as *casa blanca*, literally "house white." Many more technical distinctions are studied in the subfields of computational linguistics (dealing, for example, with voice recognition software and machine translation) and clinical linguistics (focusing on speech pathologies, such as a lisp). These rely further on research into the mechanisms for producing sounds in human speech, the patterns of those sounds, or even the internal structures of words (the subfields of phonetics, phonology, and morphology, respectively).

As for *quantifying* the distance between languages and intelligibility, one approach is that of genealogy: this is the approach adopted by David Laitin in his article "Language Conflict and Violence," which coded languages as more closely or more distantly related depending on how many branches separated each tongue from another (Laitin 2000). Yet this is clearly problematic regarding mutual intelligibility since linguistic genealogy is not a reliable indicator of comprehension. Not surprisingly, linguists from Denmark, Norway, and Sweden are especially interested in measuring the degree to which people from different ethnolinguistic communities can nonetheless understand some of each other's language without study. This phenomenon, called *receptive multilingualism*, was the focus of a large research project, Linguistic Determinants of Mutual Intelligibility in Scandinavia, funded by the Netherlands Organization for Scientific Research.[3]

Returning to the question of dialect versus language, the taxonomists at the leading comprehensive language research operation, called Ethnologue, offer a mea culpa by acknowledging "the definition of language one chooses depends on the purpose one has in identifying a language. Some base their definition on purely linguistic grounds. Others recognize that social, cultural, or political factors must also be taken into account. . . . Languages are more often continua of features that extend across both geographic and social space" (Lewis 2009). Yet because the whole point of Ethnologue is to classify and catalogue all known varieties of spoken and written communication, certain

criteria for determining the difference between dialect language are nonetheless applied as follows:

1. If speakers of separate varieties *can* understand each other "at a functional level" *and* without having to learn the other variety, then those
   varieties are dialects of the same language.
2. If speakers of separate varieties *can* understand each other *but* are members of separate "well-established distinct ethnolinguistic identities,"
   then those varieties are not dialects of the same language and are classified as different languages.
3. If speakers of separate varieties *cannot* understand each other *but* share
   "a common literature" or "common ethnolinguistic identity with a central variety that both can understand," then those varieties are dialects
   of the same language.

In other words, mutual intelligibility is not sufficient to unite two varieties
as dialects of the language and mutual *un*intelligibility is not sufficient to divide two varieties as separate languages. What is sufficient to make this determination is whether or not the speakers are members of the same or different
ethnolinguistic identity. Hence, in the simplest possible terms,

1. Varieties of speech are *dialects of the same language* if the speakers *share*
   the same ethnolinguistic identity.
2. Varieties of speech are *separate languages* if the speakers *do not share*
   the same ethnolinguistic identity.

Thus, the question of classifying a language versus dialect hinges on "social,
cultural, or political factors" of ethnolinguistic identity, factors that are more
commonly addressed by sociologists, anthropologists, and political scientists.
Yet without the technical mastery of linguistics proper, these separate fields
could miss essential elements of interpretation and causal analysis. Hence, a
new discipline was invented to straddle the methodological divide.

Sociolinguistics

As the study of language in relation to society, sociolinguistics considers technical variations in language as concomitant to variations in social context.

Two names are invariably associated with the launch of this discipline in the 1960s. Bill Labov began by studying class and speech on Martha's Vineyard and in New York City (his master's and doctorate respectively), and achieved broad recognition for his work on American "Black English vernacular," a work that presaged the debate over "Ebonics" in the schools of Oakland, California, by fifteen years (Labov 1966, 1972). Labov's brilliant work on varieties of English is both unparalleled and prodigious, as demonstrated by his atlas of North American English (Labov, Ash, and Boberg 2006). Yet for international and comparative work, the research of Joshua Fishman is more frequently applied and, therefore, particularly appropriate for this project. The same year Labov published his text on English in New York, Fishman published his book (1966) on the death and/or survival of "non-English mother tongues" in the United States, including Yiddish and Hungarian, among others. Yet in studying the processes by which a language dies or persists in response to contact or competition with other languages, Fishman recognized quickly the overarching *role of the state* in aiding or hindering these processes.

In particular, *nationalism* was viewed as responsible for selecting, processing, and eventually producing particularly resilient linguistic material to strengthen the social and political structures of a modernizing state. In this regard, the citizen's mother tongue, the vernacular, "is the medium of nationalism" as it "forged a new bond with language," a "mass consensus" that is essential to political stability (Fishman 1973, 40, 42–43). Hence, education in the vernacular is "crucial . . . for the arousal and maintenance of nationalism." In support of this point, Fishman cites Gellner's earliest work on the subject: "modern loyalties are centered on political units whose boundaries are defined by the language . . . of an educational system" (Gellner 1964, 163; cited in Fishman 1973, 43).

As an instrument of state policy, an educational system presents a range of problems for a vernacular that may or may not be written in a standard form, or may vary widely across territory in a *dialect continuum*, that is, "a progressive shift from one form of speech to another across a territory, such that adjacent varieties are mutually intelligible, but those at the extremes are not" (Matthews 1997). For Fishman, "the organized pursuit of solutions to language problems" is *language planning* (1973, 55), a field that he devoted much of the past three decades to advancing and explaining, especially in regard to developing languages and multilingual populations. The mechanics of language planning are technical and jargon-laden, though three components are typically cited as necessary (but not sufficient) parts of a functioning language policy: corpus planning, status planning, and acquisition planning. Adding to the complexity, of course, is politics, as "competition between languages represents competition between groups" (Millar 2005, 30).

Language Planning: Corpus, Status, and Acquisition

Language planning is a political exercise. Formally, it is "any attempt by a government etc. to favor one language, or one form of a language, over another" (Matthews 1997). Why a government should favor one form of a language over another is answered by the much broader political sociology of modern nationalism, though parsing the process as language planning aids greatly in a more clear discussion of language politics in general (Liddicoat 2007).

The classic formulation of language planning charts three branches of development: corpus planning, status planning, and acquisition planning. All three branches are shaped by subjective determinations of socioeconomic value and political utility. *Corpus planning*, as one would expect, determines the precise form or *body* of the linguistic species: just as a cat should not have scales and gills, neither should a fish have fur and whiskers. This selection of what is right or wrong in terms of language is the job of corpus planners. Technically, it is the "creation of new forms, the modification of old ones, or the selection from alternative forms in a spoken or written code" (Cooper 1989, 31). It involves decisions about grammar, orthography (including alphabets, ideograms and punctuation), lexicon, and phonology. But corpus planning is more art than science. Its practitioners subjectively decide "what is 'incorrect' or 'impure,' and what is 'correct' or 'pure'; they decide what is the 'best' usage for a language, ideologically and linguistically" (Millar 2005, 67).

Status planning describes a conflict: if there is only one variety of a single language in a given community, then there is no question as to which language is *most* important and therefore suited to elevation and recognition as an official language. Yet this scenario is hypothetical: most states are home to many dialects of the same language (a distinction that is in itself a matter of status planning) and many are home to more than one language. Unlike corpus planning, status planning is less concerned with grammar and phonology than with which language is written on a country's currency or, more pointedly, a high school diploma. Status planners, therefore, address efforts to control which language is used in specific contexts, especially contexts imbued with import or power, including the dominant language(s) of commerce, government, the media, and, above all, education. Yet the distinction between corpus planning and status planning is now perceived as largely synthetic.[4] If a language is of low status, then why should any effort be expended to develop its corpus? Fishman's later work is unequivocal in arguing that corpus planning invariably "has a status planning agenda" (Fishman 2004, 92–93).[5]

To reiterate, language planning, including both corpus and status agendas, is a synthetic and instrumental effort by a government to develop and promote a particular language within its borders. *Language standardization*, on the other hand, is a more organic phenomenon. While corpus planning and status planning are matters of state policy in the public sphere, standardization also includes personal acceptance and/or rejection of actual usage. The classic definition of language standardization is Ferguson's: "the process of one variety of a language becoming widely accepted throughout the speech community as a supra-dialectical norm—the 'best' form of the language—rated above regional and social dialects, although these may be felt to be appropriate in some domains" (Fishman, Ferguson, and Dasgupta 1968, 31). The signal word in the above definition is "felt" in that standardization is in many ways an internalized process not completely under the control of state corpus planners. A truly successful language planner will endow future generations with a vernacular, a mother tongue, that is itself the product of careful corpus planning, so that the official language of the state and the standardized language of its citizens are naturally congruent. This is the mandate of *acquisition planning*, that is, language policies that determine how a language is learned, spread, and maintained, including incentives, disincentives, and the allocation of resources. In practice, acquisition planning is therefore synonymous with *education policy*: both the spoken language of classroom instruction and the written language of textbooks are addressed by acquisition planners. Literacy is necessarily linked to a specific language with a well-defined corpus and, above all, high status (Ferguson 2006).

When effective, a state language planning program—including corpus, status, and acquisition planning—succeeds in maintaining, protecting, and advancing not only a language but the nation-state itself. William Safran, one of the few contemporary political scientists who has advanced our understanding of this question, rightly describes the relationship between states and languages as "reciprocal." Nationalist leaders may adopt an extant language for "political mobilization that leads to the creation of a state; but once established, the state manipulates the language so that it can be used effectively to make citizens and disseminate national values" (Safran 2004, 8). In this sense, language manipulation is effected through the laws, policies, and accepted practices of language planning.

Language and Politics

At this point, there is a need to distinguish clearly between the *language of politics* and the *politics of language*. The former is a subject with a pedigree that includes George Orwell, not only in *Nineteen Eighty-Four* (1949), but also more critically in his earlier *Politics and the English Language* (Orwell and Rogers 1947). This book follows the latter, that is, the politics of language, as related to the comparative conflicts of specific Muslim peoples. Yet as a project of political science undertaken in the United States, the incorporation of language planning literature makes this project somewhat unorthodox. The view from outside the discipline (and outside the country) is that political scientists are essentially deaf to questions of language: "In view of the widespread agreement that linguistic identity is of central importance for the individual, the group, and the state and that language is a major defining characteristic of ethnicity, one might be forgiven for thinking that language policy must be of central concern to sociology and political science, the disciplines that are particularly concerned with societal power and institutions. This would be a misconception" (Phillipson 1999, 94). Language in the preponderance of political science literature is often the conceptual equivalent of cosmic background radiation; it is assumed to exist, but only as an echo of the big bang of state formation, when raw political stuff cooled and coalesced into fixed bodies. This book makes no such assumptions and self-consciously applies the lessons of language planning and policy to the test a political theory, namely that Muslims are exceptionally resistant to ethnolinguistic nationalism.

Language and Nationalism

In the broader literature of ethnicity and nationalism, a central question regarding the role of language in the genesis and evolution of a nation is not *whether* language matters, but *how*. Most notably, the structuralist account of Ernest Gellner (1983), the constructivist view of Benedict Anderson (1983), the historical religious route of Adrian Hastings (1997), and the historical economic model of Eric Hobsbawm (1962, 1990) all emphasize the essential role of a common language that unifies previously disparate peoples in a fundamental new way. This is not to say that two communities who share a polity but not a common tongue will inevitably clash. More often than not, a national language is a consolidation and standardization of many local vernaculars. For Gellner, this process is an accidental effect of urbanization, modernization, and—eventually—the efforts of a state to homogenize its people through public education and therefore literacy, which itself is a necessary condition of a viable economy and competitive country. For Anderson, the process is an accidental effect of supply and demand: as printing technology makes books and newspapers available at low cost, a market emerges for material printed in the language of its consumers. For Hastings, the process is an accidental effect of proselytizing, whereby priests come to rely on vernacular texts as an effective means of spreading the gospels.

For Hobsbawm, the process is more deliberate but not dissimilar in its emphasis on language as a critical element of group cohesion: a bourgeoisie will struggle to displace a small ruling elite that is likely to use a High Culture language distinct (in a word, foreign) from the vernacular of the masses. Through education, members of a nascent middle class begin to enter the ranks of power, so "the progress of schools and universities measures that of nationalism." When the newly expanded educated class reaches sufficient size, it "imposes itself" as a national language: "Hence the moment when textbooks or newspapers are written, or when that language is first used for some official purpose, measures a crucial step in national evolution" (Hobsbawm 1962, 135).

A notable exception in the literature is, again, the rational choice work of James Fearon and David Laitin (2003), which claims to falsify these many theoretical studies linking language and nation. Their robust quantitative analysis argues that for any given pair of ethnic communities, the greater the linguistic difference between them, the lower the probability of intergroup violence. In other words (pun intended), a theoretical expectation that language difference should correlate with conflict is not only wrong, but also backward (Laitin 2000). Their operationalization of language, however, is deeply flawed. It claims to measure relative language *difference* when it actually measures only language *distance*, which in this case means a closer or more distant *relation* in the genetic sense: Spanish and Italian both share a recent common ancestor, that is, Latin; Spanish and Hindi also share a common ancestor—what linguists call the prehistoric Proto-Indo-European language—but that relationship is much more distant.

The trouble here is that this is the only measure of language comparison employed by Fearon and Laitin, dismissing all other elements of language, including morphology, syntax, lexicon, orthography, and status. As I have written elsewhere (2011, 196–97), the perspective of evolutionary biology is helpful in illustrating why ancestral *distance* is a very poor proxy of current *difference*.

Consider the relationships between and among sharks, dolphins, and dogs. On a phylogenetic tree, i.e. a "tree of life," one common ancestor shared by all three (and our own species) is the progenitor of the Gnasthostomata branch of the group Vertebrata, of the group Craniata, of the group Chordata, and so on back in time. The gnathostomes, as they are called, were dominant in the Middle Devonian age some 380 million years ago. About 20 million years later the Sarcopterygii branched off and ultimately diverged into all four-limbed creatures, including dogs and (before their return to the sea) dolphins. According to the ancestral distance scheme, dogs and dolphins are *more related*, and therefore *more similar*, than sharks and dolphins. The many, many differences separating dogs and dolphins (fur, tails, panting, etc.) are ignored in this classification, as are the many similarities of sharks and dolphins (fins, swimming, piscivory, etc.). The only thing that matters here is when the lineage split.

Yet there is an empirical language difference that—with sufficient hours of research, coding, and funds—can be quantified. Moreover, it is a characteristic of language phenomena shared by *all* of the influential accounts of nationalism and language outlined above: *printing*. In the (now) classic equations of language and nation outlined above, all explicitly detail the emergence of a shared language printed—and not just written—on paper. It is not merely the similarity or dissimilarity of a spoken language that may or may not be shared by a community; it is the preservation and dissemination of a shared voice that is captured and replicated mechanically (and affordably) in print.

On the face of it, this is in no way surprising. If a community develops a shared national language, how else would that language survive, thrive, and expand without a written form that is reproduced on an industrial scale? If nothing else, it is the *volume* of text made possible by print technology that speeds the convergence and consolidation of a community. The concept that words can be dangerous and destabilizing is as old as writing, though typically it is not the words themselves that are dangerous, but the ideas they contain. Yet I argue here that once a vernacular language is printed the words themselves become politically combustible, not for the ideas they contain, but for their form and function. A printed language invites group conflict in three ways. First, a print language exists in opposition to any rival form of the same language: this is the familiar process of standardization and rationalization pursued by state builders who consequently become nation builders, as was the case with the French language in premodern France (Weber 1976). In this case, the conflict is between regional vernaculars in competition with the vernacular of the capital. Second, a print language exists in opposition to any other print language: in fourteenth-century Europe, the mother tongues of the Flemish, Germans, and Italians were moot since there was only one print language of any consequence whatsoever: Latin. By the end of the sixteenth century, each of these languages existed not only in opposition to Latin, but also in opposition to each other (Febvre and Martin 1976; Hirschi 2012).

Third, and most important in contemporary politics, a printed language serves not only to include members of a language community, but also to *exclude* anyone else. In Anderson's model, readers of a shared print language "gradually become aware of the hundreds of thousands, even millions, of people in their particular language-field, and at the same time that *only those* hundreds of thousands, or millions, so belonged" (Anderson 1983, 44). In this way, a printed language conveys the sense of an imagined political community that is sovereign but "inherently limited" (Anderson 1983, 6).

Hence, I argue literacy is not a sufficient condition for the emergence or consolidation of a national identity. Rather, it is literacy in the *vernacular* of a language community that supports the emergence of a national identity. In other words, printing is not enough; the words themselves must be printed in the mother tongue, a symbolic representation of speech inked permanently into paper by an industrial press. Therefore, I also argue that language difference should correlate with group conflict if and only if the contrasting languages maintain distinct print cultures. By extension, if a print language is fundamental to the self-identification of a unique nation, then the relative strength of that national identity should correlate with the relative strength of that nation's print culture.

National Literacy Versus a National Language

The role of *literacy* surfaces perennially as a necessary condition of a modern and successful society, replete with liberal freedoms and a healthy middle class, that is concomitant with democracy (Lipset 1959; Rustow 1970).[6] Why? In what amounts to conventional wisdom in political science, an informed electorate is an effective electorate, and literacy is a magnificent conduit of information. Armed with knowledge, an educated citizenry is harder to manipulate instrumentally and more likely to organize its own political bodies in the space between the private sphere and the government, that is, civil society (Milner 2002). Moreover, in some cases this knowledge conveys normative ideas about justice and political legitimacy. Importantly, however, in this scenario it is not the medium that matters but the message.

It is this perspective that informs an influential account of how and why some post-Soviet states chose to *elect* leaders closely associated with the communist era who, unsurprisingly, instituted regimes more authoritarian than democratic. Keith Darden and Anna Maria Grzymała-Busse argue effectively that the relationship between literacy rates in pre-Soviet states correlated inversely with support for illiberal parties, typically the rumps of what had been the Communist Party operation of a titular Soviet Republic. Why is this so? "The ultimate roots of the explanation lie in precommunist schooling, which fomented and fostered nationalist ideas that led to the delegitimation of communist rule. . . . [There is] a causal chain linking the introduction of mass schooling, subsequent ideas about the nation and its legitimate authority, the rise of anticommunist opposition, and the communist exit" (2006, 84).[7] Hence, those states with a literate population before the Bolshevik Revolution— including the Czech Republic, Estonia, Latvia, Poland, Slovakia, Slovenia, Hungary—overwhelmingly elected "noncommunists." On the other hand, in Azerbaijan, Belarus, and all five Central Asian Republics, pre-Soviet literacy was nominal, as were the number of parliamentary seats taken by noncommunists in the first post-Soviet elections (2006, 91). Again, the explanation is that precommunist literacy afforded "the easy dissemination of ideas" and specifically aided in "transmitting, replicating, and sustaining nationalist ideas" that resurfaced after 1989 (2006, 98–99).

While the authors' correlation of literacy and post-Soviet nationalism is unimpeachable, the authors' causal link is not. Methodologically, there are multiple references to the relative amount "nationalist content" in school curricula, though the term is nowhere defined or sourced. More problematically, *literacy itself is not defined by language*. In other words, in the last years of the Austro-Hungarian Empire, was literacy in Prague defined by the ability to read and write in Czech or—as was far more typical of the time—in the language of the empire, that is, German? Inexplicably, this information is absent, and no references are cited.

Nonetheless, there is an implicit assumption—correctly or incorrectly— that *literacy* is taken to mean the ability to read and write the titular language of the country (or socialist republic) in question. This is gleaned from references to the illiterate populations of Azerbaijan and the Central Asian states, where precommunist (in this case Romanov dynasty) literacy was no more than 30 percent, arguably because education "was almost exclusively in Russian" rather than a titular language. Similarly, in reference to outliers where precommunist education did not cultivate nationalism, literacy is defined in terms of the dominant language: "Macedonians were educated in Serbo-Croatian and told they were Serbs. Most schools in the Russian Empire were Russophone and Russophile. For example, Russian was the language of schools in Belarus and Ukraine, and students were taught that they were Russian." Elsewhere, the authors acknowledge that in some states literacy rates varied dramatically by region, as in the case of Serbia where precommunist literacy around Belgrade was near universal but exceptionally low in Kosovo (Darden and Grzymała-Busse 2006, 96, 114, 97). The fact that Kosovo was (and is) populated by Albanians who speak Albanian is somehow elided. Is it possible that at least some of the Kosovars were literate in their own language but not in Serbo-Croatian, and were therefore not counted among the literate?

The point of these criticisms is to demonstrate that for Darden and Grzymała-Busse, precommunist populations of literate citizens were exposed to "notions of statehood and legitimate governance" but that the medium through which these notions were conveyed was *not* a causal factor in determining the relative appeal of a national identity in post-Soviet states and satellites (2006, 90). This is not at all the lesson of Gellner, Anderson, Hastings, or Hobsbawm, all of whom are explicit in their identification of a variegated speech community that evolves a shared print *vernacular*. In other words, it is the phenomenon of reading within a unique language community that strengthens dramatically the national bond. In short, the medium is the message. From this perspective, the argument of Darden and Grzymała-Busse is right—literacy aids nationalism and nationalism trumps communism—but for the wrong reasons. It is not the spread of nationalism as an *idea* that matters nearly as much as the spread of a nation's *language*.[8]

In the course of building a nation, it is not enough that everyone should come to speak the same language with the same sounds; rather, it is the introduction of writing that forces a community to recognize a shared syntax, lexicon, and orthography; thereafter (or simultaneously) it is the introduction of print technology that endows a necessarily conscribed written language with a more widely disseminated *print culture*. This term applies to the *social* practice of reading, writing, and printing a language no matter the content. A print culture may include some or all of the following: the use of religious texts in worship; the artistic expression of song, poetry, prose, or play; the documentation of legal or commercial transactions; the recording of events; and, most broadly, the exchange of ideas as in philosophy or politics. The term *print culture* does not necessarily specify a medium of exchange, a scale of production, or a relative rate of literacy, though it does consider the social effects of specific scenarios (Boureau and Chartier 1989). In the former German Democratic Republic, for example, literacy was very high, but printed material used in religious observances was uncommon because religion was *verboten*. The supply of available books was not driven by the demand of readers but rather the goals of the Communist Party.

Yet variations in specific print cultures should not be interpreted as falsifications of the linkage between print language and national identity formation. Of course, not everyone agrees with this position. Anderson's model, for example, has been targeted specifically for a kind of literary chauvinism. Peter Wogan, an anthropologist, argues the broad appeal of *Imagined Communities* can be attributed to a kind of self-congratulatory latter-day Orientalism that implicitly endorses a "linguistic ideology," which marginalizes the place of oral language. Wogan also takes exception with "Anderson's argument that print reading allows/causes people to think differently—to change their conception of time, to visualize a different community" (Wogan 2001, 411). This is an interesting charge, since it begs the question, does *reading* change how people think? Wonderfully, the answer is yes. Cognitive science and brain imaging experiments demonstrate that the brains of literates and illiterates differ not only in function—measurements of brain activity—but in form: a part of the brain that connects the two hemispheres is visibly thicker in literate people (Castro-Caldas et al. 1999). As a result, "When children learn to read, they return from school 'literally changed.' Their brains will never be the same again" (Dehaene 2009, 210).

Print culture should also be distinguished from other stages in the evolution of *text*. Following the evolution of human speech, the communication of songs and stories, as well as their symbology relative to a specific language community, is typically labeled *speech culture*. Over time, a speech culture may transmit an *oral tradition* often maintained by specialized members of a community (e.g., bards in medieval England, or the Kyrgyz *manaschi* who are trained from childhood in the *Epic of Manas*, a national origin mythology that describes a hero's struggle against a perennial foe, the Chinese).

A speech culture is changed fundamentally by the introduction of writing, if for no other reason than language has suddenly incorporated another dimension of *sight* as the eyes are incorporated into aural communication (Ong [1982] 2002). This is the necessary condition for *scribal culture* that again depends on language specialists, typically linked to a system of belief, for example, the scribes who literally penned religious manuscripts in the Vedic, Hebrew, Christian, and Islamic traditions, inter alia. A scribal culture is a necessary condition for the development of a print culture, though the two may emerge symbiotically when the language of speech culture suddenly evolves into a standardized print language. This has occurred many times when Christian missionaries encounter indigenous populations that have only a speech culture. Since the Christian Bible is explicit in its emphasis on spreading the word of God by any means necessary (as evidenced by the miracle of "speaking in tongues"), the necessity of vernacular Bibles required the invention of a written and printed form of a speech culture's language.

Curiously, there are some cases when a speech culture and a print culture are standardized simultaneously. Famously the Finnish, who were ruled for centuries from Stockholm by the Kingdom of Sweden and then, in the nineteenth century, from Moscow by the Romanov Empire, developed their *printed* language as an explicit symbol of a unique national identity. This print culture emerged from the oral tradition of Finland, including folktales and poetry, which in turn led to the development of a scribal culture in the seventeenth century. It was not until the nineteenth century, however, that a Finnish doctor, Elias Lönnrot, compiled these works into the first volume printed for a mass market: the Kalevala (1835), an epic poem that became a pillar of Finnish national identity.[9] However, because there were (and are) Eastern and Western dialects of Finnish, there was a parallel need to standardize their speech culture, especially after Finland won its independence in 1917. As a result, "the move towards an independent Finland and the rise of a nationalistic sentiment was also instrumental in the institutionalization of the teaching of speech" (Wilkins and Isotalus 2009, 1). The simultaneity of this processed ensured the result was a standardized vernacular, that is, mother tongue, print culture.

A print culture is best understood as a scribal culture that discovers a more efficient way of writing, such as the *xylography* of Chinese woodblock printing beginning in the seventh century, though this does not necessarily require industrial production. The volume of material produced using this technology—what was literally a *handicraft*—is a matter of scholarly debate, though it is clear there was a market for the texts produced. This market expanded exponentially in the late nineteenth and early twentieth centuries when new technologies raised production and cut costs, specifically lithography—which, like woodblock, could reproduce calligraphy though at a much greater economy of scale—and moveable cast type. To this end, Sinologist and historian Christopher Reed argues this era should be given its own label of *print commerce*.[10]

The most important shift in the evolution of text, however, is the introduction of the printing press, a relatively simple advance in technology that revolutionized entire societies; by incentivizing literacy and consolidating language communities, the press promoted the development of mass cultures at a scale and level of participation previously impossible. Certainly the press allowed for a much greater dissemination of information. However, by *fixing* information and ideas on paper, the printing press also led to the preservation and standardization of human knowledge. This social and *metaphysical* effects of this transition, to the extent that it changed ideas about the character of humanity and its relationship with nature and the divine, amounted to what Elizabeth Eisenstein called an "unacknowledged revolution" (Eisenstein 1979). The relative importance of this revolution, particularly in regard to the history of science, thereafter developed into a forum of robust academic debate (McNally 1987; Eisenstein 2002).

If we are to consider a more explicit function of print in the development of a national identity, the term *print culture* is joined most frequently by Anderson's term *print capitalism*. The latter term incorporates two important elements: the first is that a book is a commodity; the second is that the spread of a printed vernacular is driven by the commercial demand of newly literate readers, so it is an invisible hand that propels the exponential growth of

Table 3.1. Evolution of Text Cultures

Language culture	Definition	Example
Oral culture	Speech without writing	*Manas* tradition of the Kyrgyz
Scribal culture	Oral culture plus writing	Medieval European religious manuscripts
Print culture	Scribal culture plus print technology	Modern Europe (sixteenth century and thereafter)

a print culture. "The Book as a Commodity" is actually the title of a chapter in another book from which Anderson borrowed heavily, *The Coming of the Book: The Impact of Printing 1450–1800*, by Lucien Febvre and Henri-Jean Martin.[11] Based on an exhaustive history of publishing and publishers in Europe, they conclude, "From its earliest days printing existed as an industry, governed by the same rules as any other industry; the book was a piece of merchandise which men produced before anything else to earn a living" (Febvre and Martin 1976, 109).

Stripped of any romantic pretensions, the book is to a publisher as shoes are to a cobbler: any decision about the numbers and kinds of shoes to make is dictated by what will or will not sell. Though "about 20 million" books had been printed in Europe *before 1500*, more than three-quarters were in Latin, with the remainder distributed across Italian, German, French, and Flemish (Febvre and Martin 1976, 248–49). Book buyers were few, but they were wealthy, so publishing supported the growth of private libraries rather than a reading public. This all changed in 1520 when Martin Luther *published* his appeal "To the Christian Nobility of the German Nation" *in German*. The response? "All Germany caught fire" (Febvre and Martin 1976, 291). Here was a work that was not only accessible, but also controversial, and its success served as a model for publishers from that century to this.

Though it is argued here that ethnolinguistic mobilization is much more probable and pronounced if a population's language maintains a print culture, this is not to say that languages without print cultures cannot serve as political shibboleths (so to speak). For example, when the Taliban seized control of the capital for the first time, the language predominant in Kabul, Dari—the mother tongue of ethnic Tajik's, who compose a quarter of the total population—was supplanted by the language of those who composed some 90 percent of the Taliban, namely the Pashto of ethnic Pashtuns. Thereafter, even *speaking* Dari became dangerous. An academic in Kabul recalls, "'During the Taliban regime, the people in their offices tried to speak Pashto.' . . . When the Taliban fell soon after the US airstrikes began in October [2002] . . . 'the people suddenly switched and spoke Dari again'" (Prusher 2002). Similarly, following the 2008 ethnic riots sparked by a suspect election in Kenya, rival tribes sought to identify friends or foes by testing their ability to speak a certain language. As a result, some who spoke Kikuyu (the dominant vernacular of Nairobi and the ruling elite) "resorted to taking crash courses in the [other] dialects . . . just in case it comes in handy" (Barasa 2008).

Nonetheless, rival print cultures can lend themselves to conflict in a way not possible between different speech communities because they offer so many *political* opportunities, as a way either to suppress a troublesome population, or to rally the mobilization of subordinate language communities against their regime. A state may ban the printing of books, texts, or newspapers in a given language, or more moderately exercise control of a lexicon or even elements of spelling.[12] A regime may switch from one script to another, as in the case of Turkish after the end of the Ottoman Empire (from Arabic to Latin) or in Azerbaijan after the end of the Soviet Union (Cyrillic to Latin) (Aytürk 2004; O'Leary 2006). That such examples occur in times of political change is not coincidental, as "scripts are prone to come into prominence as political symbols in times of crisis, since script choice is easily instrumentalized for ideological purposes" (Coulmas 2000, 50). The political significance of language choice generally is the focus of the chapters that follow (see Table 3.1).

CHAPTER 4

Modern Standard Arabs

Without school or book, the making of a nation is
in modern times inconceivable.
—George Antonius, *The Arab Awakening*

The literature on Arab nationalism, however defined, is very broad, very deep, and very muddy.[1] Much of it is dedicated to the singular problem of defining "Arab" and consequently "Arab nationalism." Some of this work developed from the study of nationalism and some of this work developed from the study of Arabs, yet the two tracks do not frequently converge. From the perspective of nations and nationalism scholarship, and aside from Ernest Gellner, of course, there are important contributions from Elie and Sylvia Kedourie, as well as John Breuilly, who argues Arab nationalism emerged first as a "sort of modern anti-colonial nationalism" against the Ottomans, catalyzed when imperial administrators in Arab lands started acting less like Ottomans and more like Turks (Kedourie 1992; Kedourie 1971; Breuilly [1982] 1993, 149–51). There is much more, however, written from the perspective of Arab and/ or Middle East studies. Because the story is so complex, and because there are many competing interpretations of key events, most monographs are histories that trace a narrative lasting generations (Ajami 1998; Choueiri 2000; Dawisha 2003; Watenpaugh 2006; Schumann 2010). More focused work tends to examine the role of nationalism in a specific territory over time, particularly Lebanon (Firro 2004), Palestine (Nafi 1998), and especially Syria (Gelvin 1998), the site of the Great Revolt that erupted between the end of rule by the Ottomans and the beginning of French rule. The importance of this violent event is not in doubt, as "there is common agreement among scholars of Arab nationalism that Greater Syria was the main arena in the development and promotion of this Arab nationalist ideology and movement" (Suleiman 2003, 70). Nonetheless, most of this work accepts the existence of "the Arabs" as prima facie, holistically a collective that is somehow greater than the sum of its heterogeneous parts.[2]

Conflicting terminology is a principal reason why much of the research on Arab nationalism is discordant. What are the precise distinctions separating Arab nationalism, pan-Arab nationalism (*Qawmiyya*), and Arab patriotism (*Wataniyya*)? In the context of specific countries, what is the difference between, for example, Egyptian nationalism and Egyptian patriotism? Or Egyptian nationalism and pan-Arab nationalism? There is also a principal reason why terminology in Arab nationalism scholarship is a Gordian knot: disagreement among Arabs themselves about these very terms. Hence, it is understandable why much of the literature is devoted to interpreting different expressions by different leaders about who is or is not an Arab, and what is or is not the Arab nation. Considering the general symbiosis of Islam and Arab culture, it seems paradoxical that many pioneering theorists of Arab nationalism were not Muslim. George Antonius (1891–1941), the author of *The Arab Awakening* (1938), was a Christian of Lebanese and Egyptian heritage born in what was then the British Mandate of Palestine. Michel Aflaq (1910–89), the ideological founder of the Ba'ath ("revival") Party, was a Greek Orthodox Christian from Damascus. This is explicable, however, because pan-Arab nationalism was crafted to unite a region of disparate peoples adhering to multiple beliefs, so the doctrine was pragmatically *secular*, and accentuated "Arabness" (*uruba*) rather than Islam. Aflaq's "spiritual guide" was the "prophet of Arab nationalism," Sati al-Husri, a former schoolteacher educated in Istanbul who later infused the educational systems of Syria, Iraq, and Egypt with his ideas about the Arab people.[3] Chief among these ideas was who qualified as an Arab: "Every Arab-speaking people is an Arab people. Every individual belonging to one of these Arabic-speaking peoples is an Arab" (cited in Dawisha 2003, 72). Therefore, the identification is based on a single shared language: "Arabic." Ah, there's the rub.

In the sections that follow, this chapter addresses the methods and meanings of determining the demographics of the Arab world, the sociolinguistics of Arabic, the remarkable but thorny relationship of language and nationalism in the Arab world, and finally the direction of Arabic language policies and politics as evidenced in recent literature on education in Arab states as well as mass media across the Arab world, including the advent of satellite broadcasting. As to whether there is evidence of ethnolinguistic nationalism in the Arab world, I argue that there is not one, but two varieties of ethnolinguistic identification. They are separated under the conditions of a sociolinguistic phenomenon called *diglossia*, a term that literally means two tongues. The parallel languages are variously positioned as High versus Low, pure versus impure, cultured versus common. In the case of Arabic, I argue that Classical Arabic is positioned above dozens of common varieties that I call *demotic Arabic*. Correspondingly, citizens of Arab states incorporate parallel but politically incompatible varieties of ethnolinguistic identification, a condition that I call *dinationalism*.

Arabs and Muslims, Rules and Exceptions

The assumption of Muslim exceptionalism, including the notion that Islam singularly suppresses ethnolinguistic nationalism, is often supported with arguments and evidence drawn specifically from the Arab world. These arguments are then projected generally on states and societies that collectively account for all the other Muslims—four out of five—who are not Arabs. This book argues that this assumption can be falsified with evidence of ethnonationalism found across the Muslim world. None of the subsequent cases in this book that are studied in detail, however, are Arab cases. There are a number of reasons for this parsing.

When considering ethnolinguistic minority populations of Muslims that claim the right to rule a specific territory—a move that may be justified either by nationalism or Islamism—there are actually very few Arab cases that meet these criteria. Yes, there are Muslim minorities politically mobilized within Arab states—Berbers in Morocco, Kurds in Iraq—but an Arab minority in an Arab state would seem to be a logical impossibility. There is, of course, a most famous example of an Arab population fighting for self-rule: Palestinians. Yet this case is nothing if not problematic as the population of Palestine in the Occupied Territories is stateless. They are also distinct from the Arab minority within the state of Israel, who are not fighting for *territorial* self-determination within Israel proper (Jamal 2011). There are also Palestinians in Jordan, who are a minority in that state, but this raises the paradox of an Arab minority in an Arab state. It is this paradox that is at the heart of the matter of Arab nationalism and therefore the focus of this chapter. Finally, while historically and strategically a critical case, the literature on Palestinians is already vast, and expanding still. Original research and the production of primary sources in other cases, many studied only peripherally in regard to ethnonationalism, is arguably a more important contribution to this body of research.[4]

If the argument that Muslims, including Arabs, are exceptionally resistant to ethnic mobilization in pursuit of national self-determination, which in turn means a state with borders that are contiguous with the distribution of a unique people, what are we to make of *twenty-one* Arab states? Muslim exceptionalism anticipates such a fractionalized collection because a nation-state is antithetical to the Islamic conception of ummah.

Sensibly, the most common explanation for the relative abundance of Arab states is the shared legacy of Ottoman, French, and British imperialism: borders were approved in Istanbul, Paris, and London irrespective of demographic facts on the ground in the Sahara or Sahel, Maghreb or Hejaz. States were created by exogenous forces, and the so-called international (more properly interstate) system sustained these entities by recognizing their sovereignty, entering into treaties, forging military alliances, and establishing economic ties. Yet the modernist paradigm of ethnonational mobilization and modularity expects states to *create nations* even where none existed. In one formulation, pan-Arab nationalism, this would be a single Arab state, extending famously "from the Gulf to the Ocean," that is home to a single Arab nation. In a contrasting formulation (for the time being consider it *mono*-Arab nationalism), separate postcolonial Arab states would engender the growth of ethnonational identities loyal to their own flag, their own nation-state. In this case, the unique national languages and cultures of distinct peoples (Lebanese, Egyptian, etc.) would be promoted, protected, and re-created by the institutions of separate states. This disconnect begs the question, "who is an Arab?"

Arab Demographics

For the same reasons that defining *nation* is a thankless task, defining *Arab* is a job for Sisyphus. Who is or is not an *Arab*? Does *Arab* define a culture, an ethnicity, a nation, or a civilization? Does the term *Arab* qualify for all, some or none of these categories? Identifying an Arab *state*, at least, is a simpler affair, since there is a precise count of twenty-one voluntary states (and the proto-state Palestinian Territories) that are members of the League of Arab

States (hereafter shortened to the conventional Arab League). Each member of the league shares two things in common: (1) Islam is the faith of the majority and (2) Arabic is (one of) the official language(s) of the state.

From this observation it would not be unreasonable to suggest that an Arab *person*, therefore, is an Arabic-speaking Muslim. This is clearly problematic. If a Palestinian Christian speaks Arabic but is not a Muslim, is he then not an Arab? If a Berber Muslim in Algeria cannot speak Arabic, is she not an Arab? Thus, we are forced to ask, what exactly is meant by the term *Arabic*, whether ancient or modern, written or spoken? These issues surface time and again (and again and again) in statistics attempting to measure Arab populations. The CIA World Factbook, for example, often attaches tortured qualifications to the term *Arab*. In the case of Algeria, for example, it records that 99 percent of the population are hybridized "Arab-Berber," but adds "almost all Algerians are Berber in origin, not Arab; the minority who identify themselves as Berber live mostly in the mountainous region of Kabylie east of Algiers; the Berbers are also Muslim but identify with their Berber rather than Arab cultural heritage."[5]

This categorization would indicate *Arab* is at once an *ethnicity*, that is, a unique people distinct from another *ethnos* Berber, and a politically salient *identity*, and a *culture* with a distinguished pedigree. This is not helpful. An alternate source for aggregate ethnicity data is the *Demographic Yearbook* issued by UNESCO. The reference compiles census data on separate ethnic populations that are furnished by member countries: it is very detailed but entirely incomplete. Of all the members of the Arab League, only Yemen and the Occupied Palestinian Territories are represented.[6] A third and often overlooked (but eminently useful) collection of state-level statistics is available from Britannica World Data, a division of *Encyclopedia Britannica* that annually estimates statistics based on its own collections of government publications, as well as public and private reports gauging social and economic indicators for 214 countries.[7] Estimates for ethnic composition—defined as the "ethnic, racial, or linguistic composition" of a country's population—are both detailed and complete.[8] In contrast with the CIA estimate for Algeria, which fudges with 99 percent "Arab-Berber," the Britannica statisticians estimate the following: "Algerian Arab 59.1%; Berber 26.2%, of which Arabized Berber 3.0%; Bedouin Arab 14.5%; other 0.2%."[9] By compiling data from both sources, including current estimates of state populations and ethnic compositions, it appears that from twenty-one states in the Arab League, the

Table 4.1. The Arab World: Arab Populations of Arab League Members, 2006

Arab League member	State population[a]	Arab (%)[b]	Arab population
1. Egypt	78,887,007	91.6	72,260,498
2. Algeria	32,930,091	76.6	25,224,450
3. Saudi Arabia	27,019,731	88.1	23,804,383
4. Morocco	33,241,259	68.0	22,604,056
5. Yemen	21,456,188	92.8	19,911,342
6. Iraq	26,783,383	64.7	17,328,849
7. Syria	18,881,361	86.2	16,275,733
8. Sudan	41,236,378	39.0	16,082,187
9. Tunisia	10,175,014	98.2	9,991,864
10. Jordan	5,906,760	97.8	5,776,811
11. Libya	5,900,754	87.1	5,139,557
12. Palestine[c]	3,889,249	89.0	3,461,432
13. Lebanon	3,874,050	84.5	3,273,572
14. Mauritania	3,177,388	70.0	2,224,172
15. Kuwait	2,418,393	74.0	1,789,611
16. Oman	3,102,229	55.3	1,715,533
17. United Arab Emirates	2,602,713	48.1	1,251,905
18. Qatar	885,359	52.5	464,813
19. Bahrain	698,585	63.9	446,396
20. Somalia	8,863,338	2.2	194,993
21. Djibouti	486,530	11.0	53,518
22. Comoros	690,948	0.1	691
Total	333,106,708		249,276,367

Source: Adapted from the CIA World Factbook (2006) and Britannica World Data (2006).
[a]Population estimates from CIA World Factbook for July 2006.
[b]Ethnic composition estimates are from Britannica World Data for 2000.
[c]Ethnic composition estimate for Occupied Palestinian Territories is from CIA World Factbook for July 2006.

aggregate population of Arabs is just under 250 million. If, as already noted in Chapter 2, one in five people on the planet adheres to Islam, and the global Muslim population is 1.5 billion, this means the "Arab world" represents just 17 percent of the "Muslim world," or not quite one in six (see Table 4.1). In the example cited above, the categorization "Algeria Arab" indicates there are sufficiently delineated *species* of the *genus* Arab to require the qualifier "Algerian" and thereby distinguish this population from any other Arab population, such as "Sudanese" or "Saudi" Arab. It rejects the notion of a single Arab ethnicity while suggesting *acculturation* can "Arabize" an ethnolinguistic minority, the Berber. Because a Berber cannot change his ethnic phenotype, the qualifier is a linguistic tag: an "Arabized Berber" is a Berber who speaks Arabic. This begs the question, "what is Arabic?"

Arabic Linguistics and Sociolinguistics

Making more precise determinations of *how different* one language is from another language, or the relative levels of comprehension among speakers of different Arabics, is a challenge not yet met by linguistics. As for the difference between naturally spoken Arabics and "Modern" or "Standard" Arabic (this distinction is examined below in detail), Harvard linguist Wheeler M. Thackston Jr., tellingly titled "Professor of the Practice of Persian and other Near Eastern Languages," famously told a reporter for the *Christian Science Monitor* that, even for Arabs, Standard Arabic "resembles what they grow up speaking at home as much as Latin resembles English" (Farah 2002).

In academic language training departments, the marginalization of spoken Arabics is the rule (Salameh 2006a). However, while spoken Arabics remain at the margins of language training in higher education, the same cannot be said of linguistics. As an academic discipline, linguistics has produced no shortage of research on the structure and substance of many different spoken Arabic languages. While relatively little is known about pre-Islamic Arabic, the advent of Islam and the resulting fixity of fourteen centuries means *written* Arabic has an exceptionally rich, well-documented heritage and a clear trajectory from the seventh century until today. But there is also a large and growing body of research on many varieties of organic *spoken* Arabic vernaculars. Most of this research is possible only through extensive fieldwork, a methodology exemplified by linguists such as Clive Holes (2004, 2001, 1990, 1987, 1984), a renowned specialist in Gulf Arabic. Publications of this type include detailed works on the grammar and lexicons of Iraqi (Al-Khalesi 2006), Algerian (Bergman 2005), Gulf (Feghali 2004), Sudanese (Bergman 2002), and Palestinian Arabics (Mohammad 2000), to name but a few.

Languages, like people, are conventionally sorted according to ancestry and their membership in a particular family. Language classifications use a Linnaean taxonomy to identify the lineage and relations of distinct ethnolinguistic populations. The standard reference for these classifications is appropriately called *Ethnologue* (Lewis 2009). Now in its sixteenth edition, it identifies 108 language families from which all other living languages—the current figure of "known languages" is 6,912—are descended. Some of the families are very large, such as the 449 members of the Indo-European clan, or the staggering 1,514 of the Niger-Congo family, while others live in near isolation: the Basque family has but three surviving members. Each language is assigned a unique three-letter code in a system managed by the International Organization for Standardization (ISO), the Geneva-based body that determines global standards for everything from the distance between threads on sheet-metal screws to the coding of transmission signals for radio and television broadcasts. In the case of languages, the relevant body of standards is labeled ISO 639. This body is now in its third incarnation, ISO 639-3: the suffix indicates a system of three-letter coding rather than two letters as in ISO 639-2.

Arabic, like Hebrew, is a member of the Semitic branch of the Afro-Asiatic family. Unlike living Hebrew, which is now the unique mother tongue of some five million people, virtually all in the Jewish nation-state Israel, Arabic is fractured into thirty-five varieties dispersed across dozens of countries (see Table 4.2). All of the varieties are mother tongues, except one. The outlier, wonderfully, is Arabic, that is, *Standard Arabic*. The formal classification is explicit on this point: "Arabic, Standard: 246,000,000 second-language speakers of all Arabic varieties. Not a first language. Used for education, official purposes, written materials, and formal speeches. Classical Arabic is used for religion and ceremonial purposes, having archaic vocabulary. Modern Standard Arabic is a modernized variety of Classical Arabic. In most Arab countries only the well educated have adequate proficiency in Standard Arabic, while over 100,500,000 do not" (Lewis 2009). Thus, *if we apply linguistic criteria* to the current question "who is or is not an Arab?" we are forced to accept that an Arab is a native *speaker* of one of the 34 living *vernaculars* that are members of the linguistic branch Afro-Asiatic/Semitic/Central/South/Arabic.

It would be simpler to assume that the other thirty-four species are "dialects," a speech variety that may be "functionally intelligible to each other's speakers because of linguistic similarity" to one common language called Standard Arabic (Lewis 2009). This is not the case. While some Arabic varieties are, as dyads, more similar than others, especially those nearer geographically, the thirty-four living varieties of Arabic are often distinguished easily because many are *not* functionally intelligible. Consider the opinion of no less a figure than Edward Said (1935–2003). As a boy, he "grew up in a family

Table 4.2. The Arabic World: Distribution of Arabic Languages, 2009

Arabic languages— First language: Rank and classification	Primary state(s)	Speakers: Primary state	Speakers: Global
1. Egyptian Spoken	Egypt	44,406,000	46,321,000
2. Algerian Spoken	Algeria	21,097,000	21,097,000
3. Moroccan Spoken	Morocco	18,800,000	19,480,600
4. Sudanese Spoken[a]	Sudan	15,000,000	18,986,000
5. Sa'idi Spoken	Egypt (southern)	18,900,000	18,900,000
6. Mesopotamian Spoken	Iraq	11,500,000	15,100,000
7. North Levantine Spoken	Syria, Lebanon	8,800,000	14,309,537
8. Najdi Spoken	Saudi Arabia	8,000,000	9,863,520
9. Tunisian Spoken	Tunisia	9,000,000	9,247,800
10. Sanaani Spoken	Yemen	7,600,000	7,600,000
11. Ta'izzi-Adeni Spoken	Yemen	6,760,000	6,869,000
12. N. Mesopotamian Spoken	Iraq	5,400,000	6,300,000
13. South Levantine Spoken	Jordan, Palestine	3,500,000	6,145,000
14. Hijazi Spoken	Saudi Arabia	6,000,000	6,000,000
15. Libyan Spoken[b]	Libya	4,200,000	4,505,000
16. Hassaniyya[c]	Mauritania	2,475,000	2,787,625
17. Gulf Spoken	Iraq, Kuwait, Qatar	744,000	2,338,600
18. Eastern Egypt Bedawi Spoken[d]	Egypt	780,000	1,610,000
19. Chadian Spoken[e]	Chad	754,590	986,190
20. Omani Spoken	Oman	720,000	815,000
21. Hadrami Spoken	Yemen	300,000	410,000
22. Maltese	Malta	300,000	371,900
23. Baharna Spoken	Bahrain	300,000	310,000
24. Judeo-Moroccan[f]	Israel	250,000	258,925
25. Algerian Saharan Spoken	Algeria	110,000	110,000
26. Judeo-Iraqi[f]	Israel	100,000	100,100
27. Dhofari Spoken	Oman	70,000	70,000
28. Judeo-Yemeni[f]	Israel	50,000	51,000
29. Judeo-Tunisian[f]	Israel	45,000	45,000
30. Judeo-Tripolitanian[f]	Israel	30,000	35,000

(continued)

Table 4.2 (*continued*)

Arabic languages— *First language: Rank* *and classification*	*Primary state(s)*	*Speakers:* *Primary state*	*Speakers: Global*
31. Shihhi Spoken	UAE	5,000	27,000
32. Tajiki Spoken	Afghanistan	5,000	6,000
33. Cypriot Spoken	Cyprus	1,300	1,300
34. Uzbeki Spoken	Uzbekistan	700	700
Total speakers, Arabic languages—First language			221,058,797

Standard Arabic— *Second language:* *Classification*	*Proficient*	*Not proficient*	*Total*
35. Arabic, Standard	131,000,000	105,000,000	
Total Speakers, Standard Arabic—Second Language			246,000,000

Source: Adapted from Lewis (2009).
[a]Also known as Khartoum Arabic.
[b]Also known as Western Egyptian Bedawi Spoken.
[c]Also known as Hasanya, Hassani, Hassaniya.
[d]Also known as Levantine Bedawi Spoken.
[e]Also known as Shuwa Arabic.
[f]The living Judeo varieties of Arabic are spoken by remnants of Jewish émigrés to Israel originating from separate language communities long resident in Morocco, Iraq, Yemen, Tunisia, and Libya, respectively.

whose spoken language was an amalgam of what was common in Palestine, Lebanon and Syria," learned to speak Egyptian Arabic in Cairo, and also studied Standard Arabic as a subject: his actual language of instruction, at Victoria College, was English. Nonetheless, Said (2004) considered his own linguistic range significantly restricted: "If I were to try to understand an Algerian I would get nowhere, so different and varied are the colloquials once one gets away from the shores of the Eastern Mediterranean. The same would be true with an Iraqi, Moroccan or a deep Gulf dialect." Why is this the case? Like ancient Hebrew writings, Arabic texts maintained a remarkable consistency over the centuries as the classical language was protected from the vagaries of time and territory. Unlike liturgical Hebrew or liturgical Arabic, living spoken Arabic continued to evolve, naturally, along ethnic and regional lines. Thus, for a traveler on the road from Marrakesh to Muscat, asking for directions grows much more difficult with each passing mile as vernaculars vary.

Classical Arabic is essentially the language of the Quran, though not necessarily identical: the sacred text employs a number of specific stylizations and formulations that are distinct from nonliturgical texts. Moreover, the Islamic doctrine of *ijaz*, or divine inimitability, prohibits attempted imitation of the holy words of the holy book, as well as the *sirfa* principle, which stipulates that even exceptional persons who may successfully imitate the language invite the wrath of God. This language calls itself *fusha*, a term that "designates the ideas of purity, clarity, eloquence, chastity and freedom from speech impediments." As such, this term is much more than a classification: it is a normative label that reflects a number of "moral dimensions" (Suleiman 2004, 58). In practice (and, obviously, in English), this written and rationalized form of the language is called Modern Standard Arabic (MSA) or simply Standard Arabic (SA). Because there is no necessary translation of MSA or SA in High Arabic, fusha is actually the right term, but the use of either SA or Classical Arabic follows conventions and flows more easily in contemporary text. As for the unmodified word *Arabic*, this, depending on context, may either be shorthand for Classical Arabic or SA or refer to *all* Arabics. Arabic is classified by ISO 639-3 as a *macrolanguage*. In this case, each language is assigned a three-letter code—for example, Algerian Arabic is ARQ and Egyptian Arabic is ARZ—but the Arabics in toto are also assigned a generic code as the macrolanguage ARA.[10] Another good example of a macrolanguage is Chinese: while most varieties share the same writing system, different languages such as Cantonese, Shanghainese, and Taiwanese are not mutually intelligible.[11] In any case, whether considered fusha, Classical, MSA, or SA, this language—in both its written and spoken forms—must be acquired through years of formal education (see Table 4.3).

If Arabic is a macrolanguage, then it may be suggested that the dozens of other Arabic tongues are microlanguages. This is not only misleading and unhelpful, but silly. At least one in four Arabs is a native speaker of Egyptian Arabic. Moreover, there is nothing microscopic about Algerian Arabic (25.2 million) or Moroccan Arabic (22.6 million). Though the term *microlanguage* is not useful here, there is still a need to parse precisely what is meant by these more specific language labels. In the case of Morocco, we may say that Moroccan Arabic is a genetic descendant of the Arabic family and a living member of the macrolanguage Arabic. But as for the general classification of Arabic mother tongues across multiple states, there are a number of unequal and competing terms. In MSA, the term for non-SA spoken Arabic is *ammiyya* or "common" language.[12] In linguistics and sociolinguistics, there are a number

Table 4.3. Conventions of Classifying Arabic(s)

High Culture/High Language/High Arabic

Quranic	The language of the holy book of Islam that dates to seventh-century Arabia; it includes some elements that are exclusive to scripture.
Classical (CA)	From Quranic Arabic, the High Culture language of Arab civilization, especially as employed in texts from the seventh to thirteenth centuries during the Umayyad and Abbasid Caliphates. In Arabic the term is *fusha*, meaning *eloquent*; the term also applies to SA and/or MSA (below).
Standard (SA)	From CA, the written form of the language in both premodern and modern times.
Modern Standard (MSA)	The conventional term in English for the standardized High Arabic that is now taught in schools, employed in all formal contexts, and recognized by all Arab states as their official language; also an official language of the United Nations.
Educated Standard (ESA)	A living form of MSA used among educated elites across many Arab states that includes some idiomatic expressions and loaned words from other sources, as well as a simplified grammar; not static. Also known as Formal Standard Arabic.

Low Cultures/Low Languages/Low Arabic(s)

Demotic	The diverse and distinct mother tongues of Arab peoples (demos); these vernaculars are typically called *dialects* or *colloquial*. In MSA the term is *ammiyya*, meaning *common*.

---

of potentially appropriate terms, including dialect, colloquial, vernacular, and demotic. While *dialect* is often used in reference to ammiyya, it is imprecise and—for the reasons outlined in Chapter 3—applied more often as a social and political evaluation than a linguistic one. *Colloquial*, from the Latin word for "speaking" (*loquium*), describes quotidian conversation, neither formal nor informal but ordinary and pedestrian.

This is appropriate insofar as ammiyya Arabics are spoken but not written, yet this term is often interpreted in the same sense as *slang*, typically understood to describe the style of a word or phrase rather than an entire language.[13] *Vernacular*, from the Latin for "native" or "indigenous" (*vernaculus*), certainly *is* appropriate as all ammiyya are mother tongues learned organically by children from their parents and family. However, because *vernacular* can also describe spoken languages that are "characteristic of non-dominant groups or classes," this is politically problematic in the case of Arabic (Matthews 1997; see also Labov 1972). In all Arab states, *all* Arabs—dominant or nondominant—are native speakers of a particular vernacular Arabic. In certain contexts, one vernacular may be more dominant politically than another. In Jordan, for example, speakers of the native Bedouin or urbane Medani vernaculars rank higher than the Fallahi variety, which is associated particularly with Palestinian refugees ejected from their homes in 1948 and 1967 (Suleiman 2004). But *all* these vernaculars are considered impure and illegitimate in contrast with MSA, which is the vernacular of nobody, but is also essentially the sacred language of the Quran. In other words, there is no necessary stigma attached to particular ammiyya speakers because, in contrast to fusha, all ammiyya are stigmatized.

This leaves the term *demotic*, a term immediately recognizable for sharing the same classical Greek root as democracy, demos, meaning "the people." Linguists, however, more often associate the term *demotic* with Modern Greek. Before 1976, the official language of Greece was *Katharevousa* ("pure") Greek, a written from standardized in Athens following the (Russian-aided) ejection of the Ottoman Turks in 1828. Seeking to purge foreign elements from the language, this literary form drew heavily on the classical language to the exclusion of the vernacular(s). Like MSA, Katharevousa Greek existed only in the context of education, while the demos continued to speak their Demotic Greek. The two varieties, called High and Low forms respectively, came into conflict in the 1880s when a modernizing "bourgeois movement" fought for "spoken Greek in the name of economic progress, social reforms, education for all, and the assimilation of linguistic minorities" (Frangoudaki 2002, 101). Despite decades of sociolinguistic tension, Katharevousa remained the official language of Greece until 1976, when a recently established (1974) democratic regime elevated Demotic Greek with the imprimatur of the state. The national language of Greece is now considered a combination of these forms known as *Koini Neoelliniki* (Pan-Hellenic Demotic Greek) or, more simply,

Standard Greek. It is in this context that I adopt the term *demotic Arabic* to describe spoken Arabic languages in general. This is especially appropriate because Greek and Arabic share the rare experience of modern *diglossia*, that is, the stable, simultaneous, and parallel existence of High and Low language varieties separated by social status and political context.[14] What makes diglossia distinct from a language/dialect scenario, wherein the High form of the language is also the mother tongue of an economically, culturally, or politically dominant group, the High form of a diglossic language must be acquired "through education" (Matthews 1997) and is not necessarily a vernacular anywhere.

Arabic is the archetype of diglossia. However, the actual term was used first in the 1880s to address the Greek language conflict outlined above (Mackey 1993). Of course, this is not to say that diglossic communities did not exist previously. Before the state of Israel, and in precisely the same fashion as demotic Arabic and Quranic Arabic, Hebrew maintained "a traditional diglossia that had lasted some two thousand years, between Jewish vernaculars and the Holy Tongue" (Fishman 2002, 96). In specific regard to Arab peoples, the term was first applied (Huebner 1996) by the French Orientalist William Marçais (1872–1956). Nonetheless, and for many good reasons, the word *diglossia* is forever associated with Charles Albert Ferguson (1921–98). This is so not only because of his unprecedented work on diglossia in general (beginning with an eponymous article in 1959) but also for a career that shaped so many scholars and students of languages, linguistics, and especially Arabic. Eminent sociolinguist Joshua Fishman, who later developed diglossia conceptually to describe the relations of bilingual populations—a model he named societal multilingualism—is unequivocal: "there is no sociolinguist whose name and whose work mean more to me than Charles A. Ferguson" (Fishman 2002, 93). More specifically, it is safe to say that "no American has had a more profound impact on Arabic linguistics" (Belnap and Haeri 1997, 2).[15]

One of Ferguson's active prodigies is Niloofar Haeri, who earned a doctorate in linguistics from the University of Pennsylvania. Haeri's dissertation committee included Ferguson (also a University of Pennsylvania graduate) as one of her external advisers. This is illuminating because Haeri, now a professor of anthropology at Johns Hopkins University, is the author of one of the best studies of Arabic sociolinguistics published to date. Her monograph *Sacred Language, Ordinary People* (2003) is a fascinating and detailed study of language in Egypt. With exacting terminology, she observes that Egyptian Arabic "unquestionably defines an Egyptian identity and a national identity" yet is paradoxically trivialized by the state (2003, 37). She asks questions that are stunning in their simplicity: "Why isn't Egyptian Arabic the medium of education? . . . Why is citizenship in part defined in relation to a language that is no one's mother tongue? What does it mean to have a divine language as the official language of a state?" (2003, x). These are current questions so fundamental to the study of society and politics in the Arab world that it is unfathomable how they remain largely unasked (and unanswered) outside of sociolinguistics (Miller 2007). In political science especially, the silence is deafening. This is not to say that outside Anglophone academia many Egyptian and Arab writers do not engage such questions—they do, frequently and vociferously—but these authors "are marginalized inside Egypt and are not read outside it" (2003, xii). The reasons behind this marginalization stem directly from the cultural and political conundrum that is the role of language in Arab nationalism.

Arabic and Nationalism

Within the Arab world, the debate over the role of demotic versus what became MSA began in earnest in the nineteenth century. But first it must be asked why separate Arabic vernaculars had not developed into literate forms in the same fashion as separate Germanic and Romance languages had developed in Europe or Turkic languages had developed in Anatolia and beyond. On this point, there is much agreement, even among scholars who may otherwise find little in common: MSA, more precisely fusha, is sacred. Hence, the status of its contemporary form, SA, is supreme.

Yasir Suleiman, a native Palestinian linguist recently appointed as the "His Majesty Sultan Qaboos Bin Said Professor of Modern Arabic Studies" at Cambridge University, puts it this way: "The fact that the Qur'an, Islam's primary sacral text, was in Arabic acted as a centripetal force of internal cohesion on the linguistic front, unlike in Europe where the Latin Bible was the source of centrifugal vernacularization. Furthermore, whereas the Latin Bible, in spite of its antiquity and textual authority, was essentially a translation, the Qur'an is not. The fact that the Qur'an is seen as the word of God verbatim meant that it was (is) considered untranslatable" (2003, 35). Because Latin was the language of the Bible and of the Catholic Church, its *status* was unmatched until the advent of commercial printing and market demand for books written in a language many more people could understand, namely their own language. Yet this is not to say that Latin was ever considered divine. As discussed in Chapter 1, the Christian Bible is explicit on this point. It is the message that matters more than the medium. In many ways, for observant Arab Muslims past and present, the medium is inseparable from the message. While there is no debate on the exquisite sophistication and eloquence of MSA, its immutability and exclusivity in the public sphere is often considered a liability—a competitive disadvantage—in an age of industrialization, modernization, and globalization. Not surprisingly, Bernard Lewis shares this view: "unlike the peoples of Western Europe, who threw off the bonds of bad Latin and raised their vernaculars to the level of literary languages, the peoples of the Middle East are still hampered by the constraints of diglossy and of an increasingly archaic and artificial medium of communication" (Lewis 1998, 51).

Of course, in this usage, the "Middle East" could not include Turkey since the post-Ottoman peoples had also developed their own print languages. In this regard, that is, the institutional assembly of separate national languages out of vernacular raw material, there is little difference between the experience of the post-Ottoman peoples and post-Westphalia Europeans. Just as the liberation of Greece led to a debate over language and its role in forging a modern Greek nation-state, the contraction of the Ottoman Empire uncovered other regional cultures and languages, all destined to develop (or try to develop) their own national identities, including but in no way limited to the Armenians, Turks, and, yes, the Arabs (Göçek 2002).[16] Of course, before the twentieth century, the "Turks" included a great number of people who are now considered distinct nationalities. In sharp distinction to post-Ottoman Arabs, these disparate Turkic peoples ultimately developed standardized languages of their own. Unlike literate Arabs, who maintained a single sacred language across and above any and all vernaculars, other Ottoman Muslims had no such qualms about writing as they spoke. Hence, because they were "free from the constraints of sanctity, they evolved several different written languages. The most important of these were Ottoman, Azeri (used in Azerbaijan), Tatar, and the literary Turkish of Central Asia, variously known as Turki and Chaghatay." The alphabet, however, came from the Quran as all these newly literate languages "were written in the Arabic script" (Lewis 1998, 53–54).

As for the Arabs, the ideology of pan-Arabism formulated by a principal nationalist progenitor, Sati al-Husri (1879–1967), ultimately cemented the place of MSA in Arab states. When stating "every Arab-speaking people is an Arab people," Arabic for al-Husri simply meant MSA. This is ironic considering his explicit point about "Arabic-speaking," which would necessarily mean a demotic Arabic. In his view, naturally spoken Arabic languages were dismissed as "so-called nation-state dialects," and considered corruptions to be corrected (Suleiman 2003, 142). In spite of the obvious hurdle that few people could actually speak, read or write MSA, the language(s) of "Arab-speaking people" was "not living Arabic; it was just incorrect Arabic." Clearly, there was an immediate and obvious political need to stifle any and all challenges to MSA: "If the Egyptians, the Syrians, the Iraqis and the rest were to develop their vernaculars into national languages, as the Spaniards, the Italians and the rest had done in Europe, then all hope of a greater Arab unity would be finally lost" (Lewis 1998, 52). This is not to say, however, that the public use of distinct vernaculars has no political utility. In an analysis of speeches by Egypt's Nasser, Iraq's Saddam Hussein, and Libya's Muammar Qaddafi, Nathalie Mazraani, a Cambridge-trained Arabic linguist, observed that Classical Arabic was employed consistently when "constructing an abstract argument, recalling historical events, expanding new political ideas and axioms" but that vernacular Arabic proved useful when a leader explained the details of "his political program, his conversations with various leaders, or his personal experience" (Mazraani 1997, 189). This was illustrated vividly during the Arab Spring, when Tunisian president Zine al-Abidine Ben Ali spoke in Tunisian vernacular for the first time when broadcasting, on January 13, 2011, that he would not run for office after his term expired in 2014 (Amara 2011). He fled the country the following day.

Yet the selective use of vernacular Arabic by a head of state is a far cry from institutional state support. Moreover, the endorsement of MSA cuts across social and political cleavages, ironically uniting secular pan-Arab nationalists with all manner of mullahs. To separate Arab peoples by their many demotic languages would mean to separate the Arabs from their one divine language: "since it is not possible to achieve this separation without causing a rupture within Islam, the basis of the religious identity of the majority of Arabic-speakers, any attempt to replace the standard by the colloquial as the marker of a particular territorial nationalism is inevitably met with religious opposition" (Suleiman 2003, 10). This is not to say attempts were not made: there were many. Suleiman's *Arabic Language and National Identity* (2003), a detailed history of Arabic language politics, shows that proponents of language reform rejected MSA for two reasons: the language was seen either as an impediment to modernization or as an impediment to an ethnonational identity (or both). Early proposed solutions to the perceived predicament included scrapping Arabic in favor of some other language of education and commerce (usually English), updating MSA with more contemporary vocabulary and simplified grammar, or simply standardizing the vernacular.

At the extreme, MSA was seen to not only impede the development of a country and its people, but to degrade them. This was the view of Egyptian (and Coptic) writer Salama Musa (1887–1958). Because the orthodox language was "steeped in the desert ethos," he argued, this "was responsible for many of the uncivilized practices found in Egyptian society, including the so-called 'honor killings' of women for pre-marital sex." Moreover, the duality of fusha and ammiyya was viewed as a kind of cognitive pathology: "the existence of diglossia in Arabic is said to create a kind of linguistic schizophrenia, whereby Arabic speakers think in one medium (the colloquial) and encode their thoughts in another (the standard). The pursuit of ornate style in Arabic is said to encourage excellence in form at the expense of excellence in content" (Suleiman 2003, 43). In terms of artistic expression, another Egyptian Copt, poet Lewis Awad, argued MSA is "foreign to Egypt" and that this explains "the inability of the Egyptians to produce great poetry in the language" (Suleiman 2003, 79). As a leading advocate of writing in demotic Arabic, he puts himself in the company of both Mark Twain—in *The Adventures of Tom Sawyer* the words of his characters are transcribed from the vernacular, that is, "yellow" is "yaller" and "licorice" is "lickrish"—and the Quebecois playwright Michel Tremblay.[17] Nonetheless, the product of all this agitation is very small. The premier *status* of MSA is unmatched. While some language reforms are suggested perennially to aid education and spread literacy, these suggestions are "mostly ignored." Even though most people "rarely use it in everyday speech," this does not "undermine the symbolic status of the language for most Arabic-speakers" (Suleiman 2003, 10). MSA continues to function as the sole language of modern communication for public, political, and commercial affairs in the Arab Middle East.

Meanwhile, outside the Arab region, the role of MSA in Muslim-majority countries is easier to understand. It is not normally the official tongue of the state nor the national tongue (viz., the mother tongue) of the population. As such, MSA—or in this case more precisely Arabic—remains a liturgical language of little use in a non-Arab society, even if that society also adheres to Islam. Even instrumental attempts to unite disparate Muslims by promoting the language failed. Just as Israel adapted the sacred language of the Jews, Hebrew, to unite polyglot immigrants to Israel, Pakistan considered endorsing the sacred language of Muslims, Arabic, to unite the polyglot populations of what was then (pre-1971) East and West Pakistan. The idea was dropped when the government of Pakistan "realized the impracticability of *using* Arabic as an official or national language because nobody, not even the religious scholars, could actually use it" (Rahman 2002, 92–93). Correspondingly, Arabic is *not* an official language in any of the non-Arab countries where most Muslims live, including Indonesia (Bahasa Indonesia), Bangladesh (Bangla), Pakistan (Urdu), Turkey (Turkish), and Iran (Persian).[18] In fact, the only non-Arab-majority countries to endorse Arabic as an official language are Comoros and Israel.

Arabic and Education

The general subject of education in the Muslim world is of special interest when the content of Islamic religious instruction has long been suspected of breeding extremism (Coulson 2004). Inside the Arab world, most *states* are secular, so "public education" and "religious education" are not synonymous. Hence, all students study Arabic but in practice not all students study Islam. Outside the Arab world, where no Arabic is spoken outside mosques, all students of Islam are also students of Arabic. This kind of education is typically conducted at institutions distinct from the state school system. In the United States, for example, students enrolled at Catholic parochial schools receive instruction in subjects both secular and sacred (at one time including lessons in Latin), but these are necessarily private institutions, not public. Similarly, in Indonesia, devout or economically disadvantaged students (fees are lower than the alternatives) may study at a *pesantren*; in Pakistan and elsewhere at a *medressah*. In these cases, the principal element of the religious curriculum *is* the study of Quranic Arabic. Yet in these countries there is no competition between Arabic and any other language as a guarantor of social mobility. Even at a pesantren in Jakarta or a medressah in Karachi, the medium of education is either the state language (Bahasa Indonesia or Urdu, respectively) or the vernacular (Sindhi or Javanese, respectively). What is exceptionally interesting in the context of Arabs, Arabic and education is the perennial but one-sided competition between MSA, the official language of all Arab states, and the many varieties of demotic Arabic, that is, the actual languages of separate and distinct ethnolinguistic populations (see Table 4.4).

Table 4.4. Literacy in the Arab World: Adults/Youth (Ages 15–24), September 2006

Region	Adult literacy rate %			Adult illiterate population		
	Total	Male	Female	Total	Male	Female
World	82.2	87.2	77.2	780,655,129	279,969,621	500,685,508
Developed countries	98.9	99.2	98.7	9,062,165	3,310,751	5,751,414
Transitioning countries	99.4	99.7	99.2	1,340,358	326,115	1,014,243
Developing countries	77.0	83.6	70.2	770,252,606	276,332,754	493,919,852
Arab states	69.7	80.2	58.9	57,812,284	19,379,404	38,432,880

	Youth literacy rate %			Youth illiterate population		
	Total	Male	Female	Total	Male	Female
World	87.3	90.5	84.1	138,972,563	53,500,559	85,472,003
Developed countries	99.4	99.4	99.4	767,619	381,628	385,991
Transitioning countries	99.7	99.7	99.8	122,322	67,880	54,442
Developing countries	85.0	88.7	81.1	138,082,621	53,051,051	85,031,570
Arab states	84.7	90.2	79.2	9,426,079	3,112,741	6,313,337

Source: Adapted from UNESCO Institute for Statistics data.
Note: "Arab states" include Algeria, Bahrain, Egypt, Iraq, Jordan, Kuwait, Mauritania, Morocco, Oman, Palestinian Autonomous Territories, Qatar, Saudi Arabia, Sudan, Syria, and Tunisia. Some other members of the Arab League are excluded, either for nonparticipation (UAE, Lebanon, Libya, Yemen) or because they are not considered ethnically Arab by UNESCO, including Comoros, Djibouti, and Somalia. In the latter cases, Arabic is an official language, but usage is sparse at best.

Literacy in the Arab world means literacy in MSA and literacy in the Arab world is low. In a 2006 estimate for fifteen Arab states by the UNESCO Institute for Statistics, the adult literacy rate of 70 percent ranked well below the rates for developing countries, at 77 percent, and 82 percent for the world. Similarly, separate data for a youth demographic, ages fifteen through twenty-four, also fell last, just below the figure of 85 percent for developing countries and 87 percent for the world. In total, UNESCO estimates a population of *more than sixty-seven million illiterate Arabs.* Of this population, two out of three are women. Note that the figure of sixty-seven million *illiterate* Arabs is lower than the Ethnologue figure (cited earlier) of more than a hundred million Arabs who do not have "adequate proficiency" in the language. To account for this discrepancy, it is important to remember that MSA *must be acquired in both its written and spoken forms.* Hence, it is likely that the thirty-three million Arabs who fall between these categories may be able to read Arabic, but cannot communicate verbally in MSA.

It is often suggested that low rates of literacy rates in the Arab world are "directly related to the complexities of the standard Arabic language used in formal schooling and in non-formal education." Mohamed Maamouri, who earned a doctorate in linguistics from Cornell University, now directs Arabic projects at the Linguistic Data Consortium of the University of Pennsylvania, but spent much of his earlier career in Tunisia working on language policy in education. In 1998, his outlook for the future of Arabic in education was not hopeful: "What is the future of Arabic diglossia? If education of common Arabs continues in the same vein and with the same low quality results, a widening of the diglossic gap is a quite reasonable possibility. . . . The impact of this on the future of Arab education cannot be considered in optimistic terms" (Maamouri 1998, 6).

Maamouri's pessimism was supported in following years by the series of Arab Human Development Reports launched by the United Nations Development Program (UNDP). According to Amat Al Alim Alsoswa, UNDP regional director for Arab states, these reports are "Arab in inspiration, authorship, and ownership" (UNDP, Regional Bureau for Arab States 2006). The 2003 report, thematically subtitled "Building a Knowledge Society," notes high rates of illiteracy are reflected in low rates of publishing: Arabs account for 5 percent of the world's population but produce only 1.1 percent of the world's books (2006, 4). High rates of illiteracy are linked directly to the "severe crisis" of the Arabic language: "The most apparent aspect of this crisis is the growing neglect of the functional aspects of [Arabic] language use. Arabic language skills in everyday life have deteriorated and Arabic . . . has ceased to be a spoken language. It is only the language of reading and writing; the formal language of intellectuals and academics, often used to display knowledge in lectures. Classical Arabic is not the language of cordial, spontaneous expression, emotions, daily encounters, and ordinary communication" (UNDP, Regional Bureau for Arab States 2006, 7). As such, it is reasonable to suggest that literacy may be improved by teaching students to read in their own language, that is, a written form of demotic Arabic, rather than learning to read in an acquired, second language, MSA. This is not the case. For Arab language and education policy reformers like Maamouri, "Arabic diglossia is a definite aggravating factor in the low results of schooling and non-formal instruction and taking care of it, if at all possible, would greatly improve the quality of education in the region" (1998, 68). *In short, a standard impediment to literacy in the Arab world is MSA.* Remarkably, this factor is not addressed in any way, by any of the authors, of any Arab Human Development Report to date. In 2005, for example, a report thematically subtitled "Towards the Rise of Women in the Arab World" repeatedly points to illiteracy as one of the most aggravating factors blocking the rise of women in the Arab world, yet makes *no mention whatsoever* of the problems associated with diglossia and the difficulty of studying a language that is not used in "daily encounters and ordinary communication" (cited in UNDP, Regional Bureau for Arab States 2006).

In explaining this lacuna it is important to note that the Arab Human Development Reports are written and published in MSA. The elites who research and draft the reports are themselves heavily invested in a language that is paradoxically at the heart of many problems they identify across the Arab region. Yet this does not explain the omission of research, some of it published in Arab countries, that does address this issue head on (Haeri 2000). Just as early Israeli state builders were forced to pull Hebrew into the twentieth century, postcolonial Arab state builders sought to expand and extend MSA as the ideological language of choice in the era of pan-Arab nationalism. This challenge "was considered a task of monumental magnitude" and, more dauntingly, many dimensions, including "Arabization (*ta'riib*), grammatical and orthographical simplification (*tabsiit*), and lexical and syntactical modernization (*tadith*)" (Haeri 2000, 71).

These problems were addressed by separate language academies (modeled after the storied L'Académie française) in Egypt, Syria, Iraq, and elsewhere. As a result, some interstate differences in MSA have been institutionalized.

There are small linguistic variations, for example, between the schoolbooks of Algeria and Jordan. Much more prominently, however, it is the *content* of High Culture that often bears the mark of a particular regime: "so pervasive has been the influence of the state in creating its own self-perpetuating dynamic that, even in the field of High Culture, Arab intellectuals now speak about the Syrian novel, the Iraqi short story, the Egyptian theatre . . . and so on" (Suleiman 2003, 228). But these examples describe style rather than substance, the message rather than the medium, which remains fusha (Suleiman and Muhawi 2006). While one in four Arabs age fifteen and older is illiterate, and 40 percent of Arabs cannot proficiently communicate in their own official language, there is, of course, an active population of many millions of educated Arabs defined by their shared language of communication and shared print culture, namely MSA. The trouble for erstwhile Arab nation-states, however, is that this population is dispersed across a score of countries. Even after many decades of trying, MSA "unites, in effect, only the region's elites" (Braude 2005).

Arabic Media

Just as many more people can read MSA than actually speak the language, the use of MSA in public (i.e., state-sanctioned) media is much greater in print than it is in broadcasting. In Egypt, the only regular television program in MSA "is the news" (Haeri 2003, 3) and even the anchors often struggle with less-than-perfect fusha.[19] The ubiquitous sound of Arabic in Egypt—on the radio, on the stage, and in the streets—is the sound of its demotic Arabic, that is, the Egyptian language. It has dominated cinema and across the Arab world since the 1930s (Armbrust 2002). Despite competing projects in other states to produce entertainment in Classical Arabic, the efforts typically fall flat because "even the most hastily put together Egyptian *musalsal* (serial) is more fun to watch than the best classical-language dramas" (Said 2004). Hence, until very recently, Egypt was unchallenged as the media capital of the Arab world, though it is no longer correct to say it is the news capital of the Arab world. That mantle has passed primarily to the Gulf, to the private satellite broadcasters Al Arabiya (based in Dubai, launched 2003), Abu Dhabi TV (United Arab Emirates, 2000), and, above all, Al Jazeera (Qatar, 1996). Al Jazeera is "the most influential and most widely viewed" player in what Marc Lynch calls the "New Arab Public" (2006, 76). This is due in part to the innovation of opening "phone lines during live broadcasts, to let ordinary Arabs into the arguments for perhaps the first time in their history" (2006, 4). His research included "a set of 976 episodes of the five most important general interest talks shows appearing on Al Jazeera between January 1999 and June 2004" (2006, 76). When discussions on these programs include calls from listeners, the callers must speak in MSA and are chided for slipping into their demotic language.[20] The numbers of imperfect speakers are not small since many—more than 40 percent—of the people reached by the channel "do not fully speak or understand the standardized Arabic language . . . that is used in broadcast news" (2006, 76). In 2005, Riz Khan, a former BBC and CNN anchor writing an opinion piece for the *Wall Street Journal*, put his finger on the most glaring international weakness of Al Jazeera: "no one outside the Arab-speaking world understands it." In 2006, to reach not only those four out of five Muslims who are not Arab but the rest of the planet as well, Al Jazeera launched an English-language channel with Khan as their star anchor.

The phenomenon of what may be understood as a very new Arab "public sphere" has emerged as the subject of pathbreaking scholarship (Eickelman 2005; Rugh 2004). What is most remarkable, however, is that "the new Arab public is actually composed of multiple, overlapping publics that should be defined not territorially but by reference to a shared identity and a common set of political arguments and concerns" (Lynch 2006, 22). This shared identity is a pan-Arab identity, which is necessarily reinforced through the exclusive use of MSA. Al Jazeera and its private sector competitors are beaming this language to far-flung corners of the Arab world where it never had much purchase outside religious observances. A correspondent for the *Economist* (2005) reporting from Western Sahara, reported that MSA "has come alive as a real spoken tongue accessible not just to the educated few, but to everyone." As a result, Dale Eickelman argues not only that "newspapers [are] lagging behind television" but also that public sector "state television and radio have lost the battle for eyes and ears" in the Arab Middle East (2005, 37).

Yet this nonterritorial public sphere walks the same razor's edge that cuts across issues of Arab nationalism. This public is not a public of citizens, but a public of abstracted viewers watching and discussing issues above and beyond their own state. "For all its newfound prominence, the Arab public sphere remains almost completely detached from any formal political institution. The political significance of a *transnational* public sphere disconnected from any effective democratic institution has hardly begun to be theorized. . . . It is not clear who this media represents, which voices dominate, or how it can act. The public arguments and debates are disembodied from any grounded political activity, and cannot easily be translated into political outcomes" (Lynch 2006, 25). In regard to questions of nationalism, patriotism, and ethnolinguistic identification in the Arab world, this MSA public sphere accentuates the disillusionment of educated citizens who find themselves resident in erstwhile nation-states devoid of a mature civil society. The result, as Lynch argues, is "frustration" and a "sense of impotence." Just as the ideology of pan-Arab nationalism failed to erase the territorial borders and avaricious ambitions of separate Arab regimes, the advent of transnational pan-Arab media cannot be expected to unite a diverse population of distinct peoples with very different ideas about their identity, citizenship, and the legitimacy of their state.

Even Bernard Lewis, a respected historian but a contemporary commentator who compulsively lumps all Muslims—Arab and non-Arab—under a single banner, argues that the strength of the social bond forged by MSA should not be overestimated: "In principle, literary, including broadcast Arabic, is the same from Morocco to the frontiers of Iran. Naturally there are some differences of usage, but these are no greater than between the various members of the other two great communities of language: the English-speaking and the Spanish-speaking worlds. If present trends continue, it seems likely that the speakers of Arabic will follow the example set by these two—a community of language, culture, heritage, and in large measure, religion, but no common national identity" (1998, 55). Yet Lewis is misleading here. When he remarks on "some differences of usage" he is commenting on "minor" variations in spoken MSA and *not* the major differences apparent across the many separate species of demotic Arabic. The experience of English and Spanish speakers is *not* comparable: a native English speaker unable to comprehend another native English speaker is a rare exception, limited perhaps to a conversation between a resident of Kingston, Jamaica, and St. John's, Newfoundland.[21] A simultaneous conversation among residents of Sydney, Seattle, Chicago, Dublin, and Liverpool—*even if none of them had ever set foot in a classroom*—would be remarkable but comprehensible. But incomprehension between native speakers of different demotic Arabics is more rule than exception. A simultaneous conversation in the mother tongues of people from Rabat, Algiers, Cairo, Sana, and Tikrit is a nonstarter. While Lewis may be right that competent speakers of MSA will not develop a "common national identity," he is wrong to disregard even the possibility of developing ethnolinguistic identities in Morocco, Algeria, Egypt, Yemen, and Oman. In other words, the strength of MSA should not be overestimated, but the potential of demotic Arabics should not be underestimated.

A compelling argument for new strength in demotic Arabic is presented in a recent analysis of "Arab news" by Noha Mellor, a native Egyptian and former journalist (at Danish Broadcasting and the BBC World Service). She posits contemporary students engage not only the diglossia of MSA and demotic Arabic, but must also navigate two other language arenas: MSA as employed by journalists, which she details at length as a *separate* and particular language, and English. (She calls these sociolinguistic conditions triglossia and quadriglossia, respectively.) Yet in competition among the four, it is her view that demotic Arabic and English are the "living languages" of choice for a new generation of Arab youth (Mellor 2005, 109–10). At the risk of stating the obvious, it should be remembered here that Al Jazeera and its rivals are not the only satellite channels available in the Middle East: CNN, BBC, and no shortage of other English-language broadcasts far outnumber the options available in MSA. As for Mellor's contention that "newspaper Arabic" should be parsed from both MSA and demotic Arabic, at least one prominent Arabic linguist is very clearly in agreement. Clive Holes calls it "a separate stylistic genre" with "syntactic and phraseological innovations" that shows "far-reaching effects on the vocabulary, grammar, and phraseology of the Arabic used by educated Arabs in many other contexts, written or spoken" (2004, 314). Others have suggested this hybridized, more fluid variety of particularly spoken Classical Arabic should be given a label of its own as a supranational "Educated Standard Arabic" or ESA (2004, 361).

Arab Diglossia and Arab Dinationalism

It is a tantalizing thought experiment to imagine the condition of the contemporary Arab world if the peoples of the region had dispersed socially in the same manner as "Occidental" Europeans after Luther and Gutenberg, or the other "Orientals" following the dissolution of the Ottoman Empire. In this imagined scenario, each separate state would have based its sovereignty *and its borders* on the doctrine of national self-determination: a state is legitimate because it exists to protect and promote a nation, that is, a unique people demanding self-rule. Instead, there exists a conglomeration of autocratic states nominally sharing the same "pan-Arab" nationality and its language, MSA. It is this link of pan-Arab nationalism and an acquired language—a medium of literacy, High Culture, and social mobility—that is central to understanding the predicament of erstwhile Arab nation-states. The sanctity and corresponding status of Classical Arabic is the principal impediment to the elevation, reformation, and standardization of demotic Arabics. This, in turn, retards the growth of separate ethnolinguistic identities and stymies the emergence of distinct ethnonational communities that claim sovereignty over a titular and unique nation-state. Instead, these communities are citizens of ill-defined "Arab" states.

The above, of course, is a generalization. Detailing the particulars of each people and each state is the mandate of dedicated area experts. Yet the general demise of pan-Arab nationalism has spurred a number of authors to pen obituaries of a failed ideology, eulogies for the death of Nasser's dream, begging the question, what can, should, or will take its place? In 2003, political scientist Adeed Dawisha, a native of Iraq, described the trajectory of Arab nationalism "from triumph to despair," an evaluation shared that year by Iranian commentator Amir Taheri: "Pan-Arabism may not be quite dead as an ideology but is certainly agonizing." Journalist Robert Kaplan argues the execution of Saddam Hussein in 2007 is a sign that the "foolish secular Arab nationalism movement" has breathed its last. Some academics view this analysis as a hostile "demonization" of a "profoundly important and evolving political force" (Coury 2005), while others are opening champagne. Franck Salameh, writing in the first French issue of *Middle East Review of International Affairs* (2006b, 52), equates the origins of pan-Arabism with the Aryan ideals of Nazis in 1930s, "whose passions had impregnated Sati' Al-Housri, Michel Aflak and all their Arabist traveling companions."[22] This charge is echoed in the work of John Myhill, a sociolinguist at the University of Haifa, who explicitly links the MSA of pan-Arab nationalism with European fascism, citing many examples of forced linguistic assimilation in the modern histories of Germany, Italy, and (to a lesser degree) France (2006; see also Hutton 1999).

In the decades since the 1959 introduction of Ferguson's diglossia, the duality of MSA as a High Language and demotic Arabics as devalued Low Languages has been the focus of anthropological, sociological, and linguistic research, but generally not a topic of interest in political science. The grand exception to this rule is Ernest Gellner, and his specific argument, first suggested in 1964 and later developed at length, that High Culture in the Arab world means Islam. In this view, the perpetuity of a sacred language means the Arab world (or in Gellner's broad-brush application the entire Muslim world) is stuck with an immutable and effectively premodern society: "A Muslim lawyer-theologian, literate in written Arabic, or a medieval clerk with his Latin, is employable, and substitutable for another, throughout the region of his religion. Inside the religious zones, there are no significant obstacles to the freedom of trade in intellect: what later become 'national' boundaries, present no serious obstacles. If the clerk is competent in the written language, say Latin or classical Arabic, his vernacular of origin is of little interest" (1964, 161). The striking similarities between the High and Low Language of Ferguson's diglossia and the High and Low Cultures of Gellner's nationalism suggest a dialogue rather than a chance parallel evolution. Curiously, however, to my knowledge there is no single reference by Gellner to the work of Ferguson. The political sociologist John A. Hall confirms (2010) that Gellner is not now known to have cited Ferguson, but notes he would certainly have read the anthropologist Robert Redfield (1897–1958). It was Redfield, in the 1950s, who described a civilization as "an interaction of many little local cultures and a 'high culture,' a 'great tradition,' that is considered, developed, and eventually written down by thinkers and teachers" (Redfield 1962, 404; cited in Wolf 1967, 460). Moreover, Gellner "came from a world in which sociolinguistics was, so to speak, *de rigueur*. [Linguist Roman] Jakobsen had happily lived in Prague, and Gellner visited him (and also came to know Chomsky) when he was a visitor in Harvard in the early 1950s." It is therefore difficult to believe that he was unaware of Ferguson's diglossia, though Hall posits Gellner's model of High and Low Cultures in the development of nationalism was probably absorbed "from practice rather than from theory."[23]

Gellner, despite "a number of grand and unexamined assertions about Islam" (Haeri 2000, 79), nonetheless emphasizes the role of MSA—and its exclusive claim on High Culture in the state institutions of modern Arab states—as the principal agent smothering the development of ethnic nationalism in the Arab world. In this regard, he is in accord with the anthropologists, linguists and sociolinguists discussed in this chapter who detail the mechanisms by which demotic Arabics are socially marginalized and politically gelded. Diglossia in Arab states is exceptionally effective in halting the evolution of ethnolinguistic identities and ethnonational movements.

How then does this fit with the (one-time) sincerity of pan-Arab nationalism, the sustained preeminent status of MSA among both elites and non-elites across the Arab world, or the current ascension of the language in the transnational public sphere of satellite broadcasting? Why are demotic Arabics perpetually disdained publicly as impure, corrupt, vulgar, and illegitimate, even though privately they are the mother tongues of all Arabs in the region? If demotic Arabics are prevented from evolving as High Culture languages, and MSA remains an acquired language shared only by the well-educated minority of disparate states that are *not* defined by specific ethnicities or cultures, what is the *nationality* of an Arab citizen in an Arab state?

I propose here that ethnic Arab *citizens* of Arab states are *dinational*, a political condition stemming from *diglossia*.

I offer the term *dinational* to describe a population composed of persons who identify politically, internally, and simultaneously, with a pair of parallel communities. One identity is ethnic: local, organic, and tactile. The other identity is supraethnic: extraterritorial, synthetic, and abstract. A native of Marrakesh, for example, is raised in a distinct culture, with a distinct language (demotic Moroccan) and distinct social practices that easily distinguish him from natives of Alexandria or Amman. At the same time, a native of Marrakesh is also taught, in public schools, to read and write a second language, MSA. His mother tongue is not written or read. His own language is not in his textbooks and it affords no benefits of social mobility, but does afford the benefit of belonging to a distinct society. Doctrinally, his *state* is not quite a nation-state because Arab citizens of Morocco are members of the "Arab nation," conceptually one people, an imagined community linked by MSA and (with some Christian exceptions) Islam, but spread across a vast terrain. Nonetheless, as a member of the "Arab nation," he may identify with pan-Arab concerns and share some common historical or political beliefs with other members of the "Arab nation" who are nonetheless citizens of other Arab states. A citizen of Morocco may be *patriotic*, loyal to his own government or his country's Olympic teams, but cannot be an ethnolinguistic nationalist in the same vein as a Catalan or Basque because his ethnicity and first language are not linked to his nationality. He is at once divided linguistically, culturally, cognitively, and politically between Moroccan and Arab. This division is dinational.

The term *dinational* is not to be confused with the term *binational*. A binational state, such as Canada (Anglophone/Francophone) or Belgium (Flemish/Walloon), is a state that is home to a separate pair of distinct societies, most often (but not always) characterized as ethnolinguistic nations. In this case, the term *binational* describes both the population—composed of two national communities—but also describes the state, which represents both nations in public institutions. A state may be binational, or even multinational, but not dinational. The two parts of a citizen's dinational identity may be incorporated *simultaneously*. In contrast, the state anthem of binational Canada may be sung in either French *or* English, but not in French *and* English *at the same time*.

Doubters should raise the objection of Greece. Here is (or was) a diglossic population of Greeks who experienced the sociolinguistic reality of diglossia between *Katharevousa* and Demotic Greek, yet the state was (and is) a nation-state, a territory made sovereign by the express wishes of a unique people who were protected and reproduced by the institutions of a state of their own. What distinguishes Arab states from Greece is that no *one* Arab state can claim to be *a* nation-state when the "Arab nation" is divided among many individual states. Each Arab state is sovereign because it is recognized by other states, and also because the regimes in each maintain (more or less) a monopoly on the use of force, but no single Arab state can claim legitimacy resting on the doctrine of national self-determination. This, sensibly, is why the dream of pan-Arab nationalism was a single entity "from the Gulf to the Ocean."

A dinational individual identifies with both the shared culture of ethno-linguistic kin and the extended culture of a supraethnic collective. In Huntington's usage this collective is a civilization, the "highest cultural grouping of people and the broadest level of cultural identity people have short of that which distinguishes humans from other species." He explicitly lists the "Arab" civilization alongside the Western, Confucian, Japanese, Hindu, Slavic-Orthodox, Latin American, and (possibly) African civilizations. (Tellingly, and incorrectly, he follows Bernard Lewis by interchanging the term *Arab civilization* with the terms *Islamic civilization* and even *Arab Islamic civilization*.) Yet a civilization—however else defined—is not only supraethnic but also supranational: there may be any number of nation-states that are all members of the same civilization. Even if one accepts the existence of a single Arab civilization, this is not the same thing as a single Arab nation. Following the doctrine of national self-determination, a nation needs a state of its own and a state is legitimate because it represents its own nation. A civilization needs neither: in Huntington's usage "a civilization is a *cultural* entity" (Huntington 1993, 24). A strictly cultural entity does not necessarily mobilize for self-rule. Unlike a state, a cultural entity does not enter into treaties, build armies, issue passports, or require recognition from other cultural entities.

The possible political futures of Arab peoples and Arab states are illuminated by opening a window on the future of the Arabic language. In one of Ferguson's final papers, presented in 1990, he clairvoyantly anticipates the current political conundrum of MSA as a transnational, extraterritorial, supraethnic language community that cannot accommodate the public and civic expressions of specific demotic Arab peoples confined by very real borders in opaque Arab states:

> Arabic is undergoing standardization on a vast scale and in an unusual language situation. It is not just the fact of diglossia, but that it is a diglossia situation *without a center* that would be a natural place for the standardizing variety to emerge and spread. In most cases where a diglossia changes into a single standard-with-variation situation there is a center—whether cultural, economic, political, communicative, or a combination of these—that becomes the chief source of the standardizing variety. Another alternative, of course, is for the language eventually to split into several different standards, as happened with Latin and the Romance languages. A number of observers have claimed that a new supradialectical norm of educated spoken Arabic (ESA) is coming into existence, and other observers have documented unmistakable trends toward diverse regional standards. Now is the time to study these conflicting trends. (Ferguson 1997, 270–71)

Ferguson's challenge was accepted by a number of social sciences, including anthropology, sociology, and linguistics, yet political scientists have not only ignored the specific challenge of studying Arabic language politics, but also neglected the importance of comparative language politics in general.

Yet it should be noted that the challenge dovetails a debate over the question of *democratic* Muslim exceptionalism. On one side are authors who point to the peculiar politics of "Arab, Not Muslim, Exceptionalism" (Stepan and Robertson 2004, 146); on the other, "The Reality of Muslim Exceptionalism" thesis argues that the politics of not just Arabs, but *all* Islamic peoples, are essentially problematic (Lakoff 2004, 133–39). Yet both of these positions elide a fundamental point: nationalism, while not necessarily liberal, *is conducive to democracy by defining the demos*. It makes plain where to draw borders because the doctrine of national self-determination requires that the limits of the nation be coterminous with the state. Nationalism sets the parameters for who is or is not a citizen, who may or may not vote, and which culture will enjoy the benefits of official status, state support, and dedicated institutions. Again, a nation-state is sovereign because it represents and protects a unique people who claim the right of self-rule. Arab states maintain a shared

High Language and literate High Culture, but exclude demotic Arabics and ethnolinguistic identifications. Arab states are not yet nation-states. Most citizens of Arab states are purportedly members of an erstwhile "Arab nation," but this grants no particular legitimacy to the regimes and institutions of any single state in the Arab world. It is debatable whether Arab regimes can claim to represent a specific nation, for example, "the Syrian nation," and instead rely on "centralized and authoritarian states" to stay in power (Tamadonfar 2002). By logical extension, it is perhaps surprising, but not unreasonable, to suggest that because Arab states suppress ethnolinguistic nationalism they also suppress democracy.

The bankrupt leadership of many Arab states is often blamed for a political vacuum that invites Islamist ideology into the public sphere. Failing to respond effectively to a "wide range of social, economic and political problems in the Arab world" has "not only jeopardized the legitimacy of the current regimes, it [has] enabled the Islamists to offer an Islamic alternative" (Tamadonfar 2002). But it is not just the lack of public services that enables Islamists to fill the nonstate space of absent institutions. Rather it is the lack of a coherent national identity. As Daniel Brumberg argues, the "absence of a consensus over national identity, rather than any particular brand of Islamism, be it moderate, radical, illiberal, or modernist, is one of the primary roots of autocracy in the Arab world" (Brumberg 2005, 105). This begs the question, why is there no alternative presented by some political entrepreneur rallying people behind their own language, their own unique culture, and promoting instead a demotic Arabic ethnolinguistic nationalism? In the case of the largest Arab state, Haeri is provocative but compelling: "most Egyptians find speaking and writing in classical Arabic difficult, especially given the dire state of precollege education. The official language thus acts as an obstacle to their participation in the political realm. There is of course no suggestion that here that this is the only reason for the absence of democracy in Egypt. But the language situation makes a strong comment on the nature of politics in that country" (2003, 151). Myhill—courting hyperbole—goes much further, arguing that a continued determination to squash demotic Arabics is "dangerous," that the linguistic unity of Arabs is "artificial," and that the instability of the Middle East is itself linked to an intolerance of difference inherent in pan-Arab nationalism (Myhill 2006, 280).

Perhaps the most eloquent exposition of the political consequences of a language barrier is in the work of Canadian political theorist Will Kymlicka. His point of origin is Canada and his conceptual development can be traced to the multilingual politics of a binational federation. At first glance, there is little overlap between a political theorist of multiculturalism and the observations of an Arabic sociolinguist. Yet there is an uncanny correlation between Kymlicka's views on the relationship between language and democracy and Haeri's analysis of Egyptian politics: "Democratic politics is politics in the vernacular. The average citizen only feels comfortable debating political issues in their own tongue. As a general rule, it is only elites who have fluency with more than one language, and who have the continual opportunity to maintain and develop these language skills, and who feel comfortable debating political issues in another tongue within multilingual settings. . . . The more political debate is conducted in the vernacular, the more participatory it will be" (Kymlicka 2001, 213–14). The politics of Arab states may be described with many terms, but until the Arab Spring of 2011–12, *participatory* was not one of them; indeed, even after the wave of public protests and toppled regimes, the erstwhile revolution is very much a work in progress, unfinished (Lynch 2012; see also Brynen 2012). One of the reasons for this democratic dormancy may have been (or will continue to be) the exclusive endorsement by Arab states of Standard Arabic in an attempt to suppress the development of ethnic identifications and erstwhile ethnolinguistic mobilizations. In the stark view of Salameh, "Modern Standard Arabic (MSA) is the imperial tool of a partisan political enterprise, not an instrument of a spoken everyday language possessing vitality and malleability, let alone functional and authentic 'national' purpose" (2010, 1). As a result, Arab citizens of Arab states have existed in a kind of political purgatory, members of *neither* a civil *nor* an ethnic nation, and continue to avoid this and other "dichotomies of choice—such as between religious vs. secular, or national vs. country (*awmiyya* vs. *wataniyya*)—in forging their political-cultural identities" (Ibrahim 1998, 235). They are consigned to citizenship in states with no self-evident raison d'être and an erstwhile nationality that is shared with millions of other people they cannot understand. This is the state-sanctioned stasis of Arab dinationalism.

CHAPTER 5

Tongue Ties: The Kurds of Iraq

We are ready to be without bread, but we are not ready
to be without education.
—Massoud Barzani, Kurdish Democratic Party, 1991

Crossing through Habur Gate, Turkey's largest border crossing with Iraq, is confusing. The route is very clear, but after stepping *into* Iraq, one finds no visible *signs* of Iraq. The flag waving over the border features a bright yellow sun instead of the three green stars of the familiar flag of Iraq. And there is no sound of Arabic. This is the Kurdistan Region of Iraq or—according to a Kurdish public relations campaign promoting international investment— the "Other Iraq." This territory, about the size of Austria, composes nearly 20 percent of Iraq's land area. It is also home to about 20 percent of Iraq's population: the Kurds.

The origins of this Indo-European people are contentious. At one time or another—over the past four thousand years—Macedonians, Persians, Arabs, Turks, and the British have all occupied the Kurdish homeland. The earliest "literary masterpieces that made the Kurdish language a symbol of collective identity, a marker of the Kurdish people" appeared in the sixteenth century. In the twentieth century, the definitive origins of a distinctly Kurdish people were largely pursued by European academics, but in the twenty-first century "the matter has been devoted greater attention within the Kurdish nationalist discourse" (O'Shea 2006, 126).

The geopolitical history of the region, however, is less opaque. For most of the twentieth century and until the present, the Kurdish people have lived divided among four states: Turkey, Syria, Iraq, and Iran. In Turkey and Iran their language was outlawed; in Syria, they were stripped of their citizenship; in Iraq they were displaced by waves of Arab migrants and were attacked with poison gas as part of Saddam Hussein's Anfal ("spoils of war") campaign. It is no surprise, then, that these four states are conventionally and colloquially called by Kurds the "four wolves."[1] In Iraq, the Ba'ath Party was "especially hostile to the Kurds, to whom it denied regional autonomy, a share in economic development, and permission to teach the Kurdish language in Kurdish schools" (Lapidus 2002, 553). Peter Galbraith finds a source for such vitriol in "Ba'thist ideology, which defined Iraq as part of the greater Arab nation and ultimately led to genocide against the Kurdish minority" (Galbraith 2005, 279).

It is therefore curious that despite a common foe in Baghdad, in the wake of the First Gulf War the Kurds fought among themselves. Rival political parties, the Kurdish Democratic Party (KDP) and the Patriotic Union of Kurdistan (PUK), clashed over control of the de facto autonomous region created as a consequence of the Allies' no-fly zone in 1991. The conflict continued from 1994 to 1998, and ended only as a result of a deal brokered in Washington. It is important to recognize that this was more than a series of skirmishes— it was a war. Thus, the rebuilding of trust between the former combatants was no small feat. Indeed, the former regional prime minister for the PUK, Barham Salih, acknowledged in a 2006 interview that "the Kurdish region has lived through a domestic war that split it in two" but quickly added "now it's time to turn that page and unite" (Karouny 2006).

The Kurdish case is of particular interest to the questions posed by this book. In the first instance, the proposal that a shared Islamic identity bridges all ethnic divides and builds a sacred body politic is, when considering the modern history of Iraq, laughable. But a more sober question arises in regard to the nature of the territorial split between the KDP and the PUK. *The divide parallels an ethnolinguistic frontier between two language communities, namely the Sorani and Kurmanji varieties of Kurdish.* Sorani enjoys higher status and is the received medium of High Culture and education. Without regular contact, a Sorani speaker finds Kurmanji difficult to understand; a Kurmanji speaker, with regular exposure to the higher-status variety, finds communication less difficult (though still not easy). While the unified Kurdish population could be expected to rationalize the vernacular into a standard, official, and national language, the fact that blood was shed on a north/ south divide that also separated rival language communities begs the question, *was ethnolinguistic difference a factor in the Kurdish Civil War?* The short answer is no. Interviews with the ministers of culture and of education, among many other officials from both the KDP and the PUK, indicate language

Figure 5.1. Iraqi Kurdistan.

hostility is reserved primarily for Arabic, and that the modern language of the Other Iraq may be a slowly evolving mix of both Sorani and Kurmanji (see Figure 5.1).

Language in Iraqi Kurdistan

Even before 1932, when Iraq won its independence from Britain and came into being as a state recognized by the erstwhile League of Nations, the question of language policy had already erupted as a source of contention between the Arabs and the Kurds. The British took notice. During the Mandate years (1920–32), "the British attempted to institutionalize Kurdish equality in the new state." Even earlier, in 1919, "the British introduced Kurdish in place of Arabic for official matters and Persian for personal correspondence" (Blau 2006, 107). Thereafter, "the provisional 1921 Iraqi Constitution asserted that Iraq was comprised of two ethnic groups, Arabs and Kurds, and that the Kurdish and Arabic languages had equal status" (Natali 2001, 259). However, there was little force behind this assertion: "Some British officials at least encouraged bilingualism in Kurdistan and education in Kurdish, though that did not ensure the bureaucratic entrenchment of these cultural rights" (O'Leary and Salih 2005, 17).

Thus, in the years leading up to independence, Arabic was in no uncertain terms the High Culture, high status language of power in the country; however, the place of the Kurdish language paralleled the "Kurdish question," that is, how to accommodate a stateless nation in a de facto Arab state. In 1926, the Anglo-Iraq Treaty stipulated that Baghdad must enact a "Local Languages Law" to accommodate the rights of minority groups, including but not limited to the Kurds. The purported goal of the law was to "determine the boundaries of the area in which the Kurdish language would be spoken as the language of administration, the courts, and the elementary schools" (Bengio 2012, 16). However, foot-dragging was manifest: for five years the law was not even been drafted, let alone enacted (McDowall 2004, 172). When it was ratified in 1931, the actual text of the law betrayed "Iraq's determination to erode the substance." For administrative and teaching posts, positions were reserved not for Kurds but for nominal "Kurdish speakers," but in practice even this requirement was waived, especially for technical posts. As a result, positions that would sensibly be filled by a Kurd were filled by an Arab instead (McDowall 2004, 177). Even after independence, the British themselves became complicit in the practice of Arabization in Iraq. According to Gareth Stansfield, "The first round of 'Arabization' in Kirkuk commenced in the 1930s as the British sought to ensure that the labor force for the increasingly prosperous and important oil sector was predominantly Sunni Arab, rather than majority Kurdish" (Stansfield 2005, 216n13; see also McDowall 2004, chap. 8).

From that point forward, regarding language policy specifically, and "in spite of international commitments and constitutional recognition of Kurdish as an official language, the various Iraqi regimes have undertaken numerous linguacidal measures" (Hassanpour 1992, 146). In short, language planning in Iraq meant planning the consolidation and expansion of Arabic at the expense of all other minority languages. And so it was for most of the twentieth century: occasionally false promises to enhance the status and support of the Kurdish language were made and broken, yet Arabization was the de facto policy of Iraq as it slowly built the institutions of a developing country. For Kurdish leaders, this was an existential threat. Ironically, however, the implicit and explicit marginalization of the Kurdish language may have actually fueled the determination of the Kurds to sustain and protect their most essential component of their culture. Indeed, "language is such a potent symbol of nationality that the official prohibition of its use has often been the prime cause of its survival. This is especially true in the Kurdish case" (Hassanpour 1992, 147).

When given the opportunity, Kurds have persistently pushed for language rights: rare moments of language policy liberalization have been seized with zeal. Thus, in 1970, a "truce between the Iraqi government and the Kurds provided the opportunity for significant development of Kurdish language and literature in Iraq." Similarly, in 1992, following the de facto emancipation of the Kurds following the First Gulf War, "77 newspapers and magazines appeared, 38 in Hawler/Arbil, 25 in Sulaimaniya, 12 in Duhok and one in Kirkuk" (Hassanpour 1992, 146). In other words, the Kurdish print culture exploded, reinvigorating a publishing heritage that saw more than two thousand Kurdish-language books printed in Iraq between 1920 and 1985 (Hassanpour 1992, 189–91). Moreover, and also in 1992, an online Kurdish Academy of Language began as a self-described "Open Global Kurdish Linguistic Network," with the standardization of Kurdish script(s) a principal goal.[2]

Following the regime change in Baghdad at the end of the Second Gulf War in 2003, the Transitional Administrative Law (TAL) of 2004 picked up where the British left off more than eight decades earlier by naming both Arabic and Kurdish as official languages of the federation. (The smaller language communities—including but not limited to Turkomen, Assyrian, and Armenian—also won formal recognition, though not as federal languages.) The language of Article 53 specifically named "administrative, cultural and political rights." In Brendan O'Leary's view, it was correct that these rights should be interpreted very broadly; the TAL permitted "national minorities self-government in their own languages, schools, and religious affairs, and access to public administration in their own languages, where their numbers mandate it" (O'Leary 2005, 49). Thereafter, on October 15, 2005, a successful referendum enshrined all of these rights in the new constitution in Article 4: "The Arabic language and Kurdish language are the two official languages of Iraq. The right of Iraqis to educate their children in their mother tongue, such as Turkmen, Syriac and Armenian, in government educational institutions in accordance with educational guidelines, or in any other language in private educational institutions, is guaranteed." Nonetheless, officials from both leading Kurdish parties complain that communication at the state level is invariably in Arabic. This is explained in part by the fact that very few Arabs in Iraq can speak or understand Kurdish. Another reason, offered by the

Kurdistan Regional Government minister of education (KDP), Sami Shorish, is instrumental marginalization: "It's clear. Baghdad itself is an Arabic government; everything [is in] Arabic and they don't want us to have links with the world."[3]

In the twenty-first century, the most important fact to consider when appraising the development and status of language communities in Iraqi Kurdistan is that there are *three* principal *language communities* in play. Arabic is but one. The other two are both varieties of Kurdish: Sorani and Kurmanji. According to sociolinguists, particularly those who compile the standard reference Ethnologue, Sorani and Kurmanji are distinct languages. However, as discussed in Chapter 3 at length, this appraisal itself is a statement about the culture and politics of identity in the region. The question of whether Sorani and Kurmanji are dialects of the same language versus completely separate languages is to be answered not by linguists, but rather by artists and writers, bureaucrats and socialites, and—most pointedly—the Kurdish nation in toto.

At the risk of oversimplification, *observers* of Kurdish culture tend to argue the two varieties are distinct languages with many dialectical distinctions, while Kurds *themselves* tend to argue there is but one language, with only a few dialectical distinctions. Mahir Aziz, at the University of Sulaimaniya, is emphatic on this point: "Contrary to much of what has been written about the language(s) of the Kurds, one thing is clear from the start. In Iraqi Kurdistan there is *one* Kurdish language—not multiple languages as many Western observers erroneously believe. What's more, there are only two dialects" (Aziz 2011, 49–50). Similarly, Fatah Zakhoy, the KRG minister of culture (PUK) in Sulaimaniya, for example, insists Sorani and Kurmanji are "two dialects, not two big languages."[4] Yet Ethnologue argues there are actually four Kurdish languages with dozens of dialects. How can this be? The short answer is that Ethnologue's classification of four separate Kurdish language tends to overshadow a much more helpful description. Like Arabic, Kurdish is classified by sociolinguists as a single *macrolanguage*, that is, an amalgamation of *many* different varieties (languages/dialects) that all share common roots and characteristics. Thus, it is possible to argue that those who speculate there is one Kurdish language and those who posit there are many Kurdish languages are *both* right (see Table 5.1).

One point that is not in dispute is that there are but two principal kinds of Kurdish, Sorani and Kurmanji. The two varieties are distinguished by differences in region, mutual intelligibility, names, script, and status. The

Table 5.1. The Kurdish Macrolanguage

Linguistic classification	Alternate names	Dialects	Countries
Kurdish, Northern	Kurmanji, Kermancî, Kirmancî, Kurdi, Kurdî, Kurmancî In Iraq: Badinani, Bahdini, Behdini, Kirmanciya Jori, Kurmanji	Boti (Botani), Marashi, Ashiti, Bayezidi, Hekari, Shemdinani (differences among dialects, but all use the same written form)	Iraq, Syria, Turkey
Kurdish, Central	Kurdi, Sorani	Hewleri (Arbili), Xoshnaw, Pizhdar, Suleimani (Silemani), Warmawa, Rewandiz, Bingird, Mukri, Kerkuki, Garmiyani	Iran, Iraq
Kurdish, Southern	Kirmashani	Kolyai, Kalhori, Garrusi (Bijari) Sanjabi, Malekshahi (Maleksh ay), Bayray, Kordali, Feyli, Luri.	Iran, Iraq
Laki	N/A	N/A	Iran, Iraq

Source: Lewis (2009).

regional dividing line runs east to west and bisects Iraqi Kurdistan. Perhaps an even more important dividing line is the Turkish-Iraqi border: the Kurds in Turkey are predominantly Kurmanji speakers. Thus, in total, there are far more Kurmanji speakers than Sorani, yet the latter enjoys far higher status (more on this below). Regarding mutual intelligibility, the historian David McDowall argues, "Grammatically, they differ from each other as much as English and German, although vocabulary differences are probably of the same order as those between Dutch and German. In both cases these two languages represent a standardized version of a multiplicity of local dialects, which still varied almost valley by valley a century ago" (McDowall 2004, 9–10). This is not to say speakers of Kurmanji and Sorani cannot communicate. According to linguist Amir Hassanpour, they can, "with difficulty, in normal conversational situations." However, unless the separate speakers have had "considerable previous contact, the speakers of Kurmanji and

Table 5.2. The Principal Kurdish Languages in Iraq, 2004

Conventional classification	Alternate names	Region	Total speakers	Speakers in Iraq
Kurmanji	Badinani	Northern Iraqi Kurdistan	9,320,240	2,800,000
Sorani	Kurdi	Southern Iraqi Kurdistan	3,712,000	462,000
Totals			13,032,240	3,262,000

Source: Lewis (2009).

Sorani are not able to communicate effectively *in all contexts*" (Hassanpour 1992, 24).

As to the question of relative size of the Kurmanji and Sorani communities, census data from Iraq are both dated and dubious. The last countrywide census was in 1987. Another census ten years later excluded the Kurdish region. In 2010, plans to conduct a complete census were derailed by sectarian strife, delaying the plan indefinitely. Moreover, while estimates are possible, "governments seek to play down the numbers, [while] Kurdish nationalists tend to inflate them" (Bengio 2012, 3). Nonetheless, the best efforts of the U.S. Central Intelligence Agency put the population of Iraq (as of July 2012) at just over 31 million, of whom 15 to 20 percent are Kurds.[5] This would put the number of Kurds at somewhere between 4.7 and 6.2 million. Currently (2013), the Kurdistan Regional Government offers an estimate of 5.2 million,[6] up from 3.8 million in 2006.[7] This is for the entire population of Iraqi Kurdistan, including the numerous minority populations, including Arabs, Armenians, Assyrians, Chaldeans, Turkmen, and Yezidis. As for the number of ethnic *Kurds* in the region, another figure is helpful insofar as the size of each language community can be gauged. According to a 2004 estimate by Ethnologue, the population of Kurmanji and Sorani speakers totaled 3.3 million. What is most striking, however, is the *ratio* between the sizes of each speech community: Kurmanji speakers purportedly outnumber Sorani speakers by six to one. This ratio is *not* conventional wisdom in Iraqi Kurdistan. In interviews with a range of government officials (2005), a typical estimate was one-third Kurmanji and two-thirds Sorani. The question itself is considered more than a little curious. The above-mentioned minister, Sami Shorish, assured me the figure was unavailable because "we didn't look for it" (see Table 5.2).[8]

Why should Kurdish officials and sociolinguists offer such starkly different views of the respective size of each language community? An answer may be the relative status of each language. In no uncertain terms, Sorani status is dominant.

For the sake of argument, let us assume the two communities are the same size. Even if this were the case, this still does not answer the question of why Sorani is the dominant language, the High Culture language, of Iraqi Kurdistan. Why should it be the case that Sorani has higher status, and is employed as the principal written language? Joyce Blau argues it is a legacy of British imperialism, and the role of British officers during the Mandate period. Specifically, "the development of the Kurdish press in the [southern] town of Sulaimaniya—by [Briton] Major E.B. Soane—facilitated the spread of Sorani Kurdish, which writers and poets renewed and perfected" (Blau 2006, 107). Thereafter, the new regime in Baghdad "required Kurdish schools to teach only one language, and thus the language of Sulaimaniya was chosen and imposed on schools in all Kurdish provinces, including Bahdinan, where the dominant language [Kurmanji] belongs to the northern group of Kurdish dialect."[9] As a result, she argues, the children in those schools "felt that they were learning a foreign language, and left school." As a result, those schools—and many others throughout the region—ultimately taught in Arabic through the 1990s (Blau 2006, 107).

The winnowing away of Arabic deserves special mention here. In the years since 1991, much has been made of the decline of Arabic in Iraqi Kurdistan, supported typically by anecdotal observations that young people no longer understand—nor care about learning—that language. Yet there is tacit recognition of this phenomenon at the highest levels of government. In the words of Shawnm Abdulkadir Muheadin, the KRG minister of education (PUK) in Sulaimaniya, Arabic "belongs in Egypt, maybe, but not here."[10] This speaks to not only matters of education policy, but also social perceptions. For younger Kurds (more than half the population is under twenty-five) they have no memory of Arabic instruction. For older Kurds, those who can speak Arabic rarely do so, "as they associated the language with the overall repression they had suffered" (McKiernan 2006, 348). Nonetheless, there is sensitivity to the regional utility of maintaining some Arabic in Kurdish classrooms, even if it is limited to just one textbook and taught solely as a subject, and never used as a language of instruction. Moreover, there is some regional political utility as well. In an Arabic-language interview with Al Jazeera in 2012, KRG president Massoud Barzani is quick to point out that "the Arabic language is studied here in the region. That is a continuation of the policies of the last thirty years. . . . Arabic *is* being studied here in schools in Kurdistan" (Al Jazeera 2012).

There is, however, an important phenomenon that will inevitably widen the divide between *readers* of Kurdish and readers of Arabic, namely the switch from the Arabic to the Latin script. Until very recently, Kurdish in Iraq was written solely in the Arabic *script* using a variation of the Persian *alphabet*, a sensible adaptation since Kurdish and Persian are both Indo-European languages with much more in common than either in relation to Arabic. The challenge of using the Arabic script, which evolved for use with a Semitic language, to write an Indo-European language, has long been apparent to language planners and politicians. The problem, in simple terms, is that the Arabic-Persian alphabet "is inadequate for transcribing Kurdish." From the earliest years of an independent Iraq, this prompted Kurdish political and cultural elites to call for the adoption of the Latin script. However, they "came up against social-political opposition: they were citizens of Iraq, an Arab state, where the knowledge and use of Arabic as well as a shared intellectual life were imposed on them." Thus, from the 1930s onward, the government of Iraq "intensified its opposition to all attempts to Latinize the Kurdish alphabet" (Blau 2006, 107).

Without the restrictions of a chauvinist Arab regime, the drive to the Romanization of Kurdish was resurrected. There are three purported advantages to the adoption of the Kurdish-Latin alphabet, known as *Hawar*. The first is linguistic: the sounds of Kurdish are more amenable to an Indo-European alphabet. (To clarify, imagine being a French speaker who was suddenly stripped of any letters with diacritical marks: how would one write *détente* without *l'accent aigu*?) The second is utilitarian: knowing how to read and write a Latin-script language makes it much easier to learn how to read and write in English, the language that has displaced Arabic as the preferred second language in the region. The third is social, cultural, and political. The Hawar script is *already* in use in Turkey (home to many more million Kurds than Iraq) and in Syria: sharing the same standard is a means of tightening bonds among the Kurdish diaspora (Blau 2006; see also Collin 2009, 253). As of 2006, there were magazines and journals that printed articles in both Hawar and the Arabic script. Yet the drive is not just a phenomenon of print commerce (Anderson 1983). There are institutional initiatives of the Kurdish government. The KRG had already developed a plan to "implement the writing of Kurdish in Latin as a unified script," a project that started in 2008 for students in primary schools (Aziz 2011, 53).

A much greater challenge for language and corpus planners, however, is the question of how to merge the two languages/dialects of Sorani and Kurmanji. The short answer is to adopt the same solution adopted by multilingual nation-states since Westphalia: standardization and institutionalization. In the case of Sorani and Kurmanji, this is precisely the view of some Kurdish administrators. For example, Abdul-Aziz Tayyib, the KRG minister of education (KDP) is unequivocal: "I think that the Badinani [Kurmanji] children should know Sorani; also, the Sorani should know Badinani. . . . Our intention for the future [is to] mix both dialects. It is a successful project, a successful experience. It is for the future. All Kurds must understand each other."[11] Tayyib's former counterpart in the PUK administration in Sulaimaniya, KRG minister of education (PUK) Shawnm Abdulkadir Muheadin, concurs. Neither does she anticipate any problems in the classroom as the varieties are melded into a new standard as students' attitude toward this question is "relaxed."[12] This process, however, will be neither simple nor quick. Fatah Zakhoy, the KRG minister of culture (PUK) in Sulaimaniya, estimates the initiative will require some ten or twenty years.[13]

Yet all of this ambition to merge the languages/dialects of Sorani and Kurmanji into a new national standard emerged *after* the Second Gulf War, and *after* the Kurdish Civil War. Is there nothing to be gleaned from the fact that the warring communities were separated not only by territory (north/south) but also by an ethnolinguistic division, an identity frontier? In Iraq, Kurds are entirely dismissive of this question. Sami Shorish, for example, is adamant: "There is not one Sorani who thinks that there is an identity problem with the Kurmanjis and no single Kurmanji will say that he thinks that there is an identity problem. No one thinks about it at all." He notes also that there is a facile argument to be made that there is solid evidence of a political division based on language. "They say '[PUK leader] Jalal Talabani is Sorani, [KDP leader] Massoud Barzani is Badinani [Kurmanji speaking]' so it must be true. No, this is not based on the linguistic differences. The political differences had social links and cultural roots."[14] This view is paralleled precisely by Shorish's former counterpart in the PUK, Fatah Zakhoy. The feud could be attributed, he says, to "different interests, not to different dialects."[15]

In short, the existence of separate languages/dialects, Sorani and Kurmanji, is considered a question of policy and planning, not ethnolinguistic rivalry. Stafford Clarry, a humanitarian affairs advisor to the Kurdistan Regional Government, works as a liaison between the KRG and foreign donors. In his view, the distance between the two language communities is nothing more than a "rivalry" on par with divided loyalties to "the Washington Redskins and the Dallas Cowboys."[16] Yet this is not to say language policy and planning is in any way unimportant. The legacy of Arabization and the existential threat of Arab institutions left deep scars in the Kurdish psyche. Language remains a critical force for pan-Kurdish unification, and Kurds remain "deeply engaged on the issue of language and insist that Kurdish and Arabic be fully equal official languages. . . . Kurds see the equality of their language as a proxy for the equality of Kurds and Arabs in the new Iraq" (Galbraith 2005, 279). Falah Mustafa Bakir, the head of the KRG's Department of Foreign Relations, echoes this point: "The issue of language is very important definitely for everybody. For example, whenever I am anywhere, [people ask] if you're writing in your own language, and I say Kurdish. Is it Arabic? And I say, no, it's Kurdish. There is a feeling inside you that causes you to say no. A strong no, because of all what happened to us and [the Kurdish] people were struggling for their national rights; they see their language as the most important element to secure them, to tell the other people that they are not weak, for example. That we are not Arabs. And we feel proud to have another language that is separate from them."[17] It is this sentiment, that Kurds in some ways define their language and themselves in opposition to the Arabs, that indicates a broader rejection of Iraq itself. In a 2007 survey, university students were asked, "How closely attached or loyal do you feel to Iraq as a whole?" The proportion of respondents who answered "not very close" or "not at all close" topped 80 percent (Aziz 2011, 125).

Islam in Iraqi Kurdistan

If language and ethnolinguistic identity are of paramount importance to the people and politicians of Kurdistan in Iraq, what then of Islam? There remains the perennial question, is not a shared faith at least equal to if not greater than a shared language as a source of social unity and political harmony? In the case of the Kurds, the short answer is no. Yet it is important to recognize when entering a discussion about Kurds and Islam, a number of questions persistently emerge. First, what is the difference between Arab Sunnis and Kurdish Sunnis? Second, are Kurds more or less secular than their Muslim neighbors? And finally, what is the risk of Islamic fundamentalism among the Kurdish population? We consider these questions in turn.

To begin, it is significant to note that both Sunni Arabs and Sunni Kurds share more in common than, for example, Kurdish Sunnis and Shia Arabs. Yet there are old and distinct differences between Kurds in Iraq with their Sunni brethren in surrounding territories, notably the point that "most Turks and the Arabs of Mesopotamia accepted the official Hanafi school of juris-prudence following the establishment of Ottoman authority in the sixteenth century; the Kurds remained adherents of the Shaf'i school which had pre-dominated in the region in preceding centuries" (McDowall 2004, 11). Other traits distinctive from Arab Sunnis in the region include the strength of Sufi brotherhoods and a more general tolerance of those practices generally as-sociated with folk Islam (or what Gellner called the Islamic Low Culture). That being said, the importance of Sufism specifically is more as a religious legacy rather than contemporary social leverage against orthodoxy, as cur-rently "most Kurds are not nowadays affiliated to Sufi networks, and are thor-oughly urban rather than rural" (Leezenberg 2006, 203).

Does this mean that Kurds are less observant or less pious Muslims than their southern Arab neighbors? The corollary to this question is whether Kurds are more or less likely to harbor elements of fundamentalist Islam. The an-swer is not a little political. Secular Kurdish nationalists tend to marginalize discussion of Islamism in the region (Leezenberg 2006, 203), while foreign observers—particularly neoconservative policy makers in the United States—are sometimes alarmist. Michael Rubin (2001), for example, wrote a few months after the September 11 attacks that Iraqi Kurdistan was a ripe target for Islamists. Yet according to Fatah Zakhoy, the KRG minister of culture (PUK) in Sulaimaniya, there may be "some" Islamists in active in southeast Kurdistan, "but I think that they cannot be a great force in Kurdistan in the future. Kurdistan will never be like Pakistan or Afghanistan."[18]

In the years since the Second Gulf War, Islamic fundamentalists have been active *in* Iraqi Kurdistan though not necessarily *of* Iraqi Kurdistan. That is to say when Islamist elements have been active, they have either been foreign (Arab) fighters or, when the Islamists were actually Kurdish, they represented a very small slice of Kurdish society. An oft-cited example is Ansar al-Islam (hereafter Ansar) and its antecedent, Jund al-Islam. (Jund al-Islam was itself formed from two other smaller groups, the short-lived Second Soran Unit and Tahwid Islamic Front.) As early as 2001, Jund al-Islam mobilized in the south-east, near the Iranian border, with between four hundred and six hundred fighters (Rubin 2001). However, even Rubin acknowledged that Kurdish fighters accounted for fewer than 10 percent of the total force, the remainder of which was Arab. However, by 2002, Jund al-Islam morphed into a new organization: Ansar al-Islam. According to the journalist Kevin McKiernan, this was a different stripe of beast altogether. The most striking difference was that Ansar was a "home grown organization, a radical offshoot of a legal Kurdish group, the Islamic Movement in Kurdistan (IMK)." Moreover, the group (by the end of 2002) had mobilized approximately seven hundred fighters, of whom "90 percent or more were Kurds . . . most had never been out of the country" (McKiernan 2006, 213). Note, however, that McKiernan's claim is in dispute. David Romano, for example, cites a PUK agent who actually lived in the area under Ansar control. According to this source, Ansar members included "Palestinians, Iranians, Jordanians, Afghans and Arabs from various countries," most of whom "held Iranian passports" (Romano 2007).

In any case, what were these fundamentalists, whether Kurdish of foreign, actually doing, actually planning and executing from their redoubt in the southeast? By the end of 2002, their most frequent activity was clashing with the Kurdish government, specifically the PUK administration based in Sulaimaniya. By the following year, however, the question of guerrilla activity was moot. Shortly before the start of the Second Gulf War in 2003, Ansar was effectively neutralized by a joint military operation conducted by PUK forces and U.S. special forces. However, this is not to say that Ansar vanished, because it then it morphed from a guerrilla organization to a terrorist group, the shadowy Ansar al-Sunnah.[19] It was this organization that took responsibility for the suicide bomb attacks in Erbil in 2004 that targeted Eid celebrations convened by the region's two main parties, the PUK and the KDP. The attacks killed more than a hundred and wounded twice as many. This devastating attack was widely condemned, both outside and (in particular) inside Iraqi Kurdistan.

This begs the question, what is the level of support for political Islam among the Kurds of Iraq? Certainly Ansar, while a security threat, does not enjoy broad appeal. According to the International Crisis Group, "there is no hard evidence to suggest that Ansar al-Islam is more than a minor irritant in local Kurdish politics," and the group generally describes the threat of Islamic fundamentalists in Iraqi Kurdistan as "the mouse that roared" (2003). Yet perhaps the best indicator is from the polls, specifically multiparty elections that include Islamist organizations. In 2009, the Islamic Movement in Kurdistan received less than 2 percent of the popular vote (see Table 5.3).

Table 5.3. Kurdistan Regional Assembly Election Results, 2009

Organization	Party	2009 results		
		Votes	%	Seats
Kurdistani list	Kurdistan Democratic Party Patriotic Union of Kurdistan	1,076,370	57.34	59
Change list	Movement for Change	445,024	23.75	25
Service and reform	Kurdistan Islamic Union Islamic Group of Kurdistan Kurdistan Socialist Democratic Party Future Party	240,842	12.80	13
IMK list	Islamic Movement of Kurdistan	27,147	1.45	2
TDM list	Turkmen Democratic Movement	18,464	0.99	3
Social Justice and Freedom	Kurdistan Toilers' Party Kurdistan Communist Party Kurdistan Independent Work Party Kurdistan pro-Democratic Party Democratic Movement of Kurdistan People	15,028	0.82	1
CSAPC	Chaldean Syriac Assyrian Popular Council	10,595	0.58	3
Turkmen Reform	Iraqi Turkmen Front	7,077	0.38	1
National Rafidain	Assyrian Democratic Movement	5,690	0.30	2
Independent Armenian	Aram Shahine Dawood	4,198	0.22	1
ET list	Erbil, Turkmen	3,906	0.21	1
Other	Other	11,923	1.16	0
Total		1,866,264	100.00	111

Another indicator is a 2007 survey that asked citizens, "Do you agree that Islam is the vital factor for Kurdish unity?" From a sample size of 450, more than 83 percent responded "strongly disagree" (Aziz 2011, 143). Why should this be the case? One argument often proposed is that Islam never saturated Kurdish society with the same political intensity and social orthodoxy as found in the Arab world: "Since Islam's arrival in the seventh century, religious belief and practice haven't meshed with politics. Religion helped to provide spiritual cohesion in a disaggregated world, but it never provided the ideological foundation for an emerging nationalist identity. Modern Kurdistani political culture is deeply rooted in national rather than religious identity . . . [because] Islam was a foreign religion that was interjected into Kurdistan by conquest, rather than by trade, with the sword, rather than by choice" (Aziz 2011, 10). While Islamist elements did surface in Kurdistan after the First Gulf War, it is important to note that the financial and logistical support for such ventures was typically imported. Covert activities are usually attributed to Tehran. Overt Islamist activity, however, is traced to a familiar source, Saudi Arabia, though their influence is now carefully monitored. Before his current position, Bakir worked as a minister without portfolio in the Office of the Prime Minister of the Kurdistan Regional Government, Nechirvan Barzani:

He [Barzani] realized the importance of not allowing the Wahhabi money to come. So before he took the office, he started—there was a college of shariah that was sponsored and financed by the prince of Saudi Arabia—so he closed that. The prince sent him a message that he is ready to pay a million or two, I don't know how much. He said, if you give me all the resources of Saudi Arabia, I'll still close your college. So, no way. That was more dangerous on our people than any other thing. So of course, now [since 2000] there are restrictions on building mosques. And the others are under consideration because we do not want our people to be educated to be terrorists in the future.

Conclusion

If we return to the question posed by this book, that is, if Muslims are exceptionally resistant to nationalism, the case of the Kurds is a potent counterfactual. In no uncertain terms, the mobilization of Kurds in Iraq is ethnonational.

And what of the corollary, that is, if the Kurds are ethnonationalists, are they necessarily resistant to Islamist politics? The short and long answer is yes. However, of particular interest in this case is the character of the Kurdish population in Iraq, and its distinct pair of ethnolinguistic communities, the Kurmanji and Sorani, who share an identity even if divided linguistically. The fact that the communities are divided regionally—north and south, respectively—correlates with the fact that the Kurdish Civil War was also fought on a north-south frontier, but correlation is not causation. What is remarkable in the case of the Kurdish parties and the Kurdistan Regional Government is the conscious recognition that the communities are destined to integrate as the area advances economically and socially. To this end, the initiative to standardize a national variety of Kurdish that blends elements from Kurmanji and Sorani is a remarkable effort of language planning that effectively illustrates how state institutions can create a unified nationality even when a community is separated by a social barrier, which in this case is linguistic.

CHAPTER 6

Natives of the "New Frontier": The Uyghurs of Xinjiang

Go west, young man, and grow up with the country.
—John Saule, *Terre Haute Express*, 1841

Great Development of the West
—Development campaign title,
People's Republic of China, 2000

The Uyghur are a people with a long history but an imperiled future.[1] Once the masters of the famed Silk Road, the Uyghur are a Turkic people with a cultural legacy that predates Genghis Khan. Yet after a thousand years of settlement in a discrete region—a remarkable terrain surrounded by mountains and centered around a hellish desert—their homeland is now a province in a far larger state: the People's Republic of China. Relations between the Uyghur and the Chinese, as neighbors over many centuries, may be characterized diplomatically as contestable. Yet it was not until 1949 and the birth of the PRC that the fate of the Uyghur became entirely contingent on the regime in Beijing. The relative interests of the Uyghur, as a small ethnic minority with a language, culture, faith—and even faces—distinct from the far, far more numerous Chinese, were marginalized against the greater state-building project of China. As a result, the Uyghur are saddled with one of the lowest standards of living in the PRC and routinely face institutional discrimination. Thus, many are quietly committed to a secessionist solution. As masters of an idealized Uyghur nation-state, what would their country look like? The short answer is a secular republic not unlike that of their cultural cousins

Figure 6.1. Xinjiang.

in Turkey. Their nationalist ambitions are indubitable, and are sometimes expressed violently. In 2014, dramatic attacks in Kunming and Urumqi left dozens dead. Nonetheless, I argue that the probability of an *Islamic* fundamentalist mobilization remains small.

Xinjiang, a vast province of northwestern China that borders eight other countries, is the ancestral home of the Uyghur,[2] who established oasis towns along the ancient Silk Road in what is now the Central Asian frontier of the People's Republic of China (see Figure 6.1). The Communist regime named this territory 新疆, or *Xinjiang*: this translates literally as "New Frontier." For the Uyghur, this is ironic, since from their view there is nothing new about their territory or their place in it, though as seen from the east, the region was new to China. The Uyghur themselves generally use some variation of the term *Turkestan*, sometimes spelled *Turkistan*. Like the Wild

West of nineteenth-century America, the region and its people were romanticized in China as a land of adventure and wild natives, a view detailed in popular Chinese novels at the turn of the last century, and again at the turn of this century (2000) in the popular martial arts film *Crouching Tiger, Hidden Dragon* (Newby 1999).

As for the term *Uyghur*, it is important to note at the outset that the spelling of the word is remarkably inconsistent. The most common spelling is *Uighur*, most likely because it is the version preferred by major news outlets, including the BBC, Reuters, and the *New York Times*, inter alia. On the other hand, the official Chinese news agency, Xinhua (meaning "new China"), employs *Uygur*. This book uses *Uyghur* because it is the spelling preferred by Uyghurs themselves, as evidenced by the name of the primary transnational advocacy group, the World Uyghur Congress, as well as the Uyghur-language broadcast service of Radio Free Asia. Additional alternate spellings include *Uigur, Uighuir, Uiguir,* and *Wiga* and are employed where appropriate, either in the names of different organizations or in direct quotes.

All the Turkic peoples of Central Asia and Anatolia share the common heritage of Mongol ancestors who swept through the region beginning in the ninth century. Their languages share common ancestry, and their religious conventions share an affinity for Sufism. However, while they are culturally linked to a greater community of Turkic-speaking peoples from Central Asia to Anatolia, the twentieth century brought formal divisions, with institutionalized concepts and polities of Kazakh, Kyrgyz, Turkmen, and Uzbeks, the generally named "Turkic" people of "Turkestan" found themselves in need for an official name separating themselves from their cousins on the Eastern side of the geographic divide. Resurrecting a "medieval Eastern-Turkic ethnonym" (Dwyer 1998, 76), the Uyghurs "acquired this name again only after a group of Uyghur migrants to the USSR officially adopted it in 1921" (Bellér-Hann 1991, 71).

An ethnolinguistically distinct Turkic population of Muslims in this region can be traced to the tenth century, when Islam spread from the khanates of Khokand and Samarkand (now in Uzbekistan) and Bukhara (Afghanistan) (Rudelson 1999, 197). Cultural and religious communication was conducted via caravans that traversed mountain passes to link distant communities along the trade route. It was not until the eighteenth century that the imperial aspirations of Qing dynasty emperor Qianlong brought the region under eastern control (Rudelson 1998, 20). Administration by the

Manchu court was, however, interrupted repeatedly by rebellions which lasted until the collapse of Qing rule and the establishment of the Republic of China in 1911. In succeeding years, as nationalists, communists, and Japanese invaders fought for control of China, continued dissent in the far west fueled a series of revolts, which led ultimately to the declaration of an independent state, the Turkish Islamic Republic of East Turkestan. Based in Kashgar (the official Chinese spelling is *Kashi*) and led by president Ali Han Töre, the republic ended after only one year (1933–34).

A second attempt at independence in 1944 was more successful: the East Turkestan Republic, based in Khulja, survived until 1949 when the People's Liberation Army, fresh from its victory over the Kuomintang, turned its sights on the rebellious Uyghurs. The territory was renamed as one of China's five autonomous regions recognizing a titular nationality, in this case the Xinjiang Uyghur Autonomous Region, often noted as XUAR.[3] The other nominally autonomous nationalities with their own regions are the Hui of Ningxia, the Zhuang of Guangxi, the Mongolians of Inner Mongolia, and the Tibetans in Tibet. The Uyghur are also one of fifty-five groups granted official status as a "minority nationality."[4] The fifty-sixth nationality is the Han, who compose about 92 percent of the 1.3 billion people living in China.

Many of the military personnel who occupied the territory were to remain for many years. Following Chairman Mao's policy of turning demobilized soldiers into workers, the Xinjiang Production and Construction Corps (XPCC) established permanent settlements in the region.[5] Beginning with a core of some two hundred thousand people, this was the beginning of three decades of government-sponsored relocations, though over time most settlers headed west on their own, searching for opportunities in the "new region" of China. Hence, "the decisive factor for migration in Xinjiang since 1949 . . . was mainly economic" (Wang 1998, 48). The result of the migration was both a population explosion and a radical reorientation of the region's demographic profile. In 1949, Xinjiang's population of 4.3 million was about 90 percent Uyghur and 8 percent Han, with the remainder split among a dozen other minority populations.[6] As of 2010, Xinjiang's population of 21.8 million is—according to government figures—about 46 percent Uyghur and 40 percent Han (see Table 6.1).[7]

In 1949, about 70 percent of the people in Xinjiang lived in the south while 25 percent lived in the north. As of 1976, more than half of Xinjiang's resi-

Table 6.1. Xinjiang Ethnic Populations, 2010

Population	Number	Percentage
Uyghur	10,467,892	46.3
Han	8,746,148	40.1
Kazakh	1,245,023	6.7
Hui	839,837	4.6
Other	511,100	2.3
Total	21,810,000	100

Source: Xinjiang Uygur Autonomous Region
Bureau of Statistics, 2011 Sixth Xinjiang Census
(2010).
Note: Figures exclude active-duty members of the
People's Liberation Army.

dents lived in the north. Since most of Xinjiang's population growth was due to migration, and because most migrants were (are) Han settling in northern urban centers, the indigenous Uyghur population is now concentrated in a small area at the westernmost tip of the territory. In a region that accounts for one-sixth of the PRC's total land area, roughly three out of four Uyghur now live in just three southern districts: Aksu, Kashgar (Kashi), and Khotan (Hetian).[8]

Demographic disparities between the north and south, which in this case is an effective disparity between the remaining Uyghur population center and the newly Sinicized cities, are apparent in most measures of social development: fertility, mortality, and illiteracy and markedly higher in the south and lower in the north (Wang 1998, 43). As a result, the tone and tenor of ethnic conflict in Xinjiang is more acute than in the other "autonomous regions" of the PRC: "While ethnic separatism is active in Tibet, Inner Mongolia, and Xinjiang, the disparity in social development in Xinjiang provides a strong justification for the Xinjiang separatists to instill anti-Han sentiment among the ethnic minorities in Xinjiang. . . . This disparity has already engendered serious concern as well as discontent among the Uyghurs" (Wang 1998, 59). This last point regarding newer Han neighborhoods in Xinjiang's urban areas reflects the general shift in the People's Republic of China from paddy to pavement. In 1990, the ratio of rural to urban was 74 percent to 27 percent; by 2001, the proportion of rural residents dropped to 62 percent while China's share of city dwellers rose to 38 percent (National Bureau of Statistics of China 2002, 30). In Xinjiang, urbanization meant a new center of demographic gravity since "historically, there were more people in the south of Xinjiang than in the north" (Wang 1998, 43).

Language in China

Of more than 1.3 billion people in China, it is estimated that some 70 percent—more than 910 million—can speak Mandarin Chinese (Gordon 2005). Also known as *putonghua* (普通话), that is, the common tongue, or *guoyu* (国语), the national language, Mandarin developed from the vernacular of high-status Manchus and spread down from the northeast during the centuries of the Qing dynasty (1644–1911). Under the modernizing drive of the Communist Party, the language was standardized and simplified—especially the notoriously complex written form, an ideographic system lacking an alphabet—in the 1950s. While the written form of the language is consistent, literate Chinese nonetheless face significant difficulties in communicating with native speakers of other varieties, such as Cantonese or Hakka. A native of Beijing and a native of Shanghai cannot communicate with each other in their respective mother tongues.[9] The same can be said of other regional populations, such as the Gan of Jiangxi, the Jinyu of Shanxi, the Wu of Jiangsu, and so forth. Thus, while seven out of ten people in China can speak Mandarin, two of those seven—20 percent of the country—speak Mandarin as a second language. The other 30 percent of the population who cannot speak Mandarin are either uneducated Chinese—the official label for this "ethnicity" is Han[10]—or are divided among the dozens of ethnic minority communities found across the country, such as the Tibetans, Mongolians, and the southeastern populations of Bai and Dai peoples.

All fifty-five officially sanctioned minority nationalities in the People's Republic of China are nominally entitled to bilingual state education. In effect since 1978, a state policy allows education in a mother tongue, though arguably the goal was never to protect speakers of a minority language. As a pragmatic policy of linguistic assimilation, bilingual education in China "really refers to transitional schooling in the native language(s) while students master the dominant language . . . the overall goal remains the same: to introduce Chinese at some point, and gradually achieve the transition from the speakers' native language to Chinese" (Dwyer 1998, 78). This policy has waxed and waned over the years, particularly the relative emphasis of integrationist versus assimilationist goals. In the case of "politically unreliable" populations (Bell-Fialkoff 1993, 111), however, the state is more likely to pursue assimilationist policies, particularly by reducing or even eliminating mother tongue instruction in classrooms at all levels (Beckett and Postiglione 2011). In this regard, the case of Xinjiang provides a vivid example.

Language in Xinjiang

Turkic-speaking peoples in the region date from the tenth to the twelfth centuries and "by the end of the eleventh century at the latest, the Turkic language had by and large spread through the entire Tarim Basin" while the distinct population that was to become the "modern Uyghur nationality can be dated from around the turn of the fifteenth and sixteenth centuries" (Geng 1984, 10, 13). The development of the language can be traced to the Soghdians, a people active in the region from the third century BC to the eighth century AD, who introduced the written word using the Orkhon script, which was derived from that of Aramaic (Millward 2006, 45). Thereafter, the use of the Arabic script to write the region's vernacular was a consequence of the Quran and the advent of Islam. However, the utility of the Uyghur language, as a means of communication with the region's ethnic majority, expanded its appeal to communities who may or may not have had knowledge of the Arabic script: "the language serves as a lingua franca among the indigenous inhabitants of most parts of the Region, and many non-Turkic individuals (e.g., Russians, as well as members of the Mongolic Dagur, of the Tungusic Sibe[-Manchu] and of the Iranic Sariquli and Wakhi 'Tajik') acquire excellent, near-native or virtually native Uyghur language proficiency. The number of its native speakers in conjunction with its interethnic currency makes Uyghur one of the most important, if not the single most important, minority language in China" (Hahn 1991, 5). As for its written form, the twentieth century was a time of great experimentation. Under the influence of Young Turks in Ankara, instrumental ideologues in Moscow, and central planners in Beijing, the Uyghur language underwent a series of modernizing efforts, which produced three separate scripts for the same spoken tongue before it reverted to its more or less original form (see Table 6.2).

    In Xinjiang, state education policy allows Uyghur children the choice, *where available*, of attending primary and secondary in school in either Uyghur or Mandarin. Technically, it is possible to secure a higher education

Table 6.2. Uyghur Orthography

Script	Text	Period
A. English	"All human beings are born free and equal in dignity and rights. They are endowed with reason and conscience and should act towards one another in a spirit of brotherhood" (Universal Declaration of Human Rights, Article I).	1948
B. Arabic	ھەممە ئادەم زانىدىنلا ئەركىن. ئىززەت-ھۆرمەت ۋە ھوقۇقتا باپبارائۇر بولۇپ تۇغۇلغان. ئۇلار ئەقىلگە ۋە ۋىجدانغا ئىگە ھەمدە بىر-بىرىگە قېرىنداشلىق مۇناسىۋىتىگە خاس روھ بىلەن مۇئامىلە قىلىشى كېرەك.	Eleventh century–1960 and 1988–present
C. Cyrillic	Һемме адем занидинла еркин, иззет-һөрмет ве һоқуқта бапбаравер болуп туғулған. Улар еқилге ве вийдан'ға иге һемде бир-бириге кэриндашлиқ мунасивитиге хас роһ билен билен муамил қилиши кэрек.	1956–60
D: Pinyin	Pinyin is the PRC's method for writing Chinese characters with a Latin alphabet, e.g., the name of China's capital, 北京, is written "Beijing" but pronounced "bay-jing." The peculiarities of a system designed for Chinese proved awkward when applied to a Turkic language such as Uyghur.	1960–69
E. Latin I	Hǝmmǝ adǝm zatidinla ǝrkin, izzǝt-hǝrmǝt wǝ hoķuķta babbarawǝr bolup tuqulqan. Ular ǝķilqɪǝ wǝ wijdanqɪa igǝ hǝmdǝ bir-birigǝ ķerindaxliķ munasiwitigǝ hax roh bilǝn mu'amilǝ ķilixi kerǝk.	1969–87
D. Latin II	Hemme adem zatidinla erkin, izzet-hörmet we hoquqta babbarawer bolup tughulghan. Ular eqilghe we wijdan'gha ige hemde bir-birige qérindashliq munasiwitige xas roh bilen muamile qilishi kérek.	2001–present

Source: Adapted from Hahn (1991).
Note: The Arabic script and the Latin script are both used widely, though the Arabic script may be considered more formal; for example, the Uyghur-language website of Radio Free Asia is in the Arabic script (http://www.rfa.org/uyghur/). Online discussion boards in Uyghur, on the other hand, favor the computer-keyboard-friendly ease of the Latin script.

without any knowledge of Chinese: some colleges and training institutes in Xinjiang offer degree course instruction in Uyghur. In practice, Uyghur parents are presented with a difficult choice for their children: assimilate into the Chinese educational system and benefit from enhanced professional opportunities among the ruling Han, or enroll in Uyghur education through secondary school, helping to safeguard their cultural identity, but at the cost of reduced social mobility. "Few young people can ever hope to gain admittance to higher education establishments . . . if they have a history of exclusively Uyghur primary and secondary education, which does not equip them with sufficient knowledge of Chinese necessary for what is basically a Chinese higher education program" (Bellér-Hann 2002, 64). Recall for a moment the standard model of modern nationalism as a conflict of culture won by whichever group controls the state, thereby protecting and reproducing members of that culture. If education is a conduit to social mobility, and education requires assimilation, then failure to assimilate precludes social mobility. In the case of the Uyghur, this cultural model of linguistic-group nationalism fits rather well.

Four out of five Uyghurs do not speak Mandarin Chinese, which is a de facto prerequisite for any salaried position, and those Uyghurs who can speak Mandarin typically have less education than the Han job seekers against whom they must compete. As a result, the Han dominate commerce in Xinjiang's urban areas and are frequently seen by the locals as having the region's best jobs in the government, the Communist Party, and the military. The Han also usually live in newer neighborhoods and go to informally segregated schools (Chung 2002, 12). Moreover, social attitudes of the Chinese in Xinjiang toward Uyghur have been described by more than one author as simply racist (Kaltman 2007). The relative life chances of Han migrants to Xinjiang are generally perceived as unequal, with Han afforded the opportunity to "bask in prosperity," though some economists have challenged this view (Jacobs 2009; Howell and Fan 2011) (see Table 6.3).

The relative status of the Uyghur language vis-à-vis Uyghur relations with the dominant Han deserves some attention. Following two years of fieldwork in Xinjiang, an American researcher reported some remarkable illustrations of interethnic tensions. Gardner Bovingdon, speaking both Uyghur and Chinese in a Xinjiang restaurant, came to the attention of a Han restaurant manager, a Mrs. Wang, who asked, "How many languages do you speak?" In Chinese, this question translates more directly as, "You can speak how many country's languages?" He answered by noting that the question

Table 6.3. Selected Ethnic Minority Groups in China: Chinese Language
Ability, 2007

Ethnic group	Mandarin fluency (%)	Minority-language fluency (%)
Miao	92.12	59.70
Yao	89.47	74.90
Dai	88.58	98.28
Korean	84.11	93.99
Yi	81.43	69.07
Zhuang	79.99	86.16
Mongol	71.38	75.52
Tibetan	· 51.87	90.40
Kazak	42.37	99.08
Uyghur	19.88	99.74

Source: PRC State Council Language Commission.

depends on whether you count Chinese and Uyghur as the languages of one country or two. This brought a spontaneous and rather reckless comment from a Uyghur patron, who volunteered, "Right, Uyghur is one country's language—Xinjiang is a country." Mrs. Wang rephrased her question to the awkward but precise, "You can speak how many *kinds* of language?" According to Bovingdon, this exchange illustrates the hypocrisy of an official policy that nominally ascribes equal status to the languages of all China's nationalities, including Han and all the officially recognized national minorities. As the anecdote illustrates, all languages are officially equal, but a language with a country of its own, that is, Chinese in China, is more equal than the others: "Wang's unreflective assumption about one-to-one correspondence between languages and countries betrayed a prior assumption about the relative status of Hans and non-Hans in China" (Bovingdon 2002, 51).[11]

Ethnolinguistic Nationalism Versus Islamic
Fundamentalism in Xinjiang

The roles of separatists in Xinjiang are difficult to gauge since the pursuit of separatism in a police state remains more a dream shared by many, but an activity carried out be very, very few. In this section, we consider the roles of erstwhile separatist organizations operating within Xinjiang as well as diaspora organizations operating outside of China. A principal question posed is this: why do these organizations seek independence (or at the very least robust autonomy) in the first place? The language (and therefore cultural) scenario is, from the Uyghur perspective, deteriorating rapidly as state policies pursue a goal of assimilation with Chinese culture by promoting Mandarin institutionally and marginalizing both the status and utility of Uyghur. Whether or not the assimilation policy will succeed is another matter, as at least one activist notes religious and linguistic differences are simply too great; in other words "the Chinese want to assimilate the Uyghur people, but they don't know how to do it!"[12]

Inside China

Within China, an impediment to Uyghur mobilization perhaps greater than state security forces is simple demographics. They number something over eight million people, though official census figures are not necessarily reliable: Uyghur activists claim the actual number is three times higher. The Uyghurs are nonetheless a tiny minority in modern China—less than 1 percent of the population—yet they perennially seek autonomy or independence from Beijing. The pursuit of this goal dates to well before the "People's Republic" was either. Since 1949, rigorous attempts to assimilate the Uyghurs through the repression of religion (especially during the Cultural Revolution, 1966–76), the right to assemble, and language rights, as well as through the systematic introduction of Han Chinese immigrants into the region, have fomented deep-rooted antiregime sentiment. Periodic uprisings against Chinese rule have erupted more frequently in recent decades, though most events are spontaneous clashes or riots in the form of "social and civil unrest by disorganized, disgruntled, fairly impulsive young men, not a widespread movement" (Smith 2001). The extent of these uprisings is difficult to confirm independently as the access of independent observers (especially international journalists) is severely restricted, though it is apparent that their frequency accelerated starting in the 1990s, and has continued unabated (see, for example, Jacobs 2014).

Violence spiked dramatically in 2014. In the space of a few months, a wave of violence attributed to ethnic Uyghurs stunned China. In Kunming, a group of knife-wielding attackers slashed and stabbed their way through a crowded train station, killing twenty-nine and injuring one hundred and forty-three.

In Urumqi, another train station was targeted, this time with a bomb that killed three people and injured more than ninety. This was followed by another attack in Urumqi, when assailants in a pair of vehicles drove into a vegetable market, hurling explosive devices, ultimately killing thirty-one people and leaving nine-four wounded. Yet what is remarkable about all three attacks is that no *group* is known to have claimed responsibility, begging the question as to whether these were essentially isolated events *not* orchestrated by a Islamic terrorist network.

Before 2001, restless Uyghurs—like their Tibetan neighbors to the south—were labeled "splittists" because they were charged with trying to "split the motherland."[13] After the events of September 11, 2001, Beijing seized an opportunity to link its own effort to contain Uyghur unrest in Xinjiang with a global effort to contain Islamist violence. Without furnishing evidence of any kind, Beijing issued a government paper linking Xinjiang to Osama bin Laden, warning of a potential holy war spreading across Central Asia (Horner 2002). The People's Republic of China made several amendments to its Criminal Law, including provisions criminalizing membership in a "terrorist organization," though a definition of such an organization is not specified. According to an Amnesty International report, at a mass "public sentencing meeting" in Xinjiang on October 15, 2001, a dozen Uyghur "separatists" were given sentences ranging from five years in prison to death.[14] Beijing then secured the support of both the United States and the United Nations in separate successful campaigns to add four Uyghur groups to their official lists of international terrorist organizations, some with purported links to al-Qaeda (Foreman 2002) (see Table 6.4).

Outside China

Challenging the allegations of both Washington and Beijing, Amnesty International reports there is a "general lack of information available on any of the groups listed above" (Amnesty International 2004, 14). Only four of the groups named appear to have surfaced publicly anywhere. There are a very few published interviews with the leadership of two of the organizations specified, namely the East Turkestan Islamic Movement (ETIM) and the East Turkestan Liberation Organization (ETLO).

Regarding the latter, there is extraordinarily little public information about the ETLO, other than its mention in the 2003 PRC document naming it one

Table 6.4. Purported Groups of Uyghur Separatist Militants/Terrorists

Organization	Claimant	Reported
World Uyghur Youth Congress: WUYC (now part of the World Uyghur Congress) East Turkestan Information Center (ETIC)	People's Republic of China: Ministry of Public Security	December 2003
East Turkestan Islamic Movement (ETIM) East Turkestan Liberation Organization (ETLO)	People's Republic of China Government Reports	2002–3
East Turkestan International Committee East Turkestan Islamic Party East Turkestan Islamic Party of Allah East Turkestan Opposition Party Islamic Holy Warriors Islamic Reformist Party Shock Brigade	People's Republic of China: Report titled "East Turkestan Terrorists"	January 2002
Free Turkestan Movement Home of East Turkestan Youth Organization for the Liberation of Uyghurstan United Revolutionary Front of Eastern Turkestan (aka United National Revolutionary Front) Uyghur Liberation Organization Wolves of Lop Nor Xinjiang Liberation Organization	U.S. Congressional Research Service	December 2001

of four Uyghur international terrorist groups. China claimed the ETLO is led by exiles Hudaberdi Haxerbik and Abulimit Turxun, as well as Dolqun Isa, who, according to the PRC, "organized and participated in all sorts of terrorist activities launched by the separatist group." Isa stated that the charges against him as well as Turxun and Haxerbik are nothing more than "propaganda," noting that no proof of any kind has been offered by China to substantiate their claims.

East Turkestan Islamic Movement

By contrast, the ETIM is raised repeatedly as an example of Uyghur Islamic fundamentalism. Indeed, of all the Uyghur groups named by the Chinese and others as advocates of waging jihad and establishing an Islamist regime in East Turkestan, certainly the most publicized is the ETIM. This claim that the ETIM is in fact an Islamic fundamentalist organization is based, however, on information that is invariably traced to Chinese sources. Of the little information available from the ETIM itself, there are but two interviews with Abudula Kariaji, the vice chairman of the organization, who was interviewed by the *Wall Street Journal* in 2004 (Cloud and Johnson). (It was later learned that the ETIM chairman, Hasan Mahsum, was already dead at the time of the interview, killed in Pakistan in October 2003: thus, Kariaji is thought to be the leader of the erstwhile group.) He confirmed that his group met with Osama bin Laden in Afghanistan and, with his permission, opened three camps that "sheltered up to 500 Uyghur families" while some of the men were trained in guerrilla fighting. However, though a few dozen trainees returned to China, he claims they carried out no attacks. Kariaji said the ETIM and al-Qaeda were "never as close as the US and China claim" and that they had "deep differences with the Arab fighters." Bin Laden spoke to them about "oppression of Muslims in Palestine, Saudi Arabia, Egypt and Chechnya [but] he didn't mention Xinjiang" (Cloud and Johnson 2004).

What is conspicuous by its absence in this rare interview is a statement regarding the actual goals of the ETIM, that is, Islamist, nationalist, or otherwise. One of the only other known interviews with Kariaji was conducted on the Uyghur-language service of Radio Free Asia that same year. While there is no transcript of this interview, Dolqun Isa recalls hearing the broadcast. Stating that the ETIM is a "small group, a very small group," he said Kariaji made no mention of an Islamic state, demanding only independence from the Chinese.[15]

To many analysts in security and counterterrorism circles, this often comes as something of a surprise because the ETIM is still cited repeatedly as a jihadist organization with close ties to al-Qaeda. For example, 2010 saw the publication of *The ETIM: China's Islamic Militants and the Global Terrorist*

Threat (Reed and Raschke 2010). Yet only one year earlier, testimony before the U.S. House of Representatives Committee on Foreign Affairs questioned whether the ETIM ever really existed as anything more than a handful of activists, not terrorists. Moreover, the decision by the United States to designate ETIM as a terrorist organization in 2002 was challenged as a cynical ploy to placate China as the United States prepared its invasion of neighboring Afghanistan. A political appointee, Randy Schriver, then serving as deputy assistant secretary of state for East Asia and Pacific affairs, testified that he found this linkage "highly problematic," and emphasized the designation named only "elements of" the ETIM had "reportedly" committed acts of terrorism. A vocal member of the Subcommittee on International Organizations, Human Rights and Oversight, Representative Dana Rohrbacher, called this parsing "weasel words."

It would be easy to dismiss this public political spat as a minor event, were it not for the fact that this designation was implemented as policy in defense operations carried out in Afghanistan. It was this designation, for example, which led to the incarceration of twenty-two Uyghurs seized in Afghanistan, nominally due to membership in the ETIM. In documents obtained by the *New York Times* regarding Uyghurs detained at Guantánamo Bay, the captives were variously described as "enemy combatants" who were members of the ETIM. In 2004, the military Combatant Status Review Board described the ETIM as "one of the most militant of the Uyghur separatist groups," and as "an Islamist extremist movement linked to al Qaida" that is "operating in the eastern region of China." It was therefore considered a separatist group seeking an Islamic fundamentalist state.

All of the men were later cleared of presenting any threat to the United States; five were released in 2006 and the release of the remainder was ordered in 2008. However, because the men could not be repatriated to China without risking their immediate execution, the U.S. government had to find host nations willing to accommodate them. Thus, the last were not released until 2012.[16]

In the simplest terms, "China is taking advantage of the international war on terrorism to attempt the eradication of a domestic problem" (Gladney 2002, 269). Yet the pathology of the problem is unclear. Many social scientists, especially anthropologists and sociologists, see an ethnic minority at odds with a dominant Chinese majority. In sharp contrast, alarmist academics like Raphael Israeli see a "rising tide of Muslim fundamentalism around the globe" that has "has given rise to fundamentalist groups among Chinese Muslims, some of them violent" (Israeli 2002, 261). In his view, "their yearning to see their identity merging into that of the greater Islamic powers" means "'ethnic nationalism' does not provide the explanation for local Muslim upheavals in various parts of China" (Israeli 2002, 275).

International reporting on Xinjiang clarifies little, as there is "a degree of confusion in news sources" (Millward 2004, 26). In his analysis of sources cited in stories about Uyghur unrest, historian James Millward found little collaboration and a dearth of firsthand facts. He concluded "the notion of an imminent terrorist threat in Xinjiang from Uyghur groups is exaggerated" (Millward 2004, 32). Though not excusable, this is explicable given China's severe restrictions on the freedom of journalists and the ethical dilemmas of interviewing subjects who, by meeting with a member of the foreign press, invite arrest and persecution. A more cautious tone adopted by *New York Times* reporter Craig Smith notes correctly "how many Uyghur separatists are operating in Xinjiang today is impossible to estimate" (Smith 2001). Nonetheless, in academic journals, especially in political science, it is conventional to address a "significant terrorist movement" in Xinjiang (Steele and Kuo 2007, 1). For its part, China also clouds the Uyghur separatist question— including the scale of activist organizations and the mobilization of any followers as either ethnic "splittists" or Islamists—by simultaneously restricting the authorized culture of the Uyghur "minority nation." One year after the attacks of September 11, the provincially preeminent Xinjiang University ended more than five decades of instruction in the Uyghur language: since September 2002, all incoming first- and second-year students are taught only in Mandarin (Wingfield-Hayes 2002).

International Pressure Groups

How important are Uyghur transnational pressure groups to politics in Xinjiang? "Both Chinese officials and a number of Uyghur independence activists have greatly exaggerated the impact of these organizations on Xinjiang's daily politics" (Bovingdon 2010, 136). Moreover, "there is no independently verifiable evidence that separatist organizations have sent members into Xinjiang, let alone directed anti-state attacks in the region" (Bovingdon 2010, 137). These groups have, however, smuggled in documents and broadcast *ideas* in support of Uyghur separatists. Moreover, there is evidence the Uyghur diaspora and transnational cultural ties also lend a degree of support to the sustainment of political activism within Xinjiang. However, the character of this support is ideological rather than tactical, and the probability of this effort in fostering tactical, kinetic acts of violence appears remote (Han 2011).

Two of the most prominent groups—the World Uyghur Congress (formerly known as the World Uyghur Youth Congress) and the East Turkestan Information Center (ETIC)—are clearly established and active in Munich, Germany, but as "legally constituted non-governmental organizations. . . . China's inclusion of these groups in its list is an attempt to curb their peaceful political and human rights monitoring activities, and to conflate peaceful political activism with violent acts of 'terrorism'" (Amnesty International 2004, 13). I interviewed the leaders of both groups regarding claims and counterclaims about their organizations, including their positions on violence, but more pointedly for this book I asked about their stated political goals, and the relative importance of either ethnolinguistic identification or Islamism as effective means of mobilization. In short, religion is noted as an existential difference separating the Han and the Uyghurs, though Islamism holds no appeal. In contrast, language emerges again and again as a principal policy demand.

World Uyghur Congress

The WUYC named in the Chinese report of December 2003 has since (2004) joined the World Uyghur Congress (WUC), an umbrella organization uniting Uyghur advocates from Turkey to Australia. It was launched in 2004 by merging the WUYC and the East Turkestan National Congress, and positions itself as an advocate of nonviolent and democratic means of determining the future of East Turkestan. The head of the WUYC named a "terrorist" in the 2003 report is Dolqun Isa. He is now the secretary general of the World Uyghur Congress. He was once a student leader at the University of Xinjiang, where he studied physics, and helped establish a Uyghur rural education advocacy group, the Students Science Cultural Association, in 1987. He was expelled in 1988 for his organization of protests in Urumqi, initially regarding inequitable education policies vis-à-vis Chinese students, but also in response to some anonymous campus graffiti and pamphlets that called for Uyghurs to leave Xinjiang, or to make Uyghur men "slaves" and women "prostitutes." He escaped from China to Poland with a forged passport and then settled in Turkey for some years before emigrating to Germany in 1995.

It is Isa's position that the Uyghur population must wait for a regime change in China, thereby allowing democratic processes to improve the life chances of his kin. He denies having any interest whatsoever in promoting Islamist politics, and cites the prime mover of his actions and efforts as a fight for "self-determination." He believes the Chinese are determined to wipe out the Uyghur language, and fears that without interference the government will exclude the language from the education system at all levels in "ten or twenty years."[17]

Another figure, Erkin Alptekin, the former president of World Uyghur Congress, is the son of Isa Yusuf Alptekin, a figure revered in the Turkic world. Yusuf was not only the general secretary of the Provincial Government of Eastern Turkestan between 1947 and 1949, but also a respected historian of the Uyghur people. Erkin Alptekin was born in Lanzhou, China, in 1939: in Uyghur, his name literally means "freedom." Ten years later, when East Turkestan was essentially independent, his family "had to flee" the advancing People's Liberation Army.[18] He spent many years in Srinagar, Kashmir, and later studied journalism in Turkey. In 1971 he came to Munich and began working for Radio Free Asia. In 1991, he launched the East Turkestan Union in Europe, which, like the WUYC, later merged with the World Uyghur Congress. The same year, he also helped found the Unrepresented Nations and Peoples Organization in the Netherlands.

Alptekin argues that East Turkestan "never surrendered our sovereignty to the Chinese" and that he advocates the "right to self-determination." He refutes any charges of organized Uyghur terrorists: in response to the list of purported groups listed above, other than the four most recent, he "had never heard of any them."[19] Importantly, he argues that Islamism is marginal because a pan-ethnic identity as Turkic peoples is prevalent, followed by a Uyghur identity in East Turkestan: "I tell you frankly, among the Turkic peoples, we have some fundamentalists . . . there's no doubt about that, but in the Turkic world, we have a different way of thinking than in the Arab world. . . . In the Turkic world, we have our Turkic-ness first. I am a Uyghur, Uyghurs are Turkic. In Eastern Turkestan, we have Buddhist Uyghurs; we have a small little community of Christian Uyghurs. We never had any problem based on religion." In regard to the Uyghur language, he argues it is "the fountain of the nation—if that fountain dries out, we think that the people will cease to exist." Separately, however, he does not believe the marginalization or even loss of the Uyghur language will allow them to be subsumed by the Chinese and that they will remain unique: "The Irish people—they lost their language, but they never lost their Irish-ness . . . even if we lose our language, our Uyghur-ness will be there—our non-Chinese-ness will be there—so it could backfire in their faces, exactly like in Northern Ireland."[20]

East Turkistan Information Center (ETIC)

Regarding the East Turkistan Information Center (ETIC), its chairman, Abduljelil Qarkash, is one of the eleven people named a terrorist by the PRC in 2003. The ETIC is not affiliated with the World Uyghur Congress (see below). He was born in Khotan, Xinjiang, in 1964; in 1987 he came to Germany, by also using a forged passport. It his position that "99 percent of Uyghurs" want independence but that there is no alternative but to wait for regime change in Beijing: because there are "very few" people active in the movement, and because "group activities" are "impossible" due to pervasive and repressive security.[21] Moreover, military mobilization would be pointless because "we have no weapons." He advocates a future peaceful and democratic transition to bona fide autonomy or independence. Charges made by China that Uyghurs are agitating for sharia and a caliphate are "propaganda" and "disinformation." He is less optimistic than his colleagues in the WUC: "Twenty years, thirty, is very long for the Uyghurs' current situation. If we still wait . . . maybe we're finished." To this end he seeks to raise the profile of Uyghurs internationally and to appeal for aid from the international community. He believes Uyghur language restrictions are a state-driven tactic of total assimilation, a method coupled with a rewriting of history to say, "this area does not belong to the Uyghurs."

Uyghur American Association (UAA)

Though not initially named by China (or any other entity) as a terrorist organization in 2001, the Uyghur American Association has since emerged as a target of Chinese indignation over its alleged support of anti-Han violence in Xinjiang. The association, led by General Secretary Omer Kanat—who is also a vice president of the World Uyghur Congress—is a nonprofit organization based in Washington, D.C., that—again, like the World Uyghur Congress— advocates a nonviolent and democratic transition in East Turkestan toward popular sovereignty and national self-determination for the Uyghur.[22] Their efforts to raise the public profile of the Uyghur issue are pursued in tandem with the World Uyghur Congress, though it is important to recognize that the Uyghur American Association is in Washington for a reason. The most important audience for their public campaigns is not the American public, but rather members of Congress who have the power to influence U.S.-China relations. According to Kanat, his organization "plays a role in the foreign policy of the US toward China—we let Congress know about what China has been doing" (Kanat 2005). To this end, a principal effort of the UAA is the Uyghur Human Rights Project, an initiative that collects, documents, and distributes alleged violations of Uyghur human rights in Xinjiang.

According to Omer Kanat, the UAA is less concerned about ethnic assimilation than eradication, as he argues intermarriage between Han and Uyghur is extremely low, but policies to eliminate Uyghur culture, language, and ethnic identity pose an existential threat. Citing language of instruction policy as a principal challenge, he believes his "language is dying" in Xinjiang, put under greater threat by the continuing migration of Han westward (Kanat 2005).

Conclusion

Despite allegations made by the People's Republic of China—and with the collaboration of the United Nations and the United States—the scale of organized Uyghur separatism anywhere—either inside or outside of China—is very small. As for fundamentalist terrorism, it seems that the only act of sustained violence conducted with any serious coordination is the collective pounding of keyboards and podiums. Interviews with the leadership of these alleged terrorist organizations actually demonstrate a stated goal of national self-determination to be achieved peaceably and in a democratic environment, without stating any interest in Islamist politics. This is a far cry from the position of the PRC, which launched, in 1996, the "Strike Hard" campaign. Drafted by the Politburo Standing Committee, "Document No. 7" detailed security policies to contain purported threats of nationalist separatism and religious extremism. However, while the document cites an emphasis on catching "criminals," it actually spends a great deal more time addressing Uyghur education and language in Xinjiang. In the view of James Millward, the preeminent historian of the region: "Document No. 7 also expressed the Party's apprehension about education in Xinjiang. In order to eliminate illiteracy, since the 1950's the national minority policies had permitted, even encouraged, education in autonomous regions in major non-Chinese languages. Uyghur-language education was available from primary through university levels in Xinjiang. However, directives in Document No. 7 to 'investigate and organize schools' and warnings about teachers and textbooks 'which inspire national separatism and publicize religious ideas' suggest that party leaders felt they had insufficient control over the Uyghur-language education system" (Millward 2006, 343). It is therefore unsurprising that language restrictions are cited as a chief grievance, particularly by the World Uyghur Conference, though the efficacy of mobilizing domestically around this issue is difficult to gauge, as the possibility of safely protesting openly in Xinjiang is effectively nil. Nonetheless, Uyghur advocates continually cite language as an existential element of their identity, while Islam is relegated somewhere below "Uyghur-ness" and "Turkic-ness."

Regarding the future of Xinjiang, the Strike Hard campaign was joined in 2000 by a parallel "Great Development of the West" campaign to accelerate economic development of the region. The region has indeed developed economically, though the benefits of this development, especially in regard to petroleum exploration and exploitation in the Tarim Basin, are afforded solely to ethnic Chinese (Goodman 2004). As for the future of the Uyghurs in Xinjiang, their struggle to secure political emancipation is pursued largely outside of China. Restrictions on even the most pacific protests render mobilization in Xinjiang beyond consideration. Outside of China, however, multiple groups continue to convene conferences and work to raise the public profile of the Uyghur case globally, including the Uyghur American Association, inter alia, and its umbrella institution, the World Uyghur Congress.

Yet even the current president of the World Uyghur Congress, Rebiya Kadeer—a perennial candidate for the Nobel Peace Prize who spent six years in prison for her advocacy of Uyghur causes—is acutely aware that her efforts are countered by China's dedicated assimilationist campaign. In her memoir, she recalls the words of a Chinese diplomat who spoke with her immediately before her 2005 release to travel to the United States on medical grounds: "Twenty years from now, [there] will not be any more people known as Uyghur" (Kadeer and Cavelius 2009, 280).

Though Kadeer is an active participant in this case and thus is subjective, her claim, though unverifiable, portrays a campaign that falls along the spectrum of ethnic cleansing. It is not a campaign countering Islamic fundamentalism, though this remains a principal justification for repeated crackdowns. The irony here is that a sustained campaign of containing and ultimately eliminating the Uyghur identity may, in fact, lead to a scenario more conducive to jihadi sensibilities. This is not to say we should expect the emergence of fundamentalist terrorist organizations, which is hard to imagine inside a police state, though it does suggest the probability of generating isolated, homegrown actors will increase (Sageman 2008). Should the PRC in fact fear the instability of an Islamist mobilization, it may be in their interest to rein in the most extreme policies of pro-Han ethnic preference in Xinjiang and allow a greater liberalization of Uyghur civil society.

However, there is a separate trajectory of probably greater consequence than any specific policy toward Uyghurs, which is the general development of China itself. As the state continues its transition from a de facto Communist regime, an ideological vacuum is being filled by a new source of political legitimacy: Han Chinese nationalism (Gries et al. 2011; Hughes 2011, 2006; Carlson 2009; Friedman 2008; Wu 2008; Gries 2005; Guang 2005; Zhao 2004; Karl 2002; Yahuda 2000; Zheng 1999). If this is the path taken, the evolution of a Chinese *nation*-state may render the interests of all China's minority nations of diminishing concern. For this reason, Omer Kanat of the Uyghur American Association believes a transition away from authoritarian rule, perhaps even to democracy, may actually prove devastating to the Uyghurs.[23]

CHAPTER 7

Print Culture and Protest:
The Sindhis of Pakistan

Of late, there has been an abundance of very
unprofitable discussion amongst the rulers of the
province [Sindh] as to the language which should be
selected for literary and official purposes.
        —Sir Richard Francis Burton, *Sindh and the Races That*
                                    Inhabit the Valley of the Indus

The territory called Sindh has been inhabited continuously for millennia, most
famously by the Indus Valley civilization and its great cities, Mohenjo-Daro
and Harappa, some five thousand years ago (see Figure 7.1). As a geographic
frontier—its once-mighty Indus River separating the Indian subcontinent
from the Near East—it has also seen no small number of massive migrations.
It was crossed by Alexander the Great, invaded by the Arabs, conquered by
the Persians, occupied by the British, and, much more recently, colonized
by migrants from the east. Nonetheless, the Sindhi people pride themselves
on their excellent hospitality. This was the case in 1947 when the creation of
the Republic of Pakistan brought waves of fellow Muslims from the north of
India to settle primarily in the province of Sindh, particularly in its largest
city, the political and commercial capital of Pakistan, Karachi.[1] The trouble,
of course, was that Sindh was already inhabited. Moreover, the indigenous
population of Sindh was and is entirely distinct—ethnically, culturally,
linguistically—from the transplants (called *Mohajirs*, meaning "migrants")
who arrived en masse. Moreover, the Sindhis were and are also distinct from
all the other communities who compose Pakistan, including the Punjabis,

Figure 7.1. Sindh.

Table 7.1. Ethnic Populations of Pakistan:
July 2012 Estimates

Ethnicity	Number	Percentage
Punjabi	85,022,076	44.68
Pashtun	29,342,892	15.42
Sindhi	26,831,049	14.10
Saraiki	15,946,397	8.38
Mohajirs	14,405,039	7.57
Baloch	6,793,393	3.57
Other	11,950,283	6.28
Total	190,291,129	100.00

Source: CIA World Factbook, https://www.cia.gov
/library/publications/the-world-factbook/geos/pk
.html (accessed February 15, 2013).

Pashtuns, and Baloch, among others (see Table 7.1). How then to accommodate such an ethnolinguistically diverse population in a new state that was founded as a de jure "Muslim nation"? The short answer is that Pakistan has not. It has not succeeded in managing the perennial and thorny growth of ethnic politics—evidenced in spectacular fashion by the emergence and exit of the Bengali nation in 1971—and continues to face existential challenges from disparate communities, including the Pashtuns and Baloch. The subject of this chapter, however, is Sindh. It addresses the origins of the conflict, and particularly focuses on the language politics of the nationalist movement. Yet what is of special interest here is the place of Islam—or lack thereof—in the broader politics of Sindhi nationalism.

Language in Sindh

The British conquered Sindh in 1843, ending the reign of the Talpurs (1782–1843), and continued to govern the territory until partition in 1947. Though the Talpurs were ethnically Baloch, they employed Persian as their High Culture language (Rahman 1996b, 103). Their most lasting legacy, however, was political rather than cultural. Upon their arrival, the British encountered the crippling legacy of inequality established by the Talpurs, built upon "one of the most repressive feudal systems in the Indian subcontinent" (A. Khan 2005, 128). The population was divided by the land-owning *waderas*—often derided as "feudal lords"—and the landless laborers—called *haris*—who in 1931 accounted for four out of five people in the territory. There was also a sectarian division at this time; the Sindhi-speaking Hindu minority was concentrated in urban areas (specifically Karachi and Hyderabad), while Sindhi-speaking Muslims were overwhelmingly rural. As a result of unequal access to education, Hindus were far more likely to be literate while the haris were almost entirely illiterate: at the end of the nineteenth century it is estimated that only 1.4 percent of the Muslim population could read or write (A. Khan 2005, 130–34).

Thus, it is all the more remarkable that the earliest agitations for Sindhi autonomy centered on the politics of language. While the British co-opted the waderas to maintain socioeconomic stability in the region, they simultaneously revolutionized the sociolinguistics of Sindhi. This began as a matter of practicality. From 1843, Sindh was governed by an administration—called a "presidency"—in Bombay. From this point onward, "Sindhi, like Bengali, enjoyed regional hegemony throughout the British era (1843–1947)" (Ayres

2009, 49). Moreover, after fifteen years the government realized that the most effective way to govern Sindh was not in Hindi or English or Persian, but in the vernacular: in 1851 all British officers assigned to Sindh were required to be proficient in "colloquial Sindhi" (Rahman 1996b, 104). Thus began the institutionalization of Sindhi in the *administration* of the territory, but also as a print language of *social mobility*. By the 1930s, Sindhi was the principal language of instruction in primary schools, a language of "official correspondence and records at the lower level," and the foundation of a Sindhi press that published eighty-seven newspapers. However, it was this ethnolinguistic distinctiveness that also led to a call for independent administration rather than from faraway Bombay: in 1936 Sindh was separated from the Bombay presidency and ruled from Karachi thereafter (Rahman 1996b, 109). By this time, Sindhi had achieved regional dominance by sustaining and promoting "a literature and a widespread presence both colloquially and administratively" (Ayres 2003, 63).

As Sindh was now home to a thriving print culture, it distinguished itself from other parts of Pakistan by maintaining the highest mother-tongue literacy rate in the country. As of 1951, Sindhis not only were five times more literate than Punjabis, Pashtuns, or Baloch, but also printed the largest number of publications, including the most indigenous language newspapers (A. Khan 2005, 143). Thus, the Sindhis could be forgiven for imagining in the 1940s that the advent of Partition in 1947 would create not only a new Muslim country, but also a supportive home for their own thriving culture, one among many, in a multiethnic Pakistan. Instead, Sindhis were more than a little "surprised to find their language had been stripped of its formal official role and would be subservient" to a nonnative tongue (Ayres 2009, 50).

Arguably the most notorious decision enacted by post-Partition Pakistan was the declaration of the north Indian tongue Urdu as its official language, despite the fact that fewer than 8 percent of the population could actually speak the language (see Table 7.2). In no uncertain terms, the imposition of Urdu was an act of astonishing hubris. It was also emblematic of an erstwhile state language planning that was and is by all accounts a spectacular failure (Ayres 2003, 51). Indeed, it is arguably the most spectacular language planning failure of post-Westphalian politics given that it directly contributed to the violent split of an entire state, namely the eventual secession of Bangladesh in 1971 and the halving of Pakistan's population (see, e.g., Uddin 2006).

This begs the immediate and obvious question: *why* Urdu? Certainly it was the mother tongue of the political elites of the Muslim League responsible

Table 7.2. Language Populations of Pakistan, 1951 Census

Language	East and West Pakistan combined (%)	West Pakistan only (%)
Bengali	56.0	0.5
Punjabi	29.0	67.1
Urdu	7.3	7.1
Sindhi	5.9	12.9
Pashto	4.9	8.2
Baloch	1.5	3.0
Brahvi	N/A	0.7

Source: Rahman (1996a).

for the creation of a *state* called Pakistan, but the decision was based as much on mythology and *nation* building as it was on preferential treatment for socioeconomic elites. In any analysis, "Urdu's emergence as the national language of Pakistan was neither obvious nor natural. That it became so marks the triumph of a particular understanding of the nation as a territory, a people, and a language in the singular" (Ayres 2009, 16). For Muhammad Ali Jinnah and Liaquat Ali Khan—the first governor general and prime minister of Pakistan, respectively—Urdu was an essential component of what Stephen Cohen calls "the idea of Pakistan," which "implied that Pakistan would be a modern extension of the great Islamic empires of South Asia, whose physical remnants still dominate the subcontinental landscape. From the Red Forts of Delhi and Agra to the Taj Mahal and the spectacular ruins of Golconda in southern India, there was compelling evidence of recent Islamic greatness" (Cohen 2004, 37). To this end, the political and cultural elites romanticized a golden age of Islamic rule, "times when Muslim/Mughal rulers spoke Urdu and Persian freely—and they consequently elevated the place of Urdu in their thinking about the future" (Ayres 2003, 56). In sharp contrast, the "non-assimilationist" Urdu-speaking Mohajirs, "proud of their urban Mughal culture of which Urdu is a symbol," resisted any and all efforts to promote the Sindhi language (Rahman 1999, 228).

In order to recapture this golden age, the Persian-based High Culture language of the Muslim Mughal Empire was supposed to serve as the unifying language of the reborn Muslim nation of Pakistan. In contrast, a language like Bengali, with a vocabulary linked to Assamese, "was deemed to be inherently

Table 7.3. Language Communities of Karachi, 1941 and 1951

Year	Population	Sindhi-speaking (%)	Urdu-speaking (%)	Other (%)
1941	364,300	90	1	8
1951	1,064,557	38	58	4

Source: Rahman (1996b, 110).

un-Islamic" (Ayres 2003, 58). This chauvinism "ultimately led Bengali Muslims to conclude that the common bond of Islam provided an insufficient basis to believe in the success of a nation" (Uddin 2006, 119). Thus, the 1952 announcement in Dhaka by Liaquat Khan's successor, Prime Minister Khawaja Nazimuddin, declaring Urdu the sole official language of government *and* higher education, was at once guileless and naïve (see Table 7.3). The reaction was explosive: students protested, a curfew was enacted and ignored, and in the chaos four students were shot and killed. The dead were quickly martyred and immortalized as symbols of what became *Ekushe*, language day, a state holiday that celebrates the Bengali *nation* as much as its tongue. Hence, in the years that led up to the war of secession, "the Bengalis of East Pakistan adopted language as the main pillar of their platform against the hegemony of West Pakistani nationalism, which was primarily based on religion" (Mohsin 2003, 81).

In West Pakistan, the response to the imposition of Urdu was slower but ultimately no less profound, and nowhere more so than in the province of Sindh. In the four years following partition, Sindhi, a language with a well-established print culture and centuries of literary heritage—including but not limited to a corpus of still revered poetry[2]—was suddenly displaced from public life in its titular homeland: between 1947 and 1951, the share of Sindhi speakers in Sindh dropped from 90 percent to 38 percent. They were also outpaced in regional rates of literacy: as of 1951, "the better-educated Mohajirs, with a 23.4% literacy rate compared with 13.2% for Sindh as a whole, took up technical, bureaucratic, and professional jobs in the province" (Rahman 1995, 1008).[3] At the same time, the economically and politically savvy Mohajirs ascended to share power at the *state* level with the Punjabis, who dominated the military (see Table 7.4).

The occasional but innocent suggestion that Sindhi shares enough similarities with Urdu—both are Indo-European languages—to accommodate a relatively minor sociolinguistic shift is a nonstarter. Sindhi is a direct descen-

Table 7.4. Ethnic Origins of Military and Bureaucratic Elite

Ethnicity	Senior military officers (1959)		Senior bureaucrats (1973)	
	Number	Percentage	Number	Percentage
Punjabis	17	35.4	1,727	48.89
Pashtuns	19	39.6	287	8.12
Mohajirs	11	23.0	1,070	30.29
Sindhis	0	0.0	90	2.50
Balochs	0	0.0	9	0.25
Bengalis	1	2.0	349	9.95
Total	48	100.0	3,532	100.0

Source: Rahman (1996b, 121).

dant of the Prakrit family of languages while Urdu is descendant of Sanskrit peppered liberally with Persian and Arabic. As a lingua franca Urdu is mutually intelligible with Hindi (despite using different scripts), but mutually unintelligible with Sindhi (Ayres 2009, 50). In addition, there are two other important distinctions that separate the languages. In Sindhi, unlike Urdu, every word must end in a vowel. Second, there are more phonemes to handle in written Sindhi, so its alphabet has fifty-two letters while Urdu employs forty-four (Bughio 2001, 49). More than twenty-six million people speak Sindhi in Pakistan and another three million in India, though this smaller Hindu community uses the Gurumukhi script (a form of the Devanagari script) rather than the Arabic. Given the size of its language community, it is not surprising that Sindhi speakers still maintain a robust language community with dozens of newspapers, most published in Hyderabad and Karachi, and also support Sindhi-language broadcasts. According to Tariq Rahman, the most prominent scholar of language politics in the country, Sindhi remains "the most developed of the indigenous languages of Pakistan" (2002, 347).[4]

Despite living for decades in an environment saturated in Urdu—the requisite language of social mobility in Pakistan—Sindhis have sustained a passionate defense of their mother tongue for all the decades since partition. As was the case in Bangladesh, university students played a critical role in amplifying the political voice of language dissenters. According to Rahman, "The Sindhi language movement, which had been going on since the anti-Bombay days, took the form of the Sindhi-Urdu controversy because of the decision taken in 1957–58, by the University of Karachi forbidding students from answering examination questions in Sindhi" (1996b, 114). Nonetheless, despite student activism, the response from the state of Pakistan could be described as malign neglect, ignoring the complaints of Sindhi intellectuals as a minor—and nominally un-Islamic—distraction. However, this changed dramatically in 1971, when Pakistan cracked and Bangladesh burst forth. For the government of Pakistan, this was especially alarming vis-à-vis Sindh, since the independence movement in Bangladesh was predicated by a social movement that started in earnest in the 1950s during the imposition of Urdu over Bengali in higher education. As it happened, the regime was correct to expect a parallel mobilization in the province as pro-Sindhi students found new inspiration from the example of Bangladesh. And it was the students who became embroiled in the most notorious violence of the 1972 language riots, and "the worst language-related conflagrations took place in the context of the university"—hundreds were killed (Ayres 2009, 54–55).

The riots themselves were the consequence of a cascade of events that began with the end of "One Unit" rule (whereby all of West Pakistan was governed from the center) in July 1970, the first general elections in Pakistan in December 1970, the declaration of an independent Bangladesh in March 1971, the rise of provincial assemblies with regional capacities, and, in the case of Sindh, the ascent of an ethnic Sindhi, Mumtaz Ali Bhutto (cousin of then Prime Minister Zulfikar Ali Bhutto, also a Sindhi), to the post of governor in December 1971. The response of the ethnic Mohajir community was literally incendiary. In an interview, he recalled that on his way to take the oath of office "there were tires burning in the streets."[5] Five months later, his role shifted to chief minister of Sindh, and it was during this period, in 1972, that Bhutto realized the deepest fears of the Mohajirs by declaring Sindhi to be an official language in Sindh.

Immediately thereafter, Mohajir students launched protests that were met in turn by those of Sindhi students. According to Bhutto, the motivation of the Mohajirs was arguably fear generated by the "hype" that had been generated by "the Urdu-speaking politicians [who claimed] that now Sindhis were to be in charge; the Urdu-speakers are going to be thrown into the sea, and you will not get jobs unless you know Sindhi and may be victimized and so on and so forth."[6] However, as discussed below, the fears of the Mohajirs were unfounded as the status and utility of Urdu remain well above that of Sindhi.

During the 1972 riots, Sindhi students were literally giving up their lives in defense of a *language policy*: how can the depth of passion be explained? According to Muhammad Qasim Bughio, a professor in Department of

Table 7.5. Language Population Proportions (Percentage): Pakistan and Sindh, 2014

Area	Urdu	Punjabi	Sindhi	Pashto	Baloch	Saraiki	Others
Pakistan	7.6	44.2	14.1	15.4	3.6	10.5	4.7
Sindh	21.1	7.0	59.7	4.2	2.1	1.0	4.9
Rural Sindh	1.6	2.7	92.0	0.6	1.5	0.3	1.3
Urban Sindh	41.5	11.5	25.8	8.0	2.7	1.7	8.8

Source: Pakistan Bureau of Statistics, Government of Pakistan, http://www.pbs.gov.pk/content/population-mother-tongue (accessed June 6, 2014).
Note: Totals may be higher than 100% due to rounding.

Sindhi at the University of Sindh and the chairman of the Sindhi Language Authority, the people are "emotionally attached to the language."[7] The head of the university, Mazahar Ulhaq Siddiqi (his formal title is vice chancellor as the formal chancellor is the governor of the province), believes that many people "have a very deep sense of injury to their pride when they feel that there are attempts . . . to relegate Sindhi to a secondary level."[8] A most emphatic (if zero-sum) elaboration on the existential importance of the language is offered by Sajjad Ali Shah, an ethnic Sindhi who assiduously ascended to the post of chief justice of the Supreme Court of Pakistan (1994–97): "The Sindhi nationalists will never give up on this issue. Our whole survival, our whole identity, as an ethnic group, as Sindhi-speaking people, depends on the language. This is our province and we don't want our language to die."[9]

The probability of Sindhi language death may be rather low, yet the status and professional utility of the language are far below that of Urdu. Whether implicit or explicit, attempts to marginalize Sindhi in favor of Urdu have been successful in many arenas, especially in regard to education. While Sindhis account for nearly 60 percent of the provincial population (see Table 7.5), the language is essentially excluded from urban classrooms. In a withering assessment by the International Crisis Group, "The overwhelming political influence of Mohajirs in Sindh has prevented the effective establishment of the Sindhi language in the education, government and commercial sectors. . . . Today there are only three Sindhi-medium schools in Karachi, the provincial capital. While public school students in the province's urban centers are still required to study Sindhi as a language up to class ten, this has been widely interpreted as mere lip service" (2004, 15). This is a point of no small dissatisfaction among Sindhis, especially those with children. According to Pakistan's

2012 Annual Status of Education Report, there is a significant disconnect between *parents'* preferences for language of instruction in high-status private primary schools and the actual language employed in the classroom: while 86 percent of students speak Sindhi at home, only 6 percent of private schools in the province employ Sindhi.[10] In a separate survey, Sindhi *students* were split between their desire for primary-language instruction and their parallel interest in the utility of English. In Tariq Rahman's survey of language attitudes in Pakistan, he asked Class Ten (sixteen-year-old) students about their preferences regarding language of instruction. Among the Sindhi students, 77 percent wanted their classes taught in Sindhi, but when asked to choose the best language of instruction for all of Pakistan, 42 percent responded English. Only 9 percent of Sindhi-speaking students expressed a desire for Urdu as the language of instruction. This preference may indicate not only an element of ethnonational resistance (Rahman 2002, 350), but also a curious element of class in Karachi: "While the English language-medium schools cater for the middle, upper-middle and upper classes, the Urdu language-medium schools are aimed at the lower-middle and working classes, and the madrassas provide education for poor, marginalized or very religious people" (Rahman 2004, 307).

An interesting point about the madrassas in Sindh, which like all madrassas focus on teaching the Arabic of the Quran, is that "the informal medium of instruction" is Sindhi. However, the other available *books* are not in Sindhi, marginalizing the importance of the language when placed in a religious context (Rahman 2002, 345). In this regard, the madrassas may parallel the view of what may be called the pan-nationalists of Pakistan, including civil servants and intellectuals, who adopted the same view as "they had in the case of the Bengali language movement and dubbed all expression of Sindhi nationalism as a communist and Indian conspiracy, while Sindhi itself was associated with Hinduism just as Urdu was associated with Islam" (Rahman 1996b, 119).

It is this nominally inverse relationship between the status of Sindhi vis-à-vis Urdu and Islam that is the focus of the second part of this chapter.

Islam in Sindh

The relationship between the state of Pakistan and Islam is existential. Founded on the doctrine of "two nations," that is, one Hindu and one Muslim,

Pakistan's founders established the new state on the principal of religious union. This, of course, was challenged almost immediately by the disenfranchised majority, the Bengalis; yet the *fact* of ethnonational disharmony was not enough to sway the *belief* of influential elites in the founding mythology of Islam. It is therefore not surprising that questions of ethnic politics, and particularly the possibility of changing borders—internal or external—are reflexively characterized as an affront to the faith. As Vali Nasr has argued, ethnic politics are either engaged or dismissed depending on the relative piety of the observer: "The Islamists and right-of-center intellectuals have since early in the country's history been a part of the project of Pakistan. They depict Pakistan as an Islamic entity, the embodiment of Islamic universalism and brotherhood. In this view, state borders are inviolable; or, anything short of that would question the universality of Islam, the faith, and truth that supersedes all other allegiances in the mind of the faithful. Questioning Pakistan's borders is therefore nothing short of infidelity to Islam" (2001, 196). On the other hand, secular intellectuals have consistently problematized the question of shifting borders, and "underscored the plurality of the Pakistan state, its lack of internal unity, the weak institutionalization of its borders, and the lack of a hegemonic notion of the state, or indeed nation" (Nasr 2001, 196).

The disjunction between Islamist and secular thinkers on questions of territory, autonomy, ethnicity, and religion is paralleled in the literature on the Sindhi (and other) nationalist movement(s). Just as the lion's share of contemporary literature on Pakistan targets the role of Islamic fundamentalism in the politics of Islamabad, the literature on Sindh is conspicuously quiet on the question of Islamism vis-à-vis separatism. It is as if the role of fundamentalism, clearly a problem in other parts of Pakistan, was irrelevant to the phenomenon of ethnonational Sindhi self-determination. And to a large extent this has been the case, and when it is mentioned it is only to highlight the incompatibility of Islamism with the ethnolinguistic narrative of Sindhi nationalists. There are three reasons for this differentiation. The first is the socialist heritage of the Sindhi political movement. The second is the tempering role of Sufism. And the third is a more fundamental challenge to Islam and its place in the narrative of the Sindhi nation.

In regard to socialism, it is important to recall that supporters of an independent Sindh "started to appear in the 1940s before Sindh became a part of Pakistan" (Siddiqi 2012, 75) and continued to grow during the heyday of secular international socialism. As Rahman argues, the separatists "were

partly inspired by socialist ideas of multinationalism" (1996b, 120). This can
be seen in the thoughts of a number of prominent Sindhi intellectuals and
political leaders, including but not limited to Ibrahim Joyo and G. M. Syed
(see below), as well as latter day figures such as Qadir Magsi, the leader of
the Sindh Taraqi Pasand (STP) party.[11] Ironically, however, while Sindhi nationalists argue political Islam was eschewed in favor of a secular goal—a Sindhi nation-state defined by ethnicity and region, not religion—Sindhi
nationalists will also frequently cite a mystical strain of Islam, Sufism, as an
important element of Sindhi identity. This is evident in the artistic heritage
of Sindh. According to Rahman, Sindhi "forms of literary expression were
honed through poetic and musical performance traditions closely associated
with the practices of Sufi religious orders" (2004, 307). However, though Sufism may fortify a shared Sindhi group identity, it is also lambasted politically for its passivity, thereby weakening the independence movement.
Ibrahim Joyo, a revered but retired Sindhi figure (b. 1915) who spent much
of his life advocating for Sindhi rights, argues Sufism explains why Sindhis
are unlikely to ever mobilize militarily. Unlike many other nationalist
movements in the region, such as the Baloch or Kashmiri, Sindhi nationalists
generally disavow violence, frequently and conventionally citing a culture infused with the ethics of Sufi tolerance. The reason is a cultural predilection
for reflection rather than fighting: for this "we blame the Sufis . . . they teach
people contentment, acceptance, passivity."[12] In parallel, University of Karachi political scientist Farhan Siddiqi argues the source of Sufi tolerance is
based on its "history of peaceful coexistence of various religions, and Sindhis
selected good points from every religion and presented them to the people in
what is known as Sufism" (2012, 86). Nonetheless, it would be disingenuous
to claim all Sindhi nationalists are pacifists. The Jeay Sindh party and the
Jiye Sindh Qaumi Mahaz (despite protests to the contrary—see below), for
example, can be characterized as militant; the same can be said of the STP.
Indeed, the latter's leader, Qadir Magsi, is widely considered responsible for
anti-Mohajir violence across Karachi in 1988.

Still, while the leadership of pro-Sindhi organizations often disagree on
the right path forward, they invariably agree on the importance of the influential legacy of religious pluralism. Frequently citing the many cultures that
have crisscrossed the territory over the millennia, Sindhis tend to celebrate
a tradition that is claimed to have successfully incorporated the best elements
of whatever other people happen to be cohabiting Sindh during any one century, whether Zoroastrians, Hindus, or Jains, though intriguingly *not always*

Arabs. This raises a third reason why the Sindhi independence movement has steered away from political Islam. It is an existential view that Sindhis are themselves defined in *opposition* to the Islam of the Arabs, who are sometimes derided as interloping invaders from the west. The views of G. M. Syed are particularly relevant here. Born Ghulam Murtaza Shah Syed (1904–95), he is credited with establishing the Jeay Sindh ("Free Sindh") movement in 1972, but his efforts at publicizing and proselytizing in favor of Sindhi independence predate this event by many decades. In the case of Syed, Siddiqi argues, "Islam in Sindh is presented as a peaceful religion mainly on account of the peaceful nature of the Sindh people, as opposed to the Arabs who are condemned as illiterate and warrior like" (2012, 86). Indeed, Syed's views go much further, decrying the influence of Arabs and their version of Islam for sullying the faith of Pakistan itself. Again, Siddiqi argues Syed sustained "a scathing critique of the Punjabi-dominated Pakistan as well as the official Islam which is celebrated and venerated by the ruling elite of the country. In this context, Syed is highly critical of Muhammad Bin Qasim, the Arab invader of Sindh regarded as a [Pakistani] national hero for introducing Islam in the subcontinent. Syed labels him as a looter and a plunderer while Raja Dahir, the Hindu ruler at the time of Bin Qasim's invasion is regarded as a hero and true patriot of Sindh" (2012, 86). It would be easy to disregard Syed's views of the Arabs as hyperbole, but his assertion that the dominance of political Islam in defining Pakistan is antithetical to the position of Sindhi nationalists cannot easily be dismissed. In this vein, consider the view of proindependence Bashir Qureshi, the late chairman of the Jiye Sindh Qaumi Mahaz (Long Live Sindh People's Movement), or JSQM: "Sindhis go to the mosque to pray, and nothing else."[13]

Political Mobilization in Sindh

Despite the widely shared feeling among Sindhis of being subordinate to both the Mohajirs and the Punjabis, Sindhi nationalist organizations have been less than successful at mobilizing broad based political support. Nowhere is this more evident than at the polls, where Sindhi nationalist parties routinely fail to capture a single seat in the assembly. There are three reasons for this unimpressive record. The first is the dominance of the Pakistan People's Party, or PPP; the second is the bitter feuding among the nationalists themselves who, as a result, remain deeply fractured. And finally there is the element of

an urban-rural class cleavage separating those who are more or less supportive of separatism.

The success of the PPP may be explained in part by the fact that the party
is *of* Sindh even if it is not always *for* Sindh, at least at the expense of the federal state. The party, created by former members of the Pakistan Socialist Party,
was established in 1967 by ethnic Sindhi Zulfikar Ali Bhutto. In the years to
come, the Bhutto clan came to dominate the PPP with what can fairly be called
a dynasty. His leadership of the PPP (1967–79) was followed by that of his wife
Nusrat Bhutto (1979–83), then his daughter Benazir Bhutto (1984–2007), and
then his grandson, Bilawal Bhutto Zardari (b. 1988). A party best described
as democratic socialist, the PPP enjoys class-based support across the country, which explains its success outside of Sindh—it was voted into power five
times since 1970[14]—but it is within Sindh where they enjoy the strongest support. This has been the case since the first general election in 1970, when Sindhi support for the PPP was "overwhelming" (A. Khan 2005, 127). At the same
time, the federalist PPP has little time for the literally provincial politics of
the Sindhi organizations. For example, Mazhar ul Haq, the leader of the PPP
in the Sindh Assembly, alleges "the nationalist parties," including the JSQM,
"are on army payrolls," and that the above-mentioned Mumtaz Bhutto, who
is also the chairman of the Sindhi Nationalist Front, "just wants to be paid
off by the army . . . that's why he wants to be seen as Number One, so he can
extort money from the military. He wants a big bribe."[15]

As for the Sindhi nationalists themselves, one of their greatest challenges
is structural: there are groups and splinters of groups, a multitude of opinions, and recurring accusations and recriminations among the elites. For example, Ibrahim Joyo, one of the founding fathers of the JSQM, is also critical
of Mumtaz Bhutto, charging that his outsized ego has led to delusions of power
as a kind of latter-day *sardar*, that is, a feudal lord of premodern Sindh.[16] Meanwhile, Qadir Magsi, chairman of the STP, finds the JSQM "obsolete."[17] Rasul
Bux Palijo, a member of the old guard who worked with G. M. Syed, said he
was disgusted with the internecine infighting and decided to quit both the
formal and informal party system in favor of a broad-based social movement
modeled on the nonviolence of Gandhi's "Quit India" campaign to oust the
British.[18] Moreover, none of this is new. As far back as the 1970s, G. M. Syed
and Palijo split ways over ideological distinctions, whereby Syed "proclaimed
a separatist political agenda as opposed to Palijo," who argued "for a recon-
stituted federal Pakistani polity" (Siddiqi 2012, 45). This intensified in
the 1980s when it was Palijo's party, the Sindhi Awami Tahreek (People's

Movement), that was separately "most responsible for confronting the state" rather than Syed's Jeay Sindh (Siddiqi 2012, 44).[19]

What is perhaps surprising here is the failure of the Sindhi nationalists to consolidate when their immediate rivals, the Mohajirs, successfully coalesced around a singularly counternationalist party, the Mohajir Qaumi Movement (Migrant National Movement), or MQM.[20] It was founded by a student at the University of Karachi, Altaf Hussain, who launched the All Pakistan Mohajir Student Organization in 1978. The MQM was "an instant hit" (Siddiqi 2012, 101), and within six years the organization had evolved into a full-fledged political machine. Its early success in Karachi was remarkable: just three years after its establishment as a bona fide party, it swept local elections in both Karachi and Hyderabad, supported in large part by working-class Urdu speakers. It has in years since retained a role as the number two party in Sindh, after the PPP.[21] Its success, however, has been marred by a reputation for ruthlessness, particularly in regard to enforcing loyalty among wavering members. Such tactics disturb the middle and upper classes of Karachi, who are especially fearful of reprisals by a party that is now associated with extortion, graft, and a predilection for violence. As the Mohajir owner of a large factory volunteered in an interview, the MQM are "nothing but a bunch of terrorists."[22] While this is the rather blunt opinion of one man, it is fair to say that the general position of MQM officials vis-à-vis the politics of Sindhi separatism is framed in zero-sum terms: any gains specifically attributed to the Sindhi-speaking population is viewed as a loss for the Urdu-speaking population. Indeed, MQM elites mirror Sindhi nationalist elites in describing the Sindhi/Mohajir divide in existential terms, though in this case as a threat to the existence of *Urdu*. For example, regarding a 2005 proposed enforcement of the 1972 Sindhi Act requiring Sindhi language examination of high school students, Nasreen Jalil, the former deputy mayor (*naib nazim*) of Karachi and a senator since 2012—as well as the longtime deputy convener of the MQM Coordinate Committee—is unequivocal: "If you ask me personally it's a conspiracy against the people who speak Urdu in this province, in Sindh province. . . . You cannot compare Sindhi and Urdu since Urdu is the national language. So you cannot replace Urdu."[23]

The suggestion that Sindhi nationalists would ever try (or wish to) erase Urdu from Sindh is prima facie far-fetched, if only because it attributes a great deal of power to the nationalists themselves. While it is fair to say the nationalists enjoy broad moral support in rural areas (even if their votes go to the PPP and the Pakistan Muslim League (Functional), abbreviated as PML

(F)), it is quiet a different scenario in urban areas. Even successful Sindhis in Karachi, for example, find the suggestion of a successful separatist movement a nonstarter. This is illustrated by the opinions of professionally successful Sindhis in Karachi. Syed Shafqat Ali Shah, the former director of Matiari Sugar Mills, argues that "Karachi is a different beast altogether," where economic opportunities and globalization render provincial concerns irrelevant. In short, he views Sindhi nationalists as rural, marginal, and misguided. Moreover, he expects little to come of their efforts: "What can they do? Come on to the streets, burn cars and buses? . . . Force and violence: it is not going to work. It has not worked, so far. The people of Sindh are basically peace-loving people."[24]

Conclusion

The Sindhi nationalist movement is both earnest and improbable. Its supporters are sincere in their belief that the Sindhis are a native people occupied and dominated by nonnative rivals who are at once dismissive and domineering. While they advocate different solutions—from communal rights to autonomy to independence—the leadership of the major nationalist organizations generally frame their grievances in the language of imperialism and colonization. They invoke the right of national self-determination for a unique people. It is improbable in that the success of a Sindhi separatist movement—barring any exogenous and catastrophic end to the state of Pakistan itself—is unlikely to succeed without a broad-based mobilization of both urban and rural citizens that cuts across social classes to form a truly unified force for change.

There is another factor, however, which suggests that support for such a mobilization is artificially weakened by an external force: the threat of state military intervention. This is not to say that the Sindhis would be successful, but the probability of violence in an unregulated Sindh remains. In the view of journalist and analyst Anatol Lieven, violence would indeed erupt without the army, even if it were in the form of spontaneous urban clashes, as opposed to militias engaged in unconventional warfare. In a rather bleak assessment, he writes, "I can state with melancholy confidence that the ability of Sindh's populations to regulate their differences peacefully in the absence of the Pakistani state would be low to non-existent" (Lieven 2011, 304). This appraisal mirrors the view of Mumtaz Bhutto of the Sindhi National

Front, who believes the actual support for Sindhi separatism is much higher across the population, but that the awareness of this support is limited because the nationalist sympathizers are largely rural and therefore out of sight of political power centers: just as the Pakistani regime "did not read the signs" warning of East Pakistan's secession, they remain "totally oblivious to what is going on in Sindh."[25]

Yet the question remains, *how* does one mobilize the population, motivate the masses to act as one? *According to Sindhi nationalists themselves, their identity is defined by their language, while religion remains a private affair divorced from politics.* Again, Ibrahim Joyo opines, "It is language that gives identity" while "religion in Sindh has played no political role communalizing."[26] As a consequence, says Palijo, the Sindhis do not fit into the broader narrative of Pakistan, which is based on the erstwhile unity of Islam and Urdu: "There lies the weakness of this country: it has got no basis, it has got no root, at all. And therefore it subsists, it lives only the basis of violence, of force: that is the army."[27] This is a view supported by Stephen Cohen, who doubts the state could effectively adapt to the reality of a disparate population composed of many distinct communities. He writes, "The army is unlikely to be able to fabricate an identity compatible with Pakistan's multiethnic, multi-sectarian realities" (Cohen 2004, 274). At the same time, however, the army is also able to block any attempts to redefine the identity of Pakistan or that of any one of its constituent peoples.

This is not to say alternative and optimistic scenarios are unavailable. Rahman suggests a more robust federal system with units bordered along the edges of ethnolinguistic populations. In this case, Pakistan would have five national languages (one for each distinct community, Punjabi, Pashtun, Sindhi, Saraiki, Balochi) and one official language, Urdu, for domestic use (and for Mohajirs) and one official language, English, for international use (Rahman 1997, 839).[28] This mirrors a proposal offered by David Laitin—originally in the context of Africa—whereby multilingual populations may successfully cohabit the same state without suffering any disadvantages of disenfranchisement vis-à-vis other groups (Laitin 1992). Yet both proposals depend on a state that is willing to adapt as its populations mobilize in different ways. To date, Pakistan cannot be described as such.

CHAPTER 8

Speaking to the Nation:
The Kashmiris of India

> Eleven persons take eleven paths.
>
> —Kashmiri proverb

Flying in from Delhi, a first view of the Kashmir Valley is magnificent: a fertile basin ringed by impossibly high Himalayan peaks. The largest city, Srinagar, was once a cool mountain retreat for colonials escaping India's oppressive summer heat. It is a beautiful place and on this point, at least, there is general agreement. Divides emerge immediately, however, on who "owns" Kashmir, and what actually happened to the place—de facto or de jure—following partition in 1947. Among elites and intellectuals, there are interminable squabbles over who said what and when and the proper legal status of the territory. The modern history of Kashmir is marked by questioned sovereignty, more than a dozen UN resolutions, interventions by Pakistan and the Organization of the Islamic Conference, and elections routinely marked by "widespread Indian chicanery" (Ganguly 2006, 46).

Proposed solutions—and there have been dozens (Yusuf and Najam 2009)—range from keeping the status quo to seceding from India and acceding to Pakistan, inter alia. There have been scores of political parties and militant organizations large and small, from both sides of the India-Pakistan border, feuding for decades over this otherwise lovely piece of real estate. As a case of separatist politics, Kashmir is "defined by a complex intersection of an international dispute with sources of conflict internal to the disputed territory and its Indian- and Pakistani-controlled parts" (Bose 2003, 207). While the wars fought between India and Pakistan over Kashmir are by and large a consequence of international relations—a perspective detailed at length elsewhere in a sea of publications (Kashmir studies has even been called an "industry"; Zutshi 2012, 1033)—this chapter considers the *internal* sources of conflict, specifically the relative importance of Islam vis-à-vis an ethnonational identity.

As is the theme of this book, the relative strength of an ethnonational identity is Kashmir is gauged by the relative strength of language politics in the mobilization of separatist parties and organizations. With the exception of Mindanao, *there is no other case in this volume where language politics are more conspicuous by their absence.* The Kashmiri vernacular is in no way the foundation for a print culture, which in the past had been the purview of Persian and then Urdu, but which currently emphasizes English above all others. The status of written Kashmiri remains that of a Low Culture language that, despite a heritage of poetry that extends back more than a few centuries, is simply no longer valued. This is the case for the erstwhile shared identity of Kashmiris—*Kashmiriyat*—whether mobilized politically around ethnicity or even Islam: "What iconic status does Kashmiri have for the identity of Kashmiriyat on either side of its Indian and Pakistan borders? In India, even those Islamic groups in Kashmir who aggressively oppose the current political status of the state, particularly that of its Kashmiri-speaking province, have articulated no serious identity with the Kashmiri language" (Kachru 2002). Why should this be the case?

One answer is the extreme diversity of the region. While more than half of the population speaks Kashmiri as their mother tongue, 45 percent do not; moreover, the minority is itself divided among nearly a dozen other languages (see Figure 8.1). Another answer is the relative importance of Islam as a more effective means of galvanizing a shared identity, but even in this case diversity among Muslims renders unity an unfulfilled goal. In such an environment, Islamism has found more political purchase among the Kashmiris than it would have otherwise.

Briefly, before entering this discussion, it is important to clarify toponyms. The term *Kashmir* is now essentially shorthand for the Indian federal state of Jammu and Kashmir, which includes the Kashmir Valley, Jammu, and Ladakh. On the Pakistan side of the de facto international border this territory is known as Indian-Occupied Kashmir, or IOK; the territory actually controlled by Pakistan is self-styled as Azad (Free) Jammu and Kashmir, or AJK. On the Indian side of the border, Azad Kashmir is known as Pakistan Occupied Kashmir, or POK.

Figure 8.1. Kashmir.

Kashmir in Context

Tracing the origins of the conflict in Kashmir is a thankless task, if only because there are many conflicting narratives, any one of which is likely to incense those who ascribe to a different explanation. Yet it is possible the range of players may agree to one claim: the struggle is *existential*, not only for the people of Kashmir, but also for the warring states that each claim the territory as their own. For Pakistan, the "loss" of Muslim Kashmir indicates a failure of the "two-nation" principle that is the raison d'être of Pakistan itself. For India, to lose Muslim Kashmir would indicate a failure of its secular ideology, which is essential to a multiethnic but inclusive India. For the Kashmiris, however, the struggle hinges less on the relative success of Islamabad or New Delhi in securing the territory, than on the struggle to define what is or is not, who is or is not, *Kashmiri*. This is due in no small part to the fact that Kashmir, as may be expected from a mountainous region, is highly diverse, divided among dozens of communities that practice different faiths and speak different languages. What then do they have in common? One (very) short answer is history.

The region of Jammu and Kashmir was united as a princely state of British India in 1846 under the Treaty of Amritsar, an agreement that—in exchange for fealty to Britain—ensconced the family of an ethnic Dogra and upper-caste Hindu maharaja, Gulab Singh, in power "forever." In this case, "forever" meant just one century, as the partition of India in 1947 rendered the treaty an artifact of colonial rule. As a Muslim-majority territory with a Hindu ruler, the princely state was faced with a dilemma: on the one hand its population was mostly Muslim (77 percent), and should therefore be expected to join Pakistan; on the other, the decision was formally left to a maharajah who was given the right to choose India, Pakistan, or independence. The clumsy machinations of Gulab Singh, who initially wavered before calling on India to repel a Pakistan-backed invasion of Muslim militants from the north, resulted in not only the first war between India and Pakistan, but also a legacy of unsettled claims and uncertain allegiances.

While the war divided the territory of Kashmir, the politics of the princely state were formally divided some years earlier. In 1932, "J&K's first political party, the All-Jammu and Kashmir Muslim Conference" (Muslim Conference) was established as a reform body targeting the malfeasance of the maharaja (Bose 2003, 20). However, as a political organization that mobilized around social reform, as well as the cross-cutting cleavage of fighting political corruption, the group later recognized that it could represent not only Muslims, but Hindu Pandits and Sikhs as well. Thus, the Muslim Conference was renamed as a secular and left-leaning organization, the National Conference (NC), in 1939. It was this party, under the leadership of a charismatic school teacher named Sheikh Abdullah, that was to define the politics of Kashmir for decades. Chief among its early actions (1944) was the drafting of its manifesto, titled *Naya Kashmir* (New Kashmir), which Sumantra Bose calls "the most important political document in modern Kashmir's history," for it not only established popular sovereignty and democracy as the foundation of its politics, but also showed an "authoritarian streak" at odds with liberalism. Despite (and perhaps enabled by) this tendency, the NC did deliver on a key promise: sweeping land reform that transferred over a million acres of land to a million landless peasants, effectively ending feudalism in the region. More than any other, it was this accomplishment that led the population to view the leader of the NC, Sheikh Abdullah, as a "messiah" (Bose 2003, 25, 27–28).

Abdullah's views on the ultimate fate of Kashmir—going with India, going with Pakistan, or going it alone—are therefore worthy of no small discussion. At the time of partition, Abdullah rejected Pakistan as a "feudal state" and—in the view of Navnita Chadha Behera—the "critical factor that swayed accession in India's favor was . . . the political conviction of the National Conference's largely Muslim leadership that Kashmir's autonomy would be better protected in a secular and democratic Indian state" (Behera 2006, 39). This conviction, however, was short-lived. A fundamental dispute quickly emerged between Abdullah and India's first prime minister, Jawaharlal Nehru: the former believed Kashmir and India should be partners; the latter believed Kashmir should be a subordinate part of greater India. Hence, Abdullah came to believe that independence would be a better option for a free and prosperous Kashmir. It was this position that led to his arrest in 1953, an incarceration that lasted eleven years. As their "messiah" was now in jail, the people of Kashmir found that their protests were met with crackdowns, their hopes for democracy squashed by the hegemony of New Delhi. A series of despotic regimes came and went over succeeding decades that came to alienate virtually every element of Kashmiri society from the state itself. While India and Pakistan continued to clash over the territory, many of the actual people of Kashmir were initially rendered passive bystanders, corralled by autocratic rulers and hundreds of thousands of soldiers who are invariably young, a long way from home and well aware they are not at all welcome (Ganguly 2006, 49). Abdul Gani Bhat, a former All Parties Hurriyat Conference leader and professor at the University of Kashmir, expresses this sentiment: "What you need to understand is that I feel deeply hurt, wounded, probably into the depths of my soul when a man from Kerala, a *soldier* from Kerala, asks me on the soil of Kashmir, 'Show me your identity card.' This is the most heinous violation of human rights: a man who does not know Kashmir, a man who was never born in Kashmir, a man who never can speak Kashmiri . . . he has the cheek, the audacity to ask me a question, 'Are you a Kashmiri? Show me your identity card,' I feel deeply hurt and I feel, collectively, deeply hurt."[1] G. M. Shah, a former chief minister of Jammu and Kashmir, is even more blunt, saying, "We are being treated just like slaves."[2] Thus, while the interstate wars were fueled by Pakistan's rhetoric of two nations, ultimately "the roots of the crisis that erupted in 1989–1990 lie in a post-1947 history of denial of democratic rights and institutions to the people of J&K" (Bose 2003, 7).

This is, of course, not the only explanation. Stephen Saideman, for example, argues that the tensions between India and Pakistan over Kashmir may have many sources, but that "unrealized irredentism is at the core of the rivalry," as Pakistan as sought again and again to "regain" its "lost" territory (2005, 203). Reeta Chowdhari Tremblay, on the other hand, focuses on the "contrasting regime types" of India and Pakistan—democracy in the former, authoritarian in the latter—with a special emphasis on Pakistan's military regimes that "create structural and normative distortions in decision-making" (2005, 225–26). However, though explanations of this kind help us understand the state-level drivers of interstate conflict, how is this supposed to converge with arguments based on the politics of Kashmiris themselves? Derided by some critics, including T. V. Paul and William Hogg, who argue that such explanations are "based on idiosyncratic variables pertaining to decision makers, nation-state, or regional level factors" (2005, 251), the arguments of authors like Bose and Sumit Ganguly (Ganguly 2001, 1997) actually help us understand the political mobilization of the people(s) of Kashmir (more on this below). Put another way, such "idiosyncratic" variables address a more fundamental question: why are Kashmiris willing to fight and die for their cause? And more to the point, *what* is their cause?

A frequent and reflexive answer in and around the region is *azadi*, which is to say "freedom,'" in this case perhaps best clarified as popular sovereignty. But this does not answer a separate existential question: *who* are these sovereign people? A simple response is "the people of Kashmir," but this is ultimately dissatisfying, in no small part because there is disagreement among the *peoples* of Kashmir on this very question.

Language in Kashmir

Kashmiri is conventionally known as a "Dardic" language, a geographical distinction denoting languages spoken in the far north of India and northwestern Pakistan. Its linguistic heritage includes the Indo-Aryan and Iranian families, though its vocabulary also includes words from Sanskrit, Punjabi, Hindi/Urdu, and Arabic. Importantly, Kashmiri is distinct among the Dardic languages for it is "probably the only Dardic language that has a written literature dating back to the 13th century, a writing script of its own . . . [and a] rich tradition of oral and written literature" (Munshi 2006, 158). The original script, called *Sharada*, is now used only for liturgical purposes among a very small number of Hindu priests. Its contemporary script is a modification of the Perso-Arabic script (called *Nastaliq*), and this is the most popular form employed, though Hindu Pandits in Jammu now use the Devanagari script—also used for Hindi—to write and read Kashmiri (Rashid 2009; see also Bukhari 2013), *if* they are among the very few who can do so. The rich heritage of their mother tongue is largely lost to modern Kashmiris as very few native speakers can read (let alone write) the language (Munshi 2006, 160). An acting director of the Government Press Office in the J&K Ministry of Information estimated "only 5 to 6 percent of all Kashmiris can read 'Kashmirian,' maybe one half of 1 percent can write it."[3]

That this should be the case is largely a function of the state—both in the colonial era and in post-1947 India—which did not standardize the language, preventing its use in commerce and, especially, classrooms. In the early decades of the nineteenth century, the neglect of Kashmiri was the practice of not only the ruling Dogra elite, but also the Muslim leadership, who met questions about language of instruction in schools with "complete silence" (Zutshi 2004, 194). Hence, it was uncontroversial that schools taught in either Hindi or Urdu, regionally foreign languages that had to be acquired to enable learning. Moreover, before 1947 most people in the region had no access to education whatsoever: literacy was a luxury few could afford. Thus, it is perhaps not surprising there was not a single newspaper to be published or printed in J&K until 1924, due in no so small part to "the mass illiteracy due to a paucity of even primary education for Muslims" (Bose 2003, 17).

Following partition in 1947, language planning was addressed in New Delhi directly with a robust scheme for what might be considered ethnolinguistic emancipation. India's constitution was drafted in 1949 and ratified in 1950: it stipulates the national language of the country is Hindi, which is currently spoken natively by 41 percent of the population, now estimated at 1.22 billion. English is recognized as an official language of the entire country as well as the twenty-eight federal states. But there are also fourteen other languages with "national" status in India: Assamese, Bengali, Gujarati, Kannada, Kashmiri, Malayalam, Marathi, Oriya, Punjabi, Sanskrit, Sindhi, Tamil, Telugu, and Urdu. Kashmiri is spoken by less that one-half of 1 percent of India's population, but it is the spoken language of the majority in Jammu and Kashmir. It is not, however, the official language of the federal state of J&K, which is Urdu, despite the fact that Urdu is the mother tongue of an

Table 8.1. Languages in Jammu and
Kashmir, 2001

Language	Population	Percentage
Kashmiri	5,425,733	53
Dogri	2,205,560	22
Hindi	1,870,264	18
Punjabi	190,675	2
Ladakhi	101,466	1
Other	350,002	3
Total	10,143,700	100

Source: India Census 2001.

unknown few in the region. This is a legacy of the Naya Kashmir manifesto: "Recognizing the multilingual character of J&K—Kashmiri being the dominant tongue only in the valley and a few areas in Jammu, while Dogri is dominant only in the Jammu plains—the manifesto designates Urdu as the official lingua franca" (Bose 2003, 25) (see Table 8.1).

Yet while Urdu was initially embraced as a symbol of Kashmir's distinctive Muslim heritage, it has faded in both utility and popularity. Importantly, it has not been supplanted by the mother tongue of the majority: English, *not* Kashmiri, is the dominant language of status and social mobility. At the University of Kashmir in Srinagar, for example, students converse with each other and their professors almost entirely in English. Despite the official status of Urdu, there is little interest in studying the language, either as a medium of instruction or as a discrete subject. Public schools still teach Urdu in grammar and middle schools, but are introduced to English in high school. In private schools, the state of Jammu and Kashmir ranks third in India (after Andhra Pradesh and Tamil Nadu) for the highest percentage of students enrolled in English-medium institutions (Pratyush 2007). Thus, while most graduates are somewhat proficient in Kashmiri, Urdu, and English, a university professor laments, "there are very few people here who are perfect in [any] one language."[4] Moreover, it is also important to recognize that graduates are a small minority in a general population, of which only two out of three people can read at all: in 2011, the literacy rate for Jammu and Kashmir was 67.2 percent.[5]

Nonetheless, there are some efforts to recognize the literary heritage of Kashmiri by raising its status to that of a "classical language," a distinction that has been granted to only five other languages in India, including Tamil, Kannada, Telugu, Sanskrit, and Malayalam (Rashid 2009; see also Warikoo 1996). This would grant some government funds to support the maintenance and promotion of the language, as well as academic efforts to maintain research. It would also support efforts to teach Kashmiri as a subject in public schools (UNI 2008). But these efforts have yet to make much progress. This is due in no small part to the fact that Kashmiri language activists are very few in number and face an uphill battle against the general indifference of most speakers. Kashmiri was and is a language of personal communication, but in the shadow or more widely established languages, it never achieved the all-important status required for the evolution of a print culture. On this point, consider the view of Kashmiri linguist, Braj Kachru, professor of linguistics emeritus and jubilee professor of liberal arts and sciences at the University of Illinois:

> The domains of function of native Kashmiri were primarily restricted to the home and non-formal interactions. The language never overcame that marginality, and never was assigned elevated or formal functions. The languages of literary culture in Kashmir at various periods of its history have been, essentially, Persian, Urdu, Hindi, and much later—and to a smaller extent—English. The Kashmiri language was never in competition with any of these "elevated" languages of wider communication. In fact, attitudinally the Kashmiri language had a lower status than other languages of power, and functionally it had very restricted domains. This linguistic choice was again a consequence of the marginality of the natives of the state, the status of their language, and indeed the attitude of Kashmiris themselves toward their own language. (Kachru 2002, 8–9)

As a result, the current language scenario has three language domains: one for Urdu, one for English, and one for Kashmiri. According to Shafi Shauq, professor of Kashmiri language at the University of Kashmir, "Urdu is just for there on the paper as the official language. Kashmiri is the mother tongue; it is the common parlance, it is the common speech of the common masses, except for . . . the new rich people in the urban areas who send their children to the English medium schools . . . Otherwise, in the rural areas [of the

Kashmir Valley], Kashmiri survives as the language of the masses, language of the 99.9 percent people. They love their language, but they are not politically conscious about language."[6] Overall, there is a consensus in the valley that *written* Kashmiri is close to functional extinction. A native resident who reports for the Associated Press simply states that printed Kashmiri "is dying," if it is not dead already.[7] Note, however, that this is not at all the case in regard to *spoken* Kashmiri, which as a mother tongue of millions "remains a pivotal element in Kashmiri identity" (Evans 2008, 721), particularly of a nascent, secular ethnonational identity called "Kashmiriyat." (This is an old term that gained new currency in late 1970s, but it was not part of the critical political dialogue of the 1930s and 1940s.) It "refers to Kashmiri identity cutting across the religious divide and defined by, above all, the key elements of the love of the homeland (*Kashir*) and common speech (*Koshur*)" (Madan 2008, 28). The political context of this identity is discussed below.

Islam in Kashmir

Islam ensconced itself in Kashmir not by conquest, but by the conversion of a Buddhist, a Tibetan fugitive named Rinchana, who became the first Muslim sultan of Kashmir in 1320. However, the process had started as a "peaceful penetration" by "traders and adventurers" centuries earlier (M. Khan 2005, 1), and would continue for centuries more as a syncretic and distinctly Sufi interpretation of Islam spread through Kashmiri society. This form of Islam adopted unique characteristics as it maintained a balance between formal and informal practices. In short, Kashmiri Islam "always maintained a somewhat uneasy relationship between the Arabic (classical) and local traditions, never deaf to the call of the former but never also in denial of the latter" (Madan 2008, 14). A critical component of this development was a reaction against the caste system perpetuated by the dominant Hindu Brahmans, one of a number of factors that led to mass conversions in Kashmir, especially from the thirteenth to the sixteenth centuries (Hangloo 2008). Indeed, as early as the fifteenth century, the majority of Kashmiris had become Muslims, principally Sunni, but with a sizable Shia minority as well (Madan 2008, 10).

The contemporary composition of religious populations in the region is, however, dangerously divided not between Sunni and Shia but between Muslim and Hindu, spatially separated by the internal boundary of Jammu and Kashmir. While the latter is almost exclusively Muslim, the former is

Table 8.2. Religions in Jammu and Kashmir

Division	Population (%)	Muslim (%)	Hindu (%)	Sikh (%)	Buddhist (%)
Kashmir	5,476,970 (53.9)	97.16	1.84	0.88	0.11
Jammu	4,430,191 (43.7)	30.69	65.23	3.57	0.51
Ladakh	236,539 (2.3)	47.40	6.22	0.00	45.87
Total	10,143,700 (100)	66.97	29.63	2.03	1.36

Source: India Census 2001.

two-thirds Hindu. (The remaining territory of Ladakh, split evenly between Muslims and Buddhists, composes less than 3 percent of the total population.) It was not always thus. Before the conflagration of 1989–90, a sizable population of Hindus lived in the Kashmir Valley, but thousands of them abandoned their homes and fled south to escape the violence, some of it targeted specifically at Hindu civilians. However, if Hindus and Muslims had previously lived side by side for centuries, and both had suffered decades of political marginalization under successive regimes characterized by corruption of all kinds, how did religion ultimately come to mobilize sectarian violence (see Table 8.2)?

In addition to the geographic divide between Jammu and Kashmir, as well as a split between Kashmiri Muslims and the broader population of Indian Muslims spread elsewhere across India, Ganguly offers two other explanations. The first is linked directly to Bose's claim that it was a lack of democracy that ultimately led to the politics of religious identity: "when secular politics fails to offer adequate channels for the expression of discontent, the only viable means that remains is the pursuit of political mobilization along ethno-religious lines." The second is Pakistan, specifically its intention to destabilize its arch enemy by funding, training, and organizing a "loose, unstructured movement into a coherent, organized enterprise," greatly facilitated by the presence of battle-hardened mujahedeen who, having defeated the Soviet Union in Afghanistan, now sought a new cause (Ganguly 1997, 40, 41). Yet this does not explain why the militant insurgency took root in Kashmir when it did; in other words, why then and there? For his part, Ganguly offers a separate answer, which hinges on demographic and social changes among the people of Kashmir. Counterintuitively, these changes were wrought by a broad expansion of education in the region—both secular and religious—and a corresponding rise in literacy, *though in languages other than their mother tongue*, that is, Urdu at first, and later English. The transformation was stunning

Table 8.3. Literacy Rates in Jammu and Kashmir, 1961–81

Year	Male %	Female %	Total %	% increase
1961	16.97	4.26	11.03	N/A
1971	26.75	9.28	18.58	68.45
1981	36.29	15.88	26.67	43.54

Source: India Census 1981, cited in Ganguly (1997, 32).

for its speed, though it should be acknowledged that the bar was initially set very low: in 1961 only 11 percent of Kashmiris could read (see Table 8.3).

As this process continued, the "electorate changed from a politically passive to an increasingly politically aware and assertive population" that came to recognize Kashmir was exceptional in India for the degree to which "elections were routinely compromised" (Ganguly 1997, 31). Thus, a nascent civil society in Kashmir came to the realization that their lot was not common, that their fate was not sealed, and that they could effect some agency going forward as political mobilization came within reach.

Yet the emergence of a civil society hinges on the existence of a people that share—or come to share—a common sense of social self, an identity around which a civil consciousness may coalesce. And this raises a separate but essential question: who are the Kashmiris? This is in no uncertain terms a thorny question, which Behera admirably takes to task. For her, "the deeply plural character of Jammu and Kashmir society is at the hear of the secessionist movement in the state and helps to account for secessionist demands as well as failures." This is a plurality that includes many diverse communities: "Gujjars, Nakkarwals, Kashmiri Pandits, Dogras, and Ladakhi Buddhisits on the Indian side; and Balti, Shina, Khowar, Burushaski, Wakhi, and Pahari-speaking people on the Pakistan side; as well as Ismaili, Sunni, Shia, and Nur Bakshi sects of Islam in Azad Kashmir and the Northern Areas. Each is struggling to nurture its sociocultural identity" (Behera 2006, 104). However, while this long list of social groups indicates the consolidation of *a* Kashmiri people, united socially but divided internationally, who can effectively claim sovereignty of *the* people is a distant possibility, the consolidation of a people composed of the Kashmir Valley appears much more probable (Evans 2008). As a territorially discrete entity, this shared sense of collective self would necessarily include the majority Kashmiri Muslims but also the other ethnicities and sects that share the Valley, including but not limited to Hindus. Thus, this identity—conventionally called Kashmiriyat—is necessarily secular. This is, in fact, the view of Shabir Ahmad Shah of the J&K Democratic Freedom Party, who states "by Kashmir, we mean people who were living and who are living, who are residing in Kashmir, including Hindus, Muslims, Sikhs, Christians, irrespective of color, caste, creed, and religion. We are basically democrats and secular."[8]

The window of opportunity for a shared secular identity for Kashmir, however, may have already closed. As Madan argues (2008, 29), "the secular concept of Kashmiriyat is in today's circumstances rather vague, it has an uncertain future, particularly because the events of the last quarter century have sharpened communal identities in all regions of the state (Jammu, Kashmir, and Ladakh)." This is due in no small part to the fact that during the 1990s Kashmiriyat came "under serious attack on the one hand by fundamentalist groups such as the Hizbul-Mujahideen and on the other by an association of the displaced Kashmiri Pandit (Hindu) community with Hindu-oriented political groups such as the BJP (Bhartiya Janata Party)" (Tremblay 1997, 473). However, over the past decade it may be more useful to supplant the term *secular* with *sectarian*, insofar as it is possible for the Muslims of the Kashmir Valley to be united as *secular Muslims* in opposition to neighboring communities. It is this mobilization that deserves special consideration.

Political Mobilization in Kashmir

At the time of writing, the separatist groups in the valley remain in the orbit of the central All Parties Hurriyat Conference (APHC), a social and political group founded in 1993 to pursue national self-determination for Kashmir.[9] The APHC is split between what may be called two "major factions" led by Syed Ali Shah Geelani and Mirwaiz Omar Farooq, respectively (Tremblay 2009, 940). In general, the schism between these leaders—at once conservative versus progressive, old versus young, Islamist versus secular—is very wide, though both express a dream of "azadi" for the "people of Kashmir." What that means, however, is entirely distinct for each man. Based on extended interviews, the following is a profile of each leader that hinges on the question of "who is a Kashmiri?" and, by extension, "who are the Kashmiri people?"

Mirwaiz Umar Farooq, the chairman of the APHC, has long had the reputation of a reformer. He is young (b. 1973) and active: Bose calls him "a moderate advocate of self-determination" who declines to "play the game" of co-optation (2003, 239). Farooq argues there are three reasons for the perennial political chaos that plagues the state of Jammu and Kashmir. The first is a matter of international relations: "Really when you talk about Kashmir, you talk about an issue and the issue is between two parties. But the problem in Kashmir is that we have three parties and that's why it makes it more complex to deal with. I mean, we have India, we have Pakistan and then we have the people of Kashmir."[10] The second issue is the geographic and demographic diversity of the territory. And the third is the question of who qualifies as a Kashmiri. While he argues there is "a definite national identity," that is, a population dedicated to self-rule, the identity itself is not yet defined: "We are neither Indians; we are neither Pakistanis and as Kashmiris we don't have a recognition as such." Moreover, the people "of Kashmir are not a homogenous body, you know. There are differences right from east to west so that's why it is basically about an identity . . . how best can we preserve the identity of Kashmir and also look into possibilities of, you know, having I would say 'associations' with both India and Pakistan. That's a very difficult question."[11]

He does not find the question of Islam difficult: "I tell you with all authority that the people of Kashmir are secular." He disregards Islamist organizations (like Geelani's, below) as principally creations of Pakistan. The cacophony of leadership, he argues, stems from the spontaneous nature of the indigenous militants who emerged in the 1980s and 1990s: "It was never talked about what we are doing. What is the direction? It was a spontaneous sort of a situation where militants started coming up and people started supporting it and then, of course, India retaliated with might. Of course, that had an impact." In recent years, however, waning militancy has turned some former militants into politicians and social activists: "people started moving on political levels, you know, more political ideologies, more to do with people than to do with guns and bombs."[12]

His proposed solution is an independent state with a federal constitution, what he calls the United States of Kashmir. Each of the five regions within Jammu and Kashmir would enjoy regional autonomy. Yet this raises the question of communication: what would be the official language(s)? Farooq is not concerned: "Before [1947] it was Persian and then it became Urdu. Now it's English. I don't think that is a real question for Kashmir."[13]

Neither it is a question for Syed Ali Shah Geelani, the former chairman of the APHC and current leader of the fundamentalist faction (Jamat-e-Islami) of the APHC. This immediately raises an important point: by any definition Geelani is an avowed Islamist. He states clearly that "Islam is a complete way of life and there is no scope or any reason that politics should be separated from the Islamic religion and Islamic basic principles." He views the "the whole ummah, which is more than one billion people at a global level" as having strayed from the true interpretation of the Quran, that is, "Islam is a complete way of life," chiefly because "nationalism is overpowering."[14] Nonetheless, he also employs the rhetoric of self-determination, democracy (i.e., majority rule), and anticolonialism to describe and justify a demand for autonomy, independence, or accession to Pakistan. For example, on self-determination he claims "the people of Jammu and Kashmir, whether they are Muslims or Hindus or Sikhs or Christians, whether they are residing in any part of Jammu and Kashmir, they should be given the right to self-determination for then they will decide their future, whether they want to be with India and accede to—or they want to accede to Pakistan." On democracy he insists majority rule will win out even if that means the people decide to stay with India, even though expects "the majority of the people of Jammu and Kashmir will want to accede to Pakistan."

Yet his consistent platform that Jammu and Kashmir should quit India and accede to Pakistan is no longer popular (if it ever really was).[15] Sumit Ganguly's analysis finds "large segments of the population, especially in the predominantly Muslim Kashmir Valley, remain profoundly alienated from Indian rule . . . [as well as] deeply skeptical of Pakistan's intentions" (Ganguly 2006, 50). Nonetheless, in Geelani's view, "there are only two options: India or Pakistan," though begrudgingly he adds, "We are not rigid that the people should accede to Pakistan." As for independence, "we will accept this also." His preference for Pakistan is justified by invoking the "two-nations" ideology of partition, recalling that in 1947 the majority of the region was Muslim: hence, they were to join Pakistan, but were prevented from doing so by the Indian military.[16]

On the question of language, Geelani echoes Gellner in discarding any question of ethnolinguistic identification challenging Islam: "We are Muslims and all affairs of our individual, our collective life, are guided by the Islamic principles. So, there is no difference on the basis of language." Rather incredibly, he maintains,

> The majority of the people of Jammu and Kashmir are speaking Urdu
> and they are writing in Urdu and they are supposed to use the Urdu

language as far as the Urdu domestic situation and domestic affairs are concerned. But as far as official communications and official business are concerned, in spite of that the official language is Urdu, the work is being done in English. So, this is unfortunate: all work, political and social affairs should be [in Urdu] because Urdu is our official language. All the business should be done in Urdu, but this is not the practical situation. Practically, it is that English is overwhelming, you see, overpowering as far as Kashmir is concerned. So the language is not a basic factor for our people.[17]

Conclusion

Sustained guerrilla activity in Kashmir has waned significantly since the 1990s (Routray 2012, 189), but intermittent violence remains a part of life in Srinagar, as do "arbitrary and unlawful detentions by the state police" (Amnesty International 2013). However, filling the vacuum once occupied by militants, political organizations are now the most prominent players in the separatist movement. These parties, however, are divided by incompatible visions of Kashmiri identity. Islamist platforms appeal to the founding principals of India and Pakistan, namely two states for two nations defined by religious affiliation. In this regard, any identity markers other than Islam are irrelevant. More progressive separatists wrestle with the broader question of Kashmiri identity, *but the low status of the Kashmiri language and the demographic complexity of a multilingual region dispel any questions of language rights as a serious political issue.*

Visions of what kind of government would be chosen and appropriate for the state population, however, remain little more than abstractions while Kashmir remains pitted between a pair of powerful antagonists: "the internal divisions between segments with conflicting notions of self-determination are real, but the major obstacle to a peace process is the abysmal relations between India and Pakistan" (Bose 2003, 218). While India's "political engagement with Pakistan remains ad hoc" (Chandran 2012), there are some unilateral efforts toward conflict resolution. India, for example, has launched a program to bring former militants still living in Pakistan to return to India. Though Pakistan is not a participant in the program, the one-time jihadi insurgents are allowed to leave Pakistan and, via Nepal, establish residence back home in Kashmir (Harris 2013). However, this is a very modest step in the context of what is widely considered the most likely option for sustained peace in Kashmir, that is, some sort of de facto regional autonomy (Routray 2012; Chandran 2012; Wirsing 2004), both as a federal state within India and as a region of three territories within Kashmir: Jammu, Kashmir, and Ladakh.

CHAPTER 9

From Nationalism to Islamism?
The Acehnese of Indonesia

Deep down it is the honor and the dignity of the
Achehnese race and Islam that is involved and being
restored here.

—Hasan di Tiro, 1977

Indonesia is home to more Muslims than any other country in the world.
Nearly 90 percent of its 251 million people practice Islam; but even though
they are nearly united in faith, Indonesians are divided socially—by ethnicity, culture, and language—and literally: from the western tip of Sumatra to
the eastern border with Papua New Guinea, the state's borders stretch across
one-eighth the circumference of the globe. While the majority of Indonesians
derive from Malay origins, there are at least four hundred different ethnic
groups, most with "indigenous languages so different that communication
between the communities is impossible" (Sundhaussen 1989, 423).[1]

At the far west of the enormous Indonesian Archipelago, on the island
of Sumatra, is the province of Aceh (see Figure 9.1).[2] There are 4.4 million
people in Aceh, who collectively account for less than 2 percent of Indonesia's
population.[3] Of this number, some four out of five are ethnically Acehnese,
a people concentrated in a single political unit, who speak their own language
and compose a formally recognized ethnic group. Many of them also fought
for independence from Indonesia in a series of bloody clashes—from 1976 to
2005—that claimed more than 30,000 lives. In the wake of the astonishing dev-
astation of the 2004 earthquake and tsunami centered off the west coast of
Aceh—which claimed nearly 170,000 lives in Aceh alone—the separatists and

Figure 9.1. Aceh.

the state came to the end of a peace process that had started years earlier. Their longtime goal of complete national self-determination was not reached, but a functioning special autonomy for the region was established, which, to date, shows no real signs of weakening. The people of Aceh are effectively at peace with Indonesia. There is, however, an important caveat to this pacification: the people of Aceh are also in a state of social and political transition.

While the concept of the Acehnese as a single ethnicity with a distinct territory of their own is conventional, the people and place are actually rather diverse, with variations in dialect, custom (*adat*), and the practice of Islam (Schroter 2010).[4] The dominant *nation*, however, is in no uncertain terms the Acehnese in toto. A major conceptual problem, however, is that the definition of this nation is perennially fluid, not only as the Acehnese see themselves, but also in how they relate to the state of Indonesia, not to mention the critical place of Islam in determining Acehnese identity. In the words of Ed Aspinall, "Although the two sides in the conflict fought with guns, fire, and bombs, their battle was fundamentally about the identity of the people at the center of the conflict, the Acehnese themselves" (2009, 3).

In this chapter I argue not only that the dynamic identity of the Acehnese has shifted from an Islamic emphasis to an ethnonational character, but also that the identity may be shifting back toward a more Islamic focus. While the sense of *being* Acehnese remains strong, the challenge of clearly *defining* Acehnese remains elusive. As already discussed at length, one reason for this identity ambiguity is the lack of a unique print culture that could otherwise unite the population as an imagined community that is both linked and limited by the extent of its own language. Instead, the Acehnese share the same print culture as that of their former antagonists, that is, the official language Bahasa Indonesia. Hence, as Aceh continues to forge its own path following the peace agreement of 2005, the people are confronted with the challenge of defining themselves *contra* the state of Indonesia and its dominant *ethnie*, the Javanese, by emphasizing some other identity marker besides the ethnolinguistic. One way to do this is by celebrating the special status of Islam in Aceh, and by claiming a heritage of piety that is separate and superior to the rest of the country.

Aceh in Context

The concept of Aceh as a special region is dated not in decades but in centuries. As the first point of contact for early Muslim traders and travelers sailing from the west, Aceh developed as the first and most important center of Islam in the archipelago, famously winning the moniker "verandah of Mecca" (Lapidus 2002). Though the arrival of Islam arguably came in waves between the seventh and twelfth centuries (Basri 2010b), the legacy of the faith in Aceh was established solidly by the great Ali Mughayat, the first sultan of Aceh (r. 1496–1530). From that time to this, it is not only a convention to equate "Acehnese" with "Muslim," but also to identify the population as especially pious when compared to their regional neighbors. This sultan also greatly expanded the territorial reach of Aceh's power, and in the process established key institutions that would come to define the region. Hence, "the Acehnese conquest of [the Portuguese and the seizure of] the all important ports of northern Sumatra was accomplished by the death of Ali Mughayat in 1530. This was the effective foundation of the Acehnese state and identity" (Reid 2006, 12; 2005).

The social structure of Aceh during the four centuries of the sultanate (1496–1903) was two-pronged. While the sultan was himself at the head of the hierarchy, there was a pair of separate elite ranks that generally maintained social and political order. This model is important to our story and is explained nowhere so succinctly as by the preeminent historian of Aceh, Anthony Reid. His view is worth quoting at length:

> Until [the social revolution of] 1946 there were two elites responsible for upholding the two normative systems, which a variety of proverbs expressed in terms of complementarity. The *ulama* were expert in Islamic law and administered it when appropriate. Adat [custom] governed the system of landholding and inheritance, however, and in such matters the village head (*keucik*) and the hereditary chief of the district (*ulèëbalang*) held authority. The sultan's court in its seventeenth century heyday patronized the ulama as a means to increase leverage against the ulèëbalang [nobility], though as its grip subsequently weakened it was often the victim of clerical criticism. Dutch abolition of the sultanate [1903] left ulèëbalang and ulama in more direct confrontation as rival authorities in defining Acehneseness. (Reid 2006, 9)

This confrontation, between powers spiritual and political, has shifted back and forth dramatically throughout the past century, though it has never been resolved completely. This confrontation continues to define the politics of identity in Aceh.

The defeat of the Dutch and the end of imperialism in Indonesia instigated, unsurprisingly, a range of structural changes as the new state built its own institutions and, under the secular leadership of Sukarno (1901–70), sought to establish a new national identity for all Indonesians. In Aceh, however, the exit of the Dutch in 1949 opened a political arena for a new period of struggle between the ulèëbalang and the ultimately victorious ulama. The outcome of this struggle would lead to another conflict, the Darul Islam rebellion (1953–59), this time pitting Islamists—led by the first governor of Aceh, Daud Beureueh (1899–1987)—against secular Indonesia.[5] While regionalism played a part in mobilizing the Acehnese against the forces of Jakarta,[6] the importance of the ascent of the ulama cannot be understated; it effectively showed the struggle within Aceh was not simply political, but essentially social: "During the Indonesian revolution (1945–49), leading ulama and their allies had seized control of the apparatus of government in Aceh. They had decisively defeated their local enemies, the aristocratic caste or ulèëbalang, in a bloody social revolution and attained virtually unfettered control over local administration. The ulama also saw Islam as the natural foundation for the new Indonesian state and society they sought to create. They were thus greatly disappointed by the failure of the central government leaders to share their Islamic goals and support implementation of Islamic law" (Aspinall 2006, 152; see also McGibbon 2006, 319). To this end, it is important to recognize that the Darul Islam rebellion should not be considered an early incarnation of Acehnese secession, as the goal of the combatants was to change the character of Indonesia itself. As Benedict Anderson and others have argued, the rebellion was a reaction to Jakarta's secular policies, and "the rebellion was intended to get these policies changed, not to separate Aceh from Indonesia" (Anderson 1999, 4; see also Aspinall 2006, 151–52; Schulze 2003, 242). This is in sharp contrast to the goals of separatists who fought for outright independence decades later (1976–2005).

However, and contra conventional wisdom, Aspinall notes there is in fact a distinct *continuity* between the Darul Islam revolt and the later revolt in Aceh insofar as the violent actions of the military unintentionally fostered a sense of common Acehnese identity that could be mollified with special autonomy. In this way, "the reaction to state violence eventually contributed to the peaceful resolution of the conflict" (Aspinall 2006, 163). Even though the Darul Islam revolt was quashed, the conflict concluded as Aceh secured a nominally autonomous status as a "special region" (*Daerah Istimewa*) in 1959. The selection of autonomy as a solution to crises in Aceh established a precedent that was followed many years later by a pair of initiatives, the 1999 Special Status on the Province of Aceh (Law No. 44) and the 2001 Special Autonomy for the Special Region of Aceh as *Nanggroe Aceh Darussalam* (Law No. 18), and ultimately the 2005 memorandum of understanding that ended the war (Miller 2006, 292; McGibbon 2004).

However, the most important *distinction* between Darul Islam and the Acehnese separatist movement was the role of Islam. Unlike the avowedly religious character of the Darul Islam rebellion, the much longer insurgency in Aceh was distinctly secular. Nowhere is this more evident than in the document that marked the "official" beginning of the war in 1976. Drafted by Hasan di Tiro (1925–2010), a veteran of the Darul Islam rebellion turned cosmopolitan diplomat, the Declaration of Independence of Aceh was remarkable for eschewing religion entirely.[7] Indeed, the 1976 manifesto "made no mention of Islam and gave no hint of what kind of government would be formed if and when the insurgents came to power. Considering Aceh's Islamic traditions as the 'veranda of Mecca,' this omission appeared to be a near revolutionary break with Aceh's past" (Means 2009, 260).[8] The document did, however, cite a distinct language as one of the criteria separating the Acehnese from the erstwhile "Indonesians," which in this case—and in every mention thereafter—are defined by di Tiro as nothing more than the dominant community, that is, the *Javanese*. Rather than citing a split between the sacred and the profane, di Tiro employed the secular language of anticolonialism, describing the Javanese as imperialists who essentially replaced the Dutch as foreign overlords in Aceh. It is this rhetoric that was trumpeted by di Tiro's separatists, thereafter known as Gerakan Aceh Merdeka (GAM) in Acehnese and the Aceh Sumatra National Liberation Front in English. It is also a rhetoric that lasted for decades. Writing in 2000, an Acehnese academic teaching at a university in Malaysia was unequivocal: "The Acehnese totally reject the notion of the alleged existence of an 'Indonesian nation' on historical, cultural, sociological, anthropological, economic and political grounds" (Thaib 2000, 106–7). Moreover, this author is typical in targeting his charges not at the Indonesian people in general but at the alleged *staatsvolk*, the Javanese, who are viewed as a new source of imperial oppression: "Indonesia is nothing but an artificial nation fabricated to serve the collective interests of the Javanese under the management of its own mercenaries" (Thaib 2000, 106–7). For Acehnese elites, the question of belonging to an Indonesia national identity is mocked as "inherently absurd and unstable, a mask for Javanese colonialism" (Aspinall and Berger 2001, 1024).

The Indonesian military suppressed the initial insurgency by 1979, but ten years later GAM was "able to launch a series of attacks on police posts and army installations, demonstrating its continued ability to threaten internal security as well as the continued potency of the separatist agenda" (Tan 2000, 278). Explaining the resurgence in violence after a decade-long hiatus, the aggressive extraction of Aceh's abundant natural resources, especially natural gas, fomented a deep-seated sense of exploitation. The Acehnese resented other Indonesians, not only because they dominated Indonesia's most important institutions (including the military and the civil service), and not only because of acts committed by Indonesian soldiers in Aceh, but also because Aceh produced "a third of Indonesia's liquefied natural gas" (Tan 2000, 281). Profits from natural gas exports were piped through the notoriously opaque offices of Jakarta, leaving very little to invest back in the province that produced those profits. This point has been cited most often as the genesis of the 1970s conflict during the initial exploration and development of substantial oil deposits in and around North Aceh. This may have been crucial to the launch of GAM in 1976 as the extraction of Aceh's natural resources "created a widespread perception that Acehnese natural wealth was being drained out of the province" (Aspinall and Berger 2001, 1016–17). There is certainly some truth to this perception. A joint project sponsored by Yale and the World Bank estimates that if Aceh were independent as of 1998, "its per capita GDP would be $1,257—about one-third higher than Indonesia's average GDP" (Ross 2003, 27).

By the late 1980s, according to Benedict Anderson, the Free Aceh Movement regained popularity "because more and more Acehnese were losing any hope and confidence that they had a share in a common Indonesian project. The astounding greed of the rulers in Jakarta, and of their provincial minions and errand boys . . . increasingly seemed to say to the Acehnese: 'We don't need you; what we need are your natural resources. How wonderful it would be if Aceh were emptied of the Acehnese'" (Anderson 1999, 4). As a result, Jakarta was considered no longer a potential partner in the state-building mission of independent postcolonial Indonesia but an adversary more dangerous than the Dutch ever were.

As a result of renewed violence in 1989, Jakarta locked down the region under a military rule that lasted nearly a decade,[9] when the country itself was in a dynamic state of democratic transition. Thus, de facto martial law was finally lifted during a tumultuous period that included not only the 1997 Asian economic crisis but also the demise of the Suharto regime in 1998. A series of negotiations launched in 2000 exploring options to end the conflict yielded a very short-lived ceasefire called the Humanitarian Pause in May of that year. Negotiations sputtered, however, owing to a fundamental problem: "The peace process broke down because the two parties were unable to agree on the fundamental issue dividing them: whether Aceh would become an independent nation or remain an integral part of the Indonesian state" (Aspinall and Crouch 2003, x). In July 2001, Megawati Sukarnoputri took office as president and publicly apologized—twice—to the people of Aceh for their suffering under past governments. During this time, however, violent clashes continued: in January 2002 GAM's military commander, Abdullah Syafei, was killed by government troops. In December 2002, a Jakarta-GAM ceasefire agreement came into effect (despite wide gaps in respective interpretations of what the agreement actually meant), but just a few months later, on May 19, 2003, the Indonesian military clamped down once more on Aceh and effectively enforced martial law, sealing the territory to outside observers, including international journalists and aid workers (Reid 2004; Drexler 2008).

The isolation of Aceh ended only with a massive earthquake and its literal waves of destruction. Hence, the disastrous events of December 26, 2004,
significantly altered the facts on the ground: the metropolis of the province,
Banda Aceh, was devastated, while innumerable communities were erased
from the coastline. Since fishing is a historic and primary component of
Acehnese subsistence, the people have always dwelled close to the ocean, com-
pounding the severity of the suffering. As Jakarta was unprepared for this
cataclysm, in early 2005 the Indonesian government lifted the two-year-old
ban on foreigners traveling into and around Aceh to allow an unimpeded flow
of international aid and rescue operations. Eventually, GAM and the Indonesian government called a new ceasefire, though initially, within days of the
tsunami—even as mass graves were being filled with the corpses of more than
one hundred thousand dead in Aceh alone—seven men were shot as GAM
sympathizers (Perlez 2005).

For Jakarta, the price of donor aid for Indonesia was peace in Aceh. Less
than nine months after the tsunami (August 15, 2005), the Indonesian government met with GAM officials in Helsinki and signed a memorandum of
understanding that ultimately led to a complete demobilization. It was a
remarkable achievement in that the 2005 peace process "required the two
parties to agree on the broad outlines of a political formula *before* a ceasefire
and related security arrangements would be put into effect" (Aspinall 2005,
viii). The diplomatic mechanics of the peace process itself have been addressed
elsewhere in great detail, and need not detain us for the purposes of the current
discussion (Kingsbury 2006, 2010; Miller 2006). Ultimately, the remarkable—
even unlikely—success of the negotiations led to the signing of the Law on
Governing Aceh in July 2006. As a result, Aceh is the only province in Indonesia with its own local political parties. Equally remarkable, in the years since
the signing of the agreement(s) the relationship between Banda Aceh and
Jakarta has been positive. Indeed, "because both sides have remained committed towards the Helsinki peace process, self-government has continued to
gain ground as a viable framework for conflict resolution in Aceh" (Miller
2012, 37; see also Mietzner 2012).

Language in Aceh

Jakarta has not been unsuccessful in constructing a new modern citizen
for the developing Indonesian state. Sukarno's nondenominational and

ethnically neutral ideology of *pancasila* fueled the progress of a new state language based on Malay, the traditional lingua franca of the region, written in a Latin script. Modern Indonesian or Bahasa Indonesia (literally the "language of Indonesia") shares about 80 percent of its cognates with Malay. Following the fall of Sukarno and the rise of Suharto's New Order in 1965, the government turned to state education policy as the "cornerstone" of its efforts to unify the country "through the promotion of Indonesian nationalism [and] the common language of Bahasa Indonesia" (Bertrand 2003, 278). This effort in Indonesia, anthropologist James Errington notes, is a page from Ernest Gellner's playbook: "Gellner's account could serve as a kind of theoretical charter for [Suharto's] New Order efforts to foster simultaneously an industrial infrastructure, and universal Indonesian competence and literacy through its state school system" (Errington 1998, 61).[10]

While Indonesia's official language is based on Malay, its evolution shows evidence of influence by the dominant ethnicity of the dominant island: Java. It is unsurprising that the construction of an Indonesian identity has drawn heavily from the single largest ethnic group in the Republic: 40 percent of the population is Javanese. Yet the adoption of Bahasa Indonesia as the national language instead of Javanese per se was a politically astute decision by the nation builders, even though their preference for the ethnic majority vernacular is apparent. The government Language Institute frequently chooses Javanese words to fill the lexicon of officially sanctioned terminology when equivalent words cannot be found in Bahasa Indonesia (Foulcher 1990). In other words, "Indonesian was intended to be ethnically neutral" but "the New Order's language policy has occasionally reflected the dominance of the Javanese" (Bertrand 2003, 287). Interestingly, this is a pattern observed elsewhere in postcolonial Southeast Asia where, in the view of Anthony Smith, a postwar plural society evolved that tended to elevate a dominant ethnic group—Burmans in Burma, for example—while stoking resentment in marginalized ethnic communities—like the Karen or Kachin (Smith 1986). That being said, given the relative size of the Javanese population, it is not unreasonable that Javanese provides a good number of loan words to Indonesian. Moreover, the official language is also pragmatic in that it incorporates words from not only Javanese, but also English and Dutch, among other languages.

Acehnese is a member of the Sundic family of languages, which includes Cham, today found primarily in central Vietnam and Cambodia. It is therefore distinct from "the natural continuum of the Sumatran sub-set of Austronesian languages," a result of the in-migration of Cham since at least the middle of the fifteenth century, as well as the influence of many other populations linked by "the maritime trade route which linked the Middle East to southern China between the eighth and fourteenth centuries" (Reid 2006, 7). Linguist Mark Durie, the most accomplished specialist on Acehnese writing in English, estimates it has been spoken as a distinct language in the region for "at least as long as a millennium" (Durie 1996, 115).[11] Traditionally, Acehnese literacy was acquired in a three-stage process: "The first stage begins in childhood, when groups of children . . . learn to pronounce the Arabic alphabet and to recite a few short but important passages from the Koran in the village classroom. They do not actually learn the Arabic language: the important thing is to be able to recite correctly." The next stage is the study of Malay,[12] the high-status print language of the wider region, though "written in the Arabic script. This is the usual language of written prose in traditional Acehnese society."[13] Finally, after learning the Arabic script as a child and later using this script to read and write in Malay "an Acehnese person could acquire the skill of reciting Acehnese from written texts" (Durie 1996, 115).

The earliest known example of written Acehnese dates from 1658. For centuries, however, written Acehnese was limited to "poetic text meant for recitation" and was not employed for quotidian communication. Indeed, Acehnese "was only written in prose by Dutch language purists in the 1930s, and more recently by some Aceh nationalist purists in the 1990s" (Reid 2006, 8). Primary *instruction* in Acehnese without preliminary education in Arabic and Malay was briefly attempted by Dutch colonial officials at the beginning of the twentieth century, but in Durie's opinion "there is not and never has been an established tradition of instruction in reading and writing Acehnese" (1996, 116). In postindependence Indonesia, state education policy is officially bilingual, meaning primary instruction is in a local language followed by higher education in Bahasa Indonesia written in the Latin script. However, the first Acehnese reader since the Dutch colonial era was not published until 1968. Titled *Geunta*, or "reverberation," the text "tells its readers that the very fact they are now reciting this textbook, Geunta, is confirmation that they share one language, Acehnese" (Shiraishi 1983, 86). Nonetheless, diglossia remains the norm as "the use of Acehnese predominates in personal or 'internal' domains such as the home and the village, whereas in contact with the outside world, in schools and in offices, Malay/Indonesian is preferred" (Durie 1996, 121; see also Daud 1997).

The status and utility of written Acehnese remain very low. It is some-times taught as a subject in elementary schools (perhaps for two or three years) but is not a part of the Acehnese core curriculum, and therefore the decision of whether to offer the subject at all is left to each primary and secondary school. Even when it is offered, according to a member of the Aceh Education Council, it is taught only twice a week with sessions that last just thirty-five minutes.[14] At the university level, it is not offered as a minor or a major, due in no small part to the fact that it is very difficult to find books—let alone textbooks—in Acehnese. This is not to say that there are no Acehnese writers—far from it—but they conventionally write in the High Culture language, that is, Indonesian.

As mentioned above, Hasan di Tiro's 1976 Declaration of Independence of Aceh cites the Acehnese language as evidence of Aceh's status as a unique nation. Indeed, in interviews with GAM leaders and laypersons in Aceh, there is a general acknowledgment of the distinctiveness of Acehnese as a language that distinguishes them from other Indonesians. In an interview with Malik Mahmud, GAM's former prime minister of the state of Aceh (in exile), he acknowledged that in regard to written Acehnese, "we don't use it much," but nonetheless "we know we need it."[15] Indeed, GAM spokesman Bakhtiar Abdullah said he expected a GAM-led government to "revise the Acehnese language in the education sector."[16] Irwandi Yusuf, a GAM intelligence officer who became the first elected governor of Aceh in 2007, regards the question of language with disinterest: "the Acehnese language is almost forgotten, at least how to write it . . . maybe throughout Aceh only ten people know how to write correct Acehnese."[17] This perhaps explains why, since the advent of real autonomy in 2006, there was and is virtually no follow-through on policies that would support the teaching and use of Acehnese (rather than Indonesian) in the public sphere. According to Mark Durie, "the GAM folks liked the idea of Acehnese as the language of print communication, but this was more in the 'nice ideas' basket."[18] At the same time, however, spoken Acehnese remains the dominant language of the public sphere, used in everything from political rallies to community meetings between the Aceh Party and local leaders. It even appears occasionally in print, used on election banners, for example, or in text messages. Yet this is a far cry from claiming Acehnese maintains anything like a formal print culture.

This raises the question of whether Acehnese may be an example of a "symbolic language," that is, a language that is valued as an element of an identity but is not itself valued for its utility. Perhaps the best-known example of this phenomenon is Irish in Ireland—both the Republic and Northern Ireland—where there is "a fairly consistent association between the language and Irish ethnic identity," even though the language is rarely utilized in print (O'Reilly 2003, 17). Yet in the case of Aceh, perhaps a better analog would be the language milieu in Italy, where standard Italian is the High Culture language of literacy, yet "mutually incomprehensible dialects are the still the language of choice [whereby] local linguistic varieties channel feelings of identity and thereby make up, to some extent, for a weak 'Italian' national identity" (Ruzza 2000, 169).

Islam in Aceh

In recent years, a number of notorious actions spawned by the expansion of sharia law in Aceh garnered a good deal of attention in the international press and among human rights activists, who often charged that such actions explicitly or implicitly targeted women (Human Rights Watch 2010; Padden 2011). For example, in 2010, Ramli Mansur, the district chief (*bupati*) of the Western Aceh (Aceh Barat) Regency, sponsored a bylaw (*qanun*) banning women from wearing tight pants.[19] Checkpoints required pants-wearing female motorists (typically riding one of the ubiquitous scooters) to pull off the road and don a long skirt over their trousers. Remarkably, Mansur himself is a former GAM guerrilla, that is, a member of an essentially secular organization. Yet when challenged by a journalist as to why he prioritized a restriction on women's clothing over other pressing needs—infrastructure, commerce, education, etc.—he responded, "This is about thorough implementation of sharia law. . . . If you're against it, you're blaspheming" (Kurniawait 2010). This action was followed in 2010 by a more general ban on the sale of tight clothing in the capital, Banda Aceh, enacted by the head of the sharia enforcement agency, Samsuddin. In defense of an unpopular move, he cited support from the incoming governor, Dr. Zaini Abdullah, GAM's former minister of foreign affairs of the State of Aceh in exile, who—according to Samsuddin—"very much supports the enforcement of Islamic law" (Pathoni 2012).[20] In 2013, another move targeting women, this time banning their straddling of motorcycles or scooters, was promulgated by the mayor of Lhoksuemawe, Suaidi Yahya, who claimed such a posture showed the curves of a woman's body, which "is against sharia" (Saragih and Simanjuntak 2013).

Also in 2013, North Aceh's bupati banned adult women from the traditional practice of dancing when welcoming guests, claiming such behavior was in violation of Islamic values.

However, it would be wrong to accept the characterization of all sharia prohibitions as gender specific. Men are also targeted routinely for violating sharia regulations: they are in fact the majority of those punished by caning. Gambling is prohibited, as is the wearing of shorts in some parts of Aceh. Other violations include drinking alcohol and failure to attend Friday prayers. Some violations may not even be religious: boys playing hooky from school may also be rounded up and driven back to class. Most infamous, however, was an incident whereby young men sporting Mohawks or colorfully dyed hair—essentially punk rock fans—were arrested: first, their heads were shaved and then they were forced to attend "educational" camps.

While these developments may seem anecdotal, in Aceh "the general religious atmosphere of the Islamic community had been pointing more and more to the demand of implementing sharia across all aspects of life" (Basri 2010a 275). It would be simple to attribute this phenomenon to the rise of the ulama following the end of the war in 2005, and the opening of a social and political space for religious leadership. This was a structural shift from earlier decades. In the years following the end of the Darul Islam revolt in 1959, the ulama remained socially significant but were less than successful in achieving political relevance. This was due in no small part to the actions of the state as it worked to consolidate Aceh as an integral part of Indonesia. Hence, "the ulama's aspirations to local leadership were thwarted by Jakarta's opposition to the Islamic agenda and by its cultivation of a new technocratic elite." Importantly, however, while "the technocrats proved to be effective local clients for three decades, they ultimately lacked popular legitimacy" (McGibbon 2006, 350). Legitimacy remained with traditional social structures that continued to play critical roles in the daily lives of average Acehnese, including the local ulama, who not only studied and taught religion, but also served as "the person to go to with various social problems or religious questions" (Basri 2010b, 200n12). However, it is also important to recognize that the ulama were (and are) far from monolithic. As Shane Barter notes, during the conflict the ulama were divided: some remained on the sidelines, some supported Jakarta, and others supported GAM (Barter 2012, 2004).

Nonetheless, in the years of the GAM insurgency, the secular elites leading GAM, many of whom were living as exiles in Sweden, were spatially and socially removed from many of the de facto leaders on the ground, who performed duties both spiritual and social. Moreover, GAM not only was divorced from the aspirations of those who personally supported political Islam, but also sought to keep them in the private sphere. Indeed, in an interview with Dr. Zaini Abdullah, he explicitly rejected any claims that GAM promoted sharia as "Indonesian propaganda."[21] This view was shared by Malik Mahmud, who said this propaganda claimed "we are going to set up a Muslim state, as Acehnese fanatical Muslims; but we are not."[22] Of course, there is a question of whether these remarks were moderated to align with the supposed views of a skeptical American political scientist. Nonetheless, the claims of both Abdullah and Mahmud may very well be (or were) sincere. As recently as 2007, Damien Kingsbury was unequivocal: "GAM is a nationalist organization the political goals of which are explicitly based on territory rather than religion. Further, explicit in the political agenda of GAM is the ending of the imposition of sharia" (2007, 166). Again, there is an audience issue here: Kingsbury is also a Western political scientist. Despite claims to the contrary, it is not correct to say that particular power brokers in Aceh do not support the imposition of Islamic law, including some former members of GAM.

How is it that a secular separatist insurgency managed to mobilize a population in support of independence without leaning on religion and suddenly found, on winning regional autonomy, that religion had returned as a powerful force in Aceh's politics?

Part of the answer stems from the fact that the imposition of sharia was actually not all that sudden, and had been building since 1999. Two initiatives enacted in the post-Suharto years actually provided for no small measure of religious authority; this was arguably an instrumental move on Jakarta's part to isolate the more secular rebels. In Law 44 of 1999, "Aceh was given authority to introduce sharia law, with cases to be tried in regular district courts," while Law 18 of 2001 allowed "creation of sharia courts with jurisdiction that included family law, property law, and also criminal cases" (Means 2009, 276). In 2002, provincial administration of religious law was assigned "to Dinas Sharia Islam (Department of Sharia Affairs), which controls the Wilayatul Hisbah, otherwise known as 'religious police' or 'the vice and virtue patrol'" (Means 2009, 277), and known more colloquially as the Wi-Ha (Marks 2010). Despite opposition from some secular elites, "provincial regulations quickly followed, mostly attempting to regulate the personal moral and religious behavior of Muslims" (Aspinall 2007, 256–57).

By 2004, sharia law came to affect "education, zakat (alms tax), proper Muslim dress for men and women, criminal justice, economic transactions, mortgages, banking, religious donations, gambling, alcohol consumption, and khalwat (illicit sex relations). In addition, Islamic criminal punishments were prescribed," from prison to fines and public canings delivered in public at mosques after Friday prayers (Means 2009, 277). In 2006, calls for further empowering the religious police were raised, including proposals to expand capital punishments for adultery, and amputating the hands of thieves.

Note, however, that, following his electoral victory in 2007, secular Governor Irwandi Yusuf (another former GAM leader) publicly opposed any attempt to implement the most extreme criminal punishments (Means 2009, 279). In 2013, the most notorious bylaw—stoning adulterers to death—though never signed, was actually removed by the Acehnese assembly (Hasan 2013).[23] Thus, for all these initiatives enacting sharia law, it would be off the mark to claim Aceh is entirely steeped in salafist Islam, a pious prison where there is no separation between the public and the private, where religion is all powerful in every social and personal domain. A Reuters photographer working in Aceh put it this way: "It gives me the feeling I'm in Lebanon or Jordan, but not Iran or Saudi Arabia: 'sharia lite,' a friend of mine suggests" (Sagolj 2012).

Political Mobilization in Aceh

Perhaps the most important question about the politics of Aceh is why, in the years following the independence of Indonesia, the population first mobilized around Islam in the Darul Islam rebellion, but in later years, from the 1970s and the rise of GAM, mobilized as a secular ethnonational community seeking national self-determination. Why, as Edward Aspinall (2007) asks, did the political pendulum in Aceh swing "from Islamism to nationalism"? This question requires an answer. But it must be followed by a second question, one that reflects the rise of sharia law in Aceh: has the pendulum swung from Islamism to nationalism and *back again*?

For Aspinall, the fact that Aceh should have ever turned away from Islamist politics is anomalous: "For reasons of history and sociology, it would appear that Aceh should be a major center for the militant Islamist groups which have recently proliferated in Indonesia. The territory has a well-established reputation for the piety of its inhabitants and a long history of

Islamic militancy. Yet the major oppositional forces in Aceh in recent years has been nationalism of an essentially secular type" (2007, 245). The explanation for this anomaly was the fact that Islam, as a *commonality* with the rest of Muslim-majority Indonesia, defeated the purposes of the Aceh *separatist* movement: "Arguments based on Islamic solidarity tended to bind the two entities together, rather than driving them apart. As a result, once Acehnese nationalist leaders made the fateful move to aim for a separate state, the logic of identity differentiation led them away from their Islamic roots. It was this logic which accounts for the secularization of dissent in Aceh" (2007, 247). However, is it not unreasonable to suggest that, following the decision to remain part of the country, "the logic of identity differentiation" now demands another marker of identity to distinguish the Acehnese from other Indonesians? Is it not possible that the "Islamic *commitment*, that all Acehnese feel is part of their identity" (Reid 2006, 9) has surfaced as a critical component of what it is to be Acehnese as opposed to the typical Indonesian (or especially Javanese)? In this view, as argued by Acehnese scholar Hasan Basri, "the application of Islamic law fulfills one of the aspirations of Acehnese people, namely a need to protect their identity" (2010a, 284). This is not to say that Islam has replaced nationalism among the political elite, but rather that it is now a necessary element of Acehnese politics.

It is remarkable that the definition of Acehnese identity is and has been a continuing struggle that echoes back to the ages of the sultans, when the pious ulama fought the aristocratic ulèëbalang, the spiritual versus the secular, the sacred versus the profane. Note, however, that this contest was and is played at a very high level. According to Chanintira Thalang, Acehnese national identity "is fluid . . . [and] this fluidity is best understood as changes in the ideological expression of Acehnese nationalism by elite leaders rather than diminished, or heightened, mass sentiments," which have remained fairly constant (2009, 319). This suggests the contest to define what (or who) is (or is not) Acehnese may be a contest played out among elites, but less so among the population as a whole. This may explain why the enforcement of sharia laws is sometimes criticized as class-based, whereby the elites remain unaffected by the proscriptions that have come to affect average citizens: "The implementation of sharia Islam has been limited to the surface level affecting only the lower classes, while the political elite and government officials have not been touched at all. . . . To them, sharia is merely political jargon to decrease the restlessness of a society that yearns for the glory of the past; a time when sharia Islam was applied effectively in the social and political lives of the Acehnese" (Basri 2010a, 283). Arguably, it is this yearning "for the glory of the past" that most solidly united the people of Aceh, yet this glorious past—the age of the sultans—was itself a time of tension between elites who claimed legitimacy either through noble status or through faith.

Conclusion

To place the case of Aceh in context, recall that a central argument of this book is that there is an inverse relationship between the strength of a specific national identity and a generic (universal) religious identity. Also recall that Muslim-minority separatist movements offer unmatched opportunities to test this proposition simply by asking whether their conflict is rooted in the politics of ethnolinguistic identity or the politics of Islam. In the case of Aceh, the answer depends on when one asks the question, as Aceh was central not only to the separatist war waged by GAM, but also to the Islamist war waged for Darul Islam in the 1950s. Why the shift?

Following Aspinall, it is sensible to conclude that the tactics of the Acehnese shifted according to whether or not the goal of the elites was autonomy or independence. If the war was to change the nature of Indonesia from secular to sacred, then remaining part of Indonesia was a priority, and the mobilization of the Acehnese was driven by a sectarian mission to purify and promulgate Islam across the entire archipelago. On the other hand, if the war was to secure a nation-state for the Acehnese, then that which separated them from the rest of the country—their secular national identity—was paramount, while the fact of being Muslim—a commonality—was rejected as impolitic.

In no uncertain terms, the organization that fought for independence and won autonomy, GAM, was a secular entity. From its founding in 1976 to the election of a GAM leader as the first governor of Aceh in 2007, GAM defined itself and the Acehnese people as a nation deserving self-determination. GAM's leaders explicitly rejected the implementation of sharia. And yet, since autonomy, Aceh's provincial assembly and (especially) regional officials have continued to endorse and implement restrictions on behavior in the name of Islam. The public face of Islam is more prevalent, and the rhetoric of Islamists more indignant. In the meantime, GAM's former leaders—now ensconced as members of the post-GAM (2008) Aceh Party (Partai Aceh)—continue to celebrate Acehnese nationalism. In 2013, Governor Zaini Abdullah signed a regulation making the once-banned flag of secular GAM the official banner of Aceh itself, thereby deploying a "potent tool for mass mobilization," which immediately sparked heated protest from Jakarta. The protest, however, was ignored. Hence, the intransigence of Abdullah and the Aceh Party may be interpreted as a sign that "the power of the GAM machinery in Aceh continues to grow" (International Crisis Group 2013, 1–2).

What Aceh's leaders have not done, however, is deliver on the one-time aspiration of their founding father—Hasan di Tiro—to elevate, celebrate, and propagate the Acehnese vernacular as a High Culture print language. Thus, what would otherwise serve as the default mechanism of a new state to build a national identity—a common print culture—was not and is not available to the provincial leaders of Aceh. Rather, the Acehnese remain defined by their centuries of shared history but divided by the role of Islam in their state and society.

CHAPTER 10

Religious Community Versus Ethnic Diversity:
The Moros of the Philippines

The so-called Moro problem is a thing of the past.
—Manuel Quezon, 1935

At the eastern edge of both Southeast Asia and the Islamic world, the southern Philippines mark the farthest reach of Muslim merchants and sailors who carried the faith overseas from its Arabian origins. The arrival of Islam in the thirteenth century preceded the arrival of Christianity by more than two centuries, though today more than more than 90 percent of the Philippines' 104 million citizens are Catholic, while only 5 percent are Muslim.[1] Thus, it is easy to assume that the Muslims of the Philippines are essentially peripheral. There is some literal truth to this assumption, insofar as the great majority of the Muslim population lives at the southern edge of the archipelago, far removed from the social and political center of the state, Manila, far to the north on the island of Luzon. However, this is not to say that the homeland of the Muslims is considered a marginal part of the Philippines. The island of Mindanao composes 28 percent of the land area of the entire country; indeed, of the three gold stars on the flag of the Philippines, one of them represents Mindanao, while the second and third represent the other largest areas of the archipelago, namely Visayas and Luzon. Mindanao is also rich in natural resources and thus an essential component of the country's economy (see Figure 10.1).

That Mindanao is an integral and inseparable part of the Philippines is therefore axiomatic in most of the country, yet this has not been the case in the historically Muslim south.[2] This region spawned the most deadly and protracted conflict in the short history of the postcolonial state, a separatist

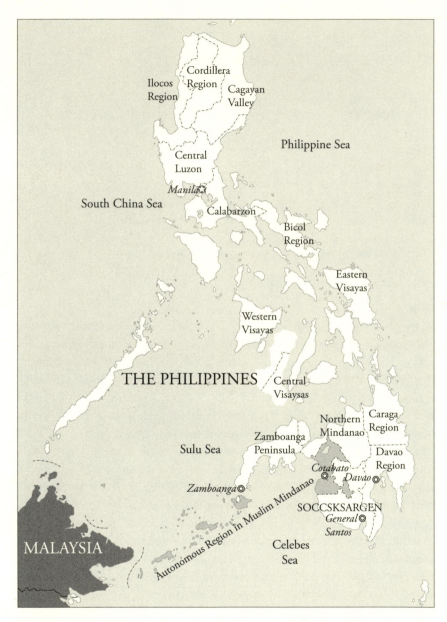

Figure 10.1. The Philippines.

insurgency that by some estimates has claimed the lives of at least 120,000 people since its ignition in the early 1970s. This conflict forms the focus of this chapter. At the heart of the discussion is the relative importance of the role of Islam as opposed to other factors, specifically the sociolinguistic diversity that is a hallmark of not only the Philippines, but also the Muslim population of Mindanao, arguably "the most diverse region in the country" (Milligan 2005b, 19). Unsurprisingly for an archipelago of more than seven thousand islands, there are at least 120 mutually unintelligible languages in the country (Gonzalez 2007, 19). Of these, thirteen ethnolinguistic populations are numbered among the Muslims of Mindanao. Therefore, given the fact that the Muslims are united not by ethnicity but *purportedly* by Islam, it is not unreasonable to suggest that the conflict is simply sectarian, pitting Christians against Muslims. This suggestion, though conventional, is nonetheless wrong.

In careful consideration of how different groups have mobilized against Manila at different points in the struggle for self-determination, it is evident that ethnicity—including its concomitant elements of clan and culture—plays no small role in the conflict. At some times weakening and at other times strengthening divisions among the Muslim population, ethnicity has been and continues to be a dynamic variable essential to understanding both the origins and evolution of the dispute. Moreover, even ethnicity may be of second order power when framed in the context of clan ties and loyalties that further disaggregate disparate groups.

Mindanao in Context

While the insurgency is conventionally dated to the early 1970s, Muslims in Mindanao are quick to challenge this claim, arguing instead that the conflict actually started centuries before. As is so often the case in separatist movements, there is a tendency to recall a golden age during which the embattled people were once masters of their own house. For the Muslims, this was the age of the sultans: the Sultanate of Sulu was established in 1457; the Sultanate of Cotabato in 1500. The rise of the sultanates paralleled those elsewhere in Southeast Asia, such as the Sultanate of Brunei, a phenomenon that highlights the fact that the southern Philippines were actually the far edge of a Muslim culture that stretched westward to the Sultanate of Aceh. It is for this reason that Theodore Friend argues the better way to think of the region is as the "Phil-Indo" Archipelago (Friend 2006; see also Gross 2007). However, it was only in the Philippines that the Catholic Christian Spanish established colonies (from 1565), starting an imperial reign that would last until the Spanish-American War in 1898. Nonetheless, while colonization developed in earnest on other islands, the Muslims of Mindanao are emphatic in their claim that they were never colonized, but rather resisted the Spanish in a perennial series of clashes that never subdued the sultans.[3] Hence, they claim, rather than the Spanish, it was the Americans who decisively ended the age of the sultans, ending four centuries of Islamic self-rule in the southern Philippines. While the islands became a self-governing commonwealth of the United States in 1935, American sovereignty continued until the Japanese invaded in 1942. Following the end of World War II, the Philippines emerged as an independent entity for the first time in 1946.

A principal challenge facing the government of the new state was to create a unified new nation, a fact that may be considered a source of "weakness" in the Philippines, "itself a product of the arbitrary imposition of colonial borders that failed to take account of the region's enormous ethno-religious diversity" (Chalk 2001, 242; Merry and Milligan 2010, 3). The two largest ethnic groups in the Philippines, both Catholic, are the Tagalog and the Cebuano at 28 and 13 percent, respectively. As for the myriad of Muslim populations, none account for more than 10 percent of the population.[4] Nonetheless, the country was consolidated under the colonial regime of the United States, and later by the autocrat Ferdinand Marcos. Yet almost from the beginning Marcos faced violent mobilizations, first by the Hukbalahap in central Luzon in the early 1950s, an experience that was to influence the state's response to such challenges in the future, specifically as it sought to diffuse the insurgents. In the 1960s, Marcos then faced not only the Moro Problem (George 1980) but also the communist insurgency waged by the New People's Army, which prompted the imposition of martial law in 1972. It was also in this year that the first Muslim insurgent organization established itself as the Moro National Liberation Front.

It is important to note that this chapter has avoided the use of term *Moro* until now. While it is conventional to speak of the Moro conflict in the Philippines, it is nonetheless important to recognize that the term and the concept of a united Muslim population sharing the same name is relatively new—at least for the Muslims themselves. Irrespective of separate ethnic or cultural identities, Muslims were collectively branded Moros, a racist slight coined by the Spanish recalling the occupation of Iberia by the Islamic Moors. However, in the 1960s "Philippine Muslim nationalists attempted to appropriate the epithetic 'Moro' and transform it into a positive symbol of collective identity" (McKenna 1998, 81).[5] This collective identity was arguably consolidated as a result of repression—social, political, and especially demographic—that began in earnest decades earlier. It is therefore best understood as a term "defined more by resistance to external powers than by Islam or, for that matter, ethnicity" (Liow 2006, 8). To this end, the term *Moro* later evolved to represent all the "original" inhabitants of Mindanao—including the non-Muslim indigenous peoples, called Lumads, as well as some long-resident Christians—and changed to "Bangsamoro," literally the "Moro People."

Following the defeat of the sultans, first the U.S. administration and then the administration in Manila began to support mass migration of Christians from north to south and provided inducements in the form of promised real estate holdings (Chalk 2001, 247; Rood 2005). As a result of this state-sponsored migration—effectively internal colonialism (Milligan 2005b, 20)—Mindanao experienced a radical restructuring of its entire population: the Moros became a minority in their own homeland. Overall, the share of Muslims on Mindanao dropped from about 75 percent at the turn of the twentieth century to about 25 percent in 1970. The dilution was especially concentrated in more developed areas: in the Cotabato of 1918, the ratio of Muslims to Christians was nearly two to one; by 1970 Christians outnumbered Muslims by a ratio of 1.68 to 1. Between the 1950s and 1970s alone, Manila sponsored forty-two separate resettlement projects that invariably granted preferred lands to settler families; the programs sponsored by the Ministry of Agrarian Reform alone transferred fifty thousand families from north to south (Tigno 2006, 45) (see Table 10.1).

In no uncertain terms, it was "Catholic transmigration from the north" that was a principal—if not the most pointed—source of resentment, as the resettlement programs "dispossessed many Muslims of what are considered to be ancient and communal land rights" (Chalk 2001, 247). This is not to say that the resentment was unidirectional: Catholics maintained decidedly pejorative views of the Moros, supporting the opinion that "their" Christian country would be better off without them. A 1975 poll showed "Filipino Muslims were consistently ranked last by other groups in terms of their desirability as neighbors, employers, employees, friends or marriage partners," since they were regarded as "lazy, hostile, unreliable, poor, proud, conservative and stingy" (Milligan 2005a, 81).

Another source of resentment among the Moros, however, was and is relative economic deprivation. In the years following independence, this

Table 10.1. Population Trends in Muslim Areas of the Philippines, 1918–70

Population	Year				
	1918	1939	1948	1960	1970
Muslim population of the Philippines (%)	4.29	4.23	4.11	4.86	4.32
Cotabato					
Muslims	110,926	162,996	155,162	356,460	424,577
Non-Muslims	61,052	135,939	284,507	672,659	711,430
Ratio	0.55	0.83	1.83	1.89	1.68
Lanao					
Muslims	83,319	162,632	237,215	412,260	497,122
Non-Muslims	8,140	80,805	106,703	236,670	308,328
Ratio	0.10	0.50	0.45	0.57	0.62
Sulu					
Muslims	168,629	230,553	226,883	310,926	401,984
Non-Muslims	4,147	16,584	1,393	15,972	23,633
Ratio	0.03	0.07	0.01	0.05	0.06
Zamboanga					
Muslims	44,789	92,028	133,348	194,444	191,527
Non-Muslims	102,544	263,956	288,593	829,389	1,251,870
Ratio	2.29	2.87	2.16	4.27	6.54

Source: Adapted from Gutierrez and Borras (2004, 14).

peripheral region was neglected in favor of more robust development on Luzon, the core of the country's economy, as well as Christian-dominated provinces on Mindanao. Hence, Mindanao suffered "from administrative neglect, and in some cases outright exploitation, as a result of development programs whose prime purpose has been to further the interests and preferences of the dominant community" (Chalk 2001, 242). A principal problem stemmed from the "modernization" of the agrarian political economy (Vellema, Borras, and Lara 2011). As Gutierrez and Borras argue, the conflict can therefore be explained by "widespread landlessness, the continuing weakness of state institutions in implementing agrarian reform and enforcing ancestral domain claims, as well as the absence of autonomous civil society" (2004, ix–x):

"Minoritized" over the decades in their homeland, the last five provinces where Muslims remain as the majority are not only the poorest provinces but also those where the quality of life is worst. These five provinces—Maguindanao, Sulu, Lanao del Sur, Basilan, and Tawi-Tawi—according to the Human Development Index ranking of Philippine provinces—have the least access to education, health, electricity, transport, water, and sanitation services—the basic infrastructure required to sustain any growth or development. Moreover, life expectancy and adult literacy are lowest in these provinces. In all, the Muslim areas of the Philippines are, generally speaking, at the bottom of the heap. (Gutierrez and Borras 2004, 2)[6]

Nonetheless, in the context of the separatist movement writ large, there is a question of correlation versus causation. Even if the Moros remained the poorest population in the Philippines, were it not for the transmigration of the Christians, the politics of Mindanao may have taken a different direction. In other words, it is important to recall Walker Connor's warning that economic deprivation is not "a necessary precondition for ethno-national tensions. Economic differentials are but one of several possible catalysts. A mass influx of outsiders into an ethnic homeland, for example, is a far more potent one" (2001, 121). Put another way, even if very poor, the Moros may not have mobilized a separatist insurgency if they had been allowed to keep their homeland and dignity intact.

While the Moros watched their territory shrink dramatically in the two decades following independence, simmering communal tensions at last came to a boil in 1968. Five years earlier, the territory of Sabah on the neighboring island of Borneo was transferred from the British to Malaysia. The Philippines objected, claiming the Sultanate of Sulu had only leased Sabah and, following decolonization, should have been returned to the Philippines. Hence, in 1967 the administration in Manila recruited Moros to form a commando force—called Jabidah—to foment rebellion in Sabah. However, in March 1968, when the Moros realized they were to fight fellow Muslims and—in the case of the Tausug—ethnic kin, they reportedly demanded their return home. Soldiers of the Armed Forces of the Philippines then allegedly executed the dozens, if not hundreds, of mutineers. The actual figure remains widely contested. What is uncontested, however, is that the Jabidah Massacre was the "turning point" that "set the fuse" of the Moro rebellion (Mercado 2007, 231). It not only triggered student protests and mobilized mass demonstrations in Manila, but also led to the formation of the Muslim

Independence Movement, a political organization that was but a prelude to the rebellion.

Four years later, in 1972, a former academic (and reputed leftist radical) at the University of the Philippines, Nur Misuari, organized the creation of the secular and separatist Moro National Liberation Front (MNLF), sparking the mobilization and deployment of a guerrilla force. This initial conflict lasted four years and, with the assistance of the Organization of the Islamic Conference, ended with a peace agreement signed in Libya. The 1976 Tripoli Agreement then held out the promise of regional autonomy for thirteen traditionally Muslim provinces (and the island of Palawan), the exact terms of which would be negotiated at a later date. However, following a series of Marcos-backed plebiscites in the 1970s, in a 1989 vote (under the first post-Marcos regime led by Corazon Aquino), only four provinces (Sulu, Tawi-Tawi, Maguindanao, and Lanao del Sur) elected to join the new entity, called the Autonomous Region in Muslim Mindanao (ARMM), the population of which is 91 percent Muslim.[7] During this period, neither the MNLF nor the government of the Philippines "fully honored the agreement" (Means 2009, 199): sporadic violence continued unabated. Hence, a Final Peace Agreement was not signed until 1996. The region expanded in 2001 when the city of Marawi and the island province of Basilan (but not its capital, Isabella City) voted to join the ARMM as well.

The original 1976 agreement between the MNLF and Manila, however, opened a rift within the Moro leadership that ultimately led to the birth of the Moro Islamic Liberation Front (MILF), an avowedly religious organization. Despite numerous ceasefires (1997, 2001, 2003) the MILF essentially continued armed struggle until 2012, when Philippine president Benigno Aquino and MILF leader Ebrahim Murad agreed to a framework peace agreement—ultimately signed in 2014 (Whaley) would establish a new autonomous region in the south, to be called "Bangsamoro," the shape and size of which are to be determined in a plebiscite by 2015.[8] Yet why were negotiations with Manila so distinct between the MNLF and the MILF? One factor is the role of third-party mediation (Harris 2010), and certainly views on Islam are a major variable in the equation. Still, it is most unclear whether the divide can be simply defined as a doctrinal disagreement. The rift also positioned ethnolinguistic groups into opposing camps, raising the question of whether ethnicity was another source of the split. This is in no uncertain terms an unsettled question, yet it is argued here that the role of ethnicity is key to not only a holistic understanding of the conflict but also preparing for the future of a multiethnic Mindanao.

Language in the Philippines

Problematic identity politics in the Philippines are in no way limited to the Moros, but are in fact a perennial issue that stems from the extreme ethnolinguistic diversity of the population. This issue was recognized during the 1935 constitutional convention, yet it proved so contentious that the resolution of the language question was left to a new National Language Institute, which was "to take steps toward the formation of a common national language." Perhaps unsurprisingly, the language of the economic and political elite of Luzon—Tagalog—was selected as the national language in 1940, at which point the name of the organization was changed to the Institute of National Language and Tagalog became a mandatory subject in all colleges and in the fourth year of high school. Hence, the blithe young state "assumed a unified curriculum and educational policies imposed throughout the country would gradually unify the disparate ethnic and linguistic communities of the archipelago into a single Filipino identity" (Milligan 2005a, 72). After independence in 1946, Tagalog became a subject for students at every grade level, though the language of instruction for all other subjects was English (Gonzalez 2007, 21). Note, however, that Tagalog is no longer an official language of the Philippines. Instead, it is called "Filipino," a form of Tagalog rebranded in 1987 as the erstwhile national language of all Filipinos.[9] Note also that what happens in classrooms is rather distinct, whereby "the teacher explains in Filipino or in English depending on the subject matter (English for science and mathematics and in English Language classes and Filipino for all other subjects); then repeats the same content in the local vernacular to make sure the students understand the material" (Gonzalez 2006, 125). Filipino (Tagalog) is the first language of some twenty-nine million people—fewer than one in three citizens—though it is the second language of many more: by some (certainly overblown) government estimates it is understood in 99 percent of households (Gonzalez 2007, 22); a more reasonable figure is 85 percent (Gonzalez 2006, 116). However, functional ability is not assimilation—even if Arabs in France can speak French it does not mean they are always considered or consider themselves French—and the fact that Filipino is a form of Tagalog remains a sore point—according to some (but not all) a "bitter debate"—in many corners of the country (Tupas 2007, 17; Gonzalez 2006; Rappa and Wee 2006). Nowhere is this bitter debate more contested than in the realm of education policy. Indeed, "the issue that could derail the widespread *acceptance* of Filipino as a national language and as the primary medium of instruction in state schools is the perception, held by many, that Filipino is based primarily on Tagalog," which it is (Hau and Tinio 2003, 347, emphasis added).

Primary education in local vernaculars is possible during the first few years of a child's schooling, though this is more a point of toleration than endorsement by state education officials. For the two-thirds of the population who are nonnative Tagalog speakers "no educational encouragement is provided for the languages which these people actually speak and use. . . . Tagalog remains the language of a minority (in terms of those speaking it as their first language) which has succeeded in having it established as both the official and national language of the country" (Smolicz and Nical 1997, 513–14). However, even though Filipino enjoys official status and is the formal and informal lingua franca, for basic education a de facto bilingual system has evolved "with English now more prominent than Filipino" (Gonzalez 2007, 22). Interestingly, the language issue remains bipolar, which is to say (with the possible exception of Cebuano) the only languages in the debate are Tagalog and English, with nonnative Tagalog speakers overwhelmingly in favor of English language instruction. In Mindanao, this is certainly the case. In interviews with numerous separatists and Muslim civil society advocates, not one of them expressed support for Filipino, but instead expressed a strong preference for English in schools. This is a key issue for Moros as "their most protracted exposure to the national culture . . . [is] during their education at state-sponsored schools" (McKenna 1998, 38–39). This is also a key issue for Manila as education and education policy have been "major tools by which successive Philippine government have tried to solve the Moro problem" (Milligan 2005b, 5).

Collectively, the Muslim peoples of the Philippines number 5.2 million—5 percent of the population—but are divided among thirteen separate and distinct ethnolinguistic groups found across the southern islands of the republic's archipelago. Three groups, however, dominate the demographic and political arena: the Maguindanao, the Maranao, and the Tausug collectively account for more than 90 percent of the Muslim population of the Philippines.[10] The Maguindanao, a name thought to mean "people of the flood plain," established a harbor and principality at the mouth of the Cotabato River Basin at least as early as 1300. Their home island of Mindanao was so named by the Spanish who took the name of the preeminent Maguindanao Sultanate, shortened it, and lent it to the island itself (McKenna 1998). The number of Maguindanao speakers is approximately one million. Also on the west coast of Mindanao, and just to the north of the Maguindanao homeland in the Lake Lanao region, are the Maranao—the "people of the lake"—who number close to eight hundred thousand. Maguindanao and Maranao are close cognate languages: it is estimated that a Maguindanaon can understand about 60 percent of Maranao while a Maranao finds about half of Maguindanaon intelligible (Lewis 2009). Both languages are members of the Davao family that collectively accounts for nearly one-half of all Muslims in the Philippines. For both groups, comprehension of Tagalog and/or Filipino is low. However, a separate group in the south, the Tausug, speak a language descended from that of a more northern population in what is now the central Philippines and therefore more closely related to Tagalog. The Tausug also number about one million and are centered on and around the island of Jolo in the Sulu Archipelago to the west of Mindanao.

In the years following the Spanish-American War, the regional and ethnic divide between the predominant Tausug and Maguindanao languages was readily apparent to the American colonial administrators who established the first secular schools in the region. As in Aceh, Muslim children would traditionally learn the Arabic script as part of their early religious instruction so that they could recite from the Quran (Hassoubah 1983). Unlike in Aceh, however, there was no Moro language linking the Muslim populations of the region, and none of the Moro languages maintained anything like a functioning print culture.[11] The erstwhile goal of American administrators was to teach local "children through the medium of their own languages. They believed that this was a more efficient and effective means for teaching American ideas and achieving literacy." As a result, two languages were established in the colonial school system employing texts "in Tausug and Maguindanao using Arabic script" (Milligan 2004, 458), though even this pedagogy was never put into practice.

Support for these printed languages, however, vanished with the exit of the Americans. Nonetheless, this did *not* spark an outcry, even though the state then made a concerted effort to marginalize the cultures (and languages) of the largest ethnic populations. In 1957, a Commission on National Integration was "tasked with fostering the development and integration of Muslim Filipinos," though assimilation would be a better term: "Whether or not it was official intent, the message was clear: to be modern Filipinos, Muslim Filipinos must stop being Maranao, Maguindanao or Tausug" (Milligan 2005a, 78–79). Nonetheless, vernacular language politics are an afterthought in

Mindanao, the primary point of contention being the preference for English and the rejection of Filipino.[12] Moreover, this is the case throughout the rest of the Philippines as well. This is curious, and it is therefore important to ask—especially in the case of Mindanao—"why such well-entrenched regionalisms in the country have not followed the direction taken by ay other societies with similar issues: to demand minority language rights" (Tupas 2007, 30). Again, in regard to Mindanao, there are two answers: first, there are no print cultures to speak of; second, among the thirteen distinct ethnolinguistic groups, there is no preferred language that could serve all as an intra-Moro tongue. This conspicuous absence is considered below in regard to political mobilization, and the lack of support for language rights among Muslim separatists.

Before continuing, however, it is important to note that there are some voices in support of using regional languages formally in a consolidated Muslim Mindanao. Shariff M. Julabbi, the chairman of a small MILF splinter group called the MILF/BMA (Bangsamoro Mujahedeen Alliance), argues Tausug alone should be used as the language of what was the Sultanate of Sulu in what is now the western part of Mindanao. "We have several ethnic languages or dialects here in Mindanao. You have the Tausug, you have the Maranao or the Maguindanao, but as far as the Sultanate of Sulu is concerned, we have only one language, and that is the Tausug."[13] In tandem, Abhoud Syed Linga, executive director of the Institute of Bangsamoro Studies in Cotabato, posits the there should (will) be three regional languages in formal use depending on locality: "Generally, the lingua franca for separate regions, Tausug for example, is understood in Tawi-Tawi, Sulu, Jolo, some parts of Basilan, some parts of Zamboanga. The Maranao is generally in Lanao and then the Maguindanaos, here. So I see three strong regional languages. When we did our training with the MILF forces together with International Committee of the Red Cross, the three participants were divided into three groups on the language proficiency, that is the Tausug speaking, the Maranao speaking and the Maguindanao speaking."[14] What remains an open issue, however, is the selection of an official language to unite all Mindanao. In the view of a former MNLF fighter, this remains "a difficulty," but in the meantime "we use Tagalog and English."[15]

Islam in Mindanao

While the history of Islam in Mindanao begins in the 1300s, the history of Islam in the Philippines' Moro *separatist* movement begins in earnest in the

1970s.[16] Previously, the Moro people fought together (with the exception of some collaborators) in opposition to successive colonial powers—the Spanish, the American, the Japanese, the Filipino—and remained so in their collective opposition to the postwar state. However, the role of Islam within the movement surfaced as a source of conflict in the early years of the insurgency, most dramatically with the split of the leadership of MNLF in 1977, and the formal birth of the MILF in 1984. To be sure, the supplanting of the term *national* with *Islamic* would seem to be a clear indication that the old group was nationalist and the new group religious, a transitional phenomenon in no way limited to Mindanao (Kepel 1994). Indeed, this is conventional wisdom, and there is no small amount of truth to support this view. However, this does not tell us *why* the movement was once united and then divided, and *who* was responsible for the split.

Part of the story can be traced to the competing visions of two men: Nur Misuari, the founder of the MNLF, and Salamat Hashim, the founder of the MILF. Unlike the secular Misuari, Salamat was a pious scholar of Islam who studied at Cairo's preeminent Al-Azhar University. The rift surfaced during the 1976 negotiations that led to the Tripoli Agreement when a faction of the MNLF charged Misuari was (1) settling for a watered down autonomy rather than full independence and (2) failing to account for Islam in the formation of the new entity (Liow 2006, 11). In 1984, Salamat formally announced in Jeddah, Saudi Arabia, that the breakaway faction of the MNLF was launching an entirely separate organization, the MILF. In no uncertain terms, the organization explicitly supported a campaign of Islamization, an agenda represented by "the thinking of its chief ideologue, Salamat Hashim," a "proponent of the Islamic state, and this, to his mind, was at the heart of the tension between the MILF and MNLF and explained the latter's 'betrayal' of the Bangsamoro cause" (Liow 2006, 12, 16–17). This view is not contested by the MNLF. Abraham "Abet" Iribani, a former MNLF spokesman and peace negotiator, stated in an interview that the MNLF "has always been secular" and this is the "main reason" for the split between Nur Misuari and Salamat.[17]

However, while the MILF cannot be called secular, there are some important distinctions that should be made regarding its relative credentials as an Islamist organization, including but not limited to the question of whether it can be viewed in the same light as a transnational jihadi organization like al-Qaeda or Jemaah Islamiyah, as is often the case in security literature and, on occasion, the Western press. In other words, is the MILF best defined as a rebel group, a terrorist network, or a nascent political party? Certainly in the wake of September 11 a great deal of international attention was focused suddenly on the MILF, primarily because of the possibility that the group could expand the reach of transnational jihad and Islamic terrorism to the farthest reaches of Southeast Asia (Abuza 2003; Ressa 2003). According to Zachary Abuza, in the 1990s the MILF "forged a tentative relationship with Al Qaeda, receiving money through Saudi charities." Moreover, there were "concerns that members of the Al-Qaeda-linked terrorist group Jemaah Islamiyah" received training in MILF camps (2005, 453). In addition, despite some assertions that the group was compromised by infighting and factionalization, Abuza claims the MILF is a "unitary organization" with effective "command and control" (2005, 458). In addition, though most of the MILF's actions could be classified as hit-and-run tactics against military and government targets, there have been many events that certainly qualify as terrorism, that is, actions directed against (predominantly Christian) civilians in order to spawn fear among a broader population, including bombings and kidnappings (Chalk 2001, 248).

Nonetheless, conceptually lumping the MILF in with al-Qaeda is intellectually lazy, for doing so misses critical differences between the two, especially regarding the specific goals of the MILF versus the universal struggle of transnational jihad. For example, Joseph Liow cautions that despite *organizational* links with al-Qaeda, the MILF *ideologically* shares "little with broader radical global Islamist and Jihadist ideologies and movements. . . . [Its character remains] primarily political, reflected in the key objective of some measure of self-determination, and local, as seen in the territorial and ideational boundaries of activism and agitation. . . . Tactical and operational cooperation [moreover] did not facilitate ideological confluence of any significant kind between the two organizations" (2006, 2, 21). Rather, the MILF has "demonstrated a capacity for pragmatism in pursuit of its objectives, and its commitment to religious ideology belies a readiness to recalibrate policies." This pragmatism led the MILF to abandon its initial demand for independence in favor of "autonomy, federalism, and commonwealth" (Liow 2006, 22).

Of course, there is another organization in Mindanao that cannot be called pragmatic insofar as it consistently maintains it is fighting a jihad for the establishment of sharia in an independent Islamic state. Started in 1991, the Abu Sayyaf Group (ASG) splintered from the MILF as "a self-styled fundamentalist insurgent movement" that operates in and around Zamboanga, Basilan, and Sulu (Chalk 2001, 249).[18] However, while the ASG is responsible for no small number of atrocities—including bombings, kidnappings, assassinations, beheadings, mass murders, and sabotage—it is a misconception that the group is ideologically coherent, or even zealous. According to a professor at the University of the Philippines, "The ASG is seen more as a criminal bandit group engaged mainly in kidnap-for-ransom activities and disguised as freedom fighters" (Tigno 2006, 25). They are perhaps better described as "entrepreneurs of violence," defined as "those who use their reputations and capacity for violence to compete for the power to make decisions affecting inhabitants of an area." While claiming to wage a transnational war, the ASG is better "known for its extremist and Islamic fundamentalist rhetoric" (Gutierrez and Borras 2004, 24, 26). Importantly, both the MNLF and the MILF are well aware of the group's reputation, and both the MNLF and the MILF "have gone to great lengths to distance themselves from the ASG" (Chalk 2001, 249; May 2012, 286). Since 2001, the decline of the ASG is attributed not only to the (more or less effective) severing of ties with both the MNLF and the MILF, but also to effective counterterrorism operations staged jointly by the Philippines and the United States. This, however, has not stopped the ASG from pursing its own interests. While the ASG is no longer considered a threat to the state itself, it continues to pose "a substantial threat to civilians, and to security forces deployed in the area, for the foreseeable future" (Jane's Intelligence 2013, 1).

Political Mobilization in Mindanao

It is noted above that the split between the MNLF and the MILF can be explained *in part* by the ideological rift between those who struggled for a secular Moro nation-state and those who sought to establish an Islamic state. To this we can add differences that were partly personal and partly strategic. Another part of the story, however, hinges on ethnic identity rather than Islam. The leadership and membership of the MNLF and the MILF essentially come from separate ethnolinguistic groups, the Tausug and the Maguindanao, respectively (Chalk 2001, 248; Means 2009, 201). Hence, between the MNLF and the MILF, "the ethnogeographic concentration of the two groups has always been different" (Chalk et al. 2009, 37), so cleavages tend to follow ethnic and linguistic lines (May 2012, 291). The relative importance of this distinction *is* a matter of debate, but what should not be missed is that this ethnic divide was (and is) part of the problem facing the Moros as they attempt—thus far without success—to come together as a united people, the *Bangsamoro*. Before the 1970s, unity was sourced in opposition to perceived imperialism, but after 1976 "the MNLF's swift decline . . . exposed the fragility of *communal identity* as both primordial tie and mobilizing symbol. There was, in fact, little basis for unity among Mindanao Muslims aside from Islam. Notably, Muslim communities spoke related but mutually unintelligible languages and differed socially and politically in significant ways" (Abinales 2000, 3).[19] Note that of the three main Muslim ethnic groups—the Tausug, Maguindanao, and Maranao—the Maranao are more closely aligned with the Maguindanao.[20] This is not only because the groups are regional neighbors on the main island, but also because they speak cognate languages. To this end, anthropologists sometimes characterize the divide as between the Tausug and the "Maranao/Maguindanao," a split that remains unresolved in the broader effort to consolidate a Moro identity: "Neither language has yielded to the other as a pan-Muslim lingua franca, a Moro language. The Tausug-Maranao/Maguindanaon linguistic divide and the identity division that goes along with it have not yet been effectively bridged, not even by the most militant insurgents. The only common languages between Sulu and Mindanao Moro leadership are Tagalog and English" (Frake 1998, 45–46). The leadership does not anticipate this scenario shifting. The MNLF's Iribani notes "the Tausug will remain Tausug forever. The Tausug language will remain Tausug; the Maguindanao with the Maguindanao; the Maranao with the Maranao."[21]

Yet despite this acknowledgment, the role of ethnicity is not publicly engaged by either organization: "It is often said that ethnicity is the main difference between the Tausug-dominated MNLF and the Maguindanao-dominated MILF. While this distinction is important, both groups have sought to downplay ethnicity while emphasizing other symbols of pan-Moro unity. The MNLF symbols are those of a secular Moro nationalism; the MILF has built its identity around Islam" (Gutierrez and Borras 2004, 50n2). To be sure, the MILF does indeed downplay ethnicity, perhaps because the group consists of both Maguindanao and Maranao forces, which is seen by the government of the Philippines as a source of factionalism and weakness (Abuza 2005, 459). The MILF is also specifically averse to questions of language policy. Eid Kabulu, the former MILF spokesman, acknowledged in conversation the mutually unintelligible communities that collectively compose the Moro people present "a problem," but he claims this issue is secondary to the "bigger problem" of negotiations toward a final settlement with Manila. In admirably evasive language, he proposed that "once we resolve the bigger problem [of a peace settlement], then comes the smaller problem [of language]; we are confident that we should be able to overcome this once we resolve the bigger problem." Among the "major ethnic groups" the selection of official languages in Mindanao will be for "the people to decide."[22]

However, even if the organizations themselves downplay ethnicity, this does not mean ethnicity is irrelevant, or will not present a barrier to unity in the future: far from it. In simple terms, "this diversity has hampered unity among Muslims" (Rood 2005, 39n3). In the view of Benny Bacani, the head of the Institute for Autonomy and Governance at Notre Dame University in Cotabato City, the Moros themselves are "in denial" about the relevance of ethnicity.[23] Consider also the view of a local third-party observer and peace activist: William Kreutz, an American Catholic priest and longtime resident of Mindanao (since 1963), a former president of the Ateneo de Zamboanga University who serves as the rector of the Jesuit Community at the Ateneo de Manila University in Katipunan in Zamboanga del Norte. When asked about the question of ethnicity vis-à-vis the Moro conflict, he argues it is a "core" issue, citing, for example, the fact that "the Maranaos look down on the Tausugs. They feel they are better people, they feel they are more Islamic," adding that this division weakens the overall effort to secure group rights: "It's like the American Indians who never got their act together." Note, however, that he quickly acknowledges, "These are the things you can't always say in conferences."[24]

Conclusion

In Mindanao, decades of separatist violence in clashes with the government of the Philippines were preceded by centuries of violent clashes with the Spanish, the Americans, and the Japanese. In the 1970s, two separatist organizations emerged to advance "Moro" independence—the MNLF and the MILF—and claimed to represent all the "native" (pre–World War II) peoples of Mindanao. The MNLF has consistently celebrated its secular orientation; the MILF initially indicated an Islamic (if not Islamist) orientation, but the organization now distances itself from this rhetoric. Importantly, the two parties are essentially divided along ethnic lines between the Tausug and Maguindanao. However, neither party expresses any interest whatsoever in mobilizing supporters of indigenous language rights. The disparate, multi-ethnic character of Mindanao's population is acknowledged, but treated as a problem that may or may not emerge in years to come. The conflict in Mindanao is framed in terms of anti-imperialism and anticolonialism, but the movement is divided on the question of what else unites the Moro peoples other than Islam and their collective resistance to Manila.

In the context of a diverse ethnolinguistic population that shares a tenuous group identity and a new degree of autonomy, an immediate and obvious suggestion to assist the building of postconflict institutions is to create a shared civil society, ideally built around a "neutral" language. Such was the case in Tanzania, for example, when Julius Nyerere decreed Swahili as the national language to unite more than a hundred distinct ethnolinguistic tribes, not to mention Sukarno's multiethnic Indonesia and the selection of Malay-based Bahasa Indonesia. In the case of Mindanao, where none of the vernaculars maintain a print culture, this language would be English. Nonetheless, even if this serves as an effective means of establishing a shared Moro print culture—an imagined Moro community—there are two obstacles that present serious challenges to long-lasting peace. The first is the Muslim-Christian communal split; the second is clan violence, known as *rido*.

In regard to bridging the sectarian divide, there is an entire industry of organizations dedicated to peace building in Mindanao. Formed over decades, the Mindanao peace movement "consists of a wide array of non-governmental organizations, 'people's organizations,' religious groups, human rights groups, and so on . . . and is one of the most active and vibrant in the whole of Asia" (Quimpo 2012, 128). Nonetheless, despite their best efforts, there is an extreme level of distrust between Muslims and Christians. Moreover, the majority Christian population is less trusting of Muslims than the minority Muslim population is of Christians, "thus the task of overcoming mutual mistrust lies largely on the Christian side of any divide" (Rood 2005, 22–23). Note, however, that different ethnic groups have different reputations; hence, the Christians in Mindanao are well aware of and attribute importance to ethnicity among the Muslim population. In a 2002 survey, for example, the Maranao were considered more trustworthy than either the Tausug or, in last place, the Maguindanao (see Table 10.2).

Yet mistrust of Muslims generally or an individual Muslim ethnic minority specifically is actually of less concern than the violence perpetuated

Table 10.2. Intercommunity Trust in Muslim
Mindanao, 2002

Muslim net trust of Christians (%)	Christian net trust of Muslim ethnic groups (%)	
34	Maguindanao	−27
	Maranao	−13
	Tausug	−21

Source: Survey cited in Rood (2005, 23).
Note: The "net trust" rating is the percentage of
respondents who express "very much" or "much"
trust minus the percentage of respondents who
express "little" or "very little" trust.

by localized actors, a phenomenon known in the Philippines as rido, defined as "a type of violent conflict variously referred to as feuding, revenge killings, blood revenge, vendetta, inter-tribal warfare, and clan conflicts. Character-ized by sporadic outbursts of retaliatory violence between families and kinship groups as well as between communities, this phenomenon fre-quently occurs in areas where government or a central authority is weak and in areas where there is a perceived lack of justice and security" (Torres 2007, 11). Rido is a particularly acute problem in regard to election violence, a "manifestation of a more general problem of persistent clan conflict . . . this problem is not unknown in the rest of the Philippines but it is worse in ARMM" (Rood 2012, 270). Critically, in a 2002 survey of Muslim areas in Mindanao, more people cited clan conflict as a source of violence compared to the actions of separatist or Islamist groups (Rood 2005, 6).

Note, however, that it is extremely difficult—if not impossible—to untan-gle the relationship between Moro politics writ large and rido conflict writ small. Put another way, in Mindanao, "many armed confrontations in the past involving insurgent groups and the military were actually triggered by a local rido," especially those involving land disputes and political rivalries (Torres 2007, 12, 16). Thus, even if the 2012 MILF peace deal holds together (Keister 2012), it would be naïve to expect the quality of life of average citi-zens in Mindanao to improve dramatically without the strengthening of gov-ernment institutions, particularly in regard to the enforcement of local laws and the deployment of peace officers who can be reliably expected to settle clan conflicts with professional neutrality (Chalk et al. 2009, 65). To this end, the multiethnic character of the Moros presents an all too common challenge faced by newly autonomous regions. This is to say not that life in Mindanao will not improve, but rather that local politics will continue to be contentious— even violent—until a common Moro identity can unite disparate peoples as citizens of a legitimate polity.

CHAPTER 11

Nationalism, Language, and Islam

Whether based on a close reading of the Quran or a careful study of Middle Eastern politics, it is a popular convention and academic conceit that Muslim politics are exceptional. Muslim exceptionalism typically describes either an aversion to democracy or a resistance to nationalism, or both. This book directly challenges the supposition that Muslims are exceptionally resistant to the most common form of nationalism, which is typically secular and based on a shared and distinct ethnolinguistic culture. This question was generated by a theoretical literature that argues Islam is more than a religion, but rather an entire blueprint for living, privately and publicly, that is exceptionally resistant not only to secular government but also to secular nations and, therefore, secular nation-states.

To answer this question, six cases of Muslim-minority separatist conflict were examined to determine whether or not their struggle hinged on Islamist politics or ethnonational mobilization (or both or neither). In addition, an in-depth examination of the Arab world was also conducted. In the case of the latter, I argue the sociolinguistic phenomenon called diglossia weakens the distinct ethnonational identity of disparate Arab peoples (Moroccans, Egyptians, Lebanese, etc.), as well as the civic identity of erstwhile patriots, rendering Arab states exceptionally more susceptible to Islamism. I call this condition Arab dinationalism. As for the greater Muslim world, an empirical test of such a broad view demands a wide range of subjects. Hence, a half dozen cross-regional examples of Muslim-minority separatists were selected as cases of Muslim societies challenging the sovereignty of their state, though the nature of the challenge was not predetermined. Vernacular language was adopted as a proxy for ethnolinguistic identification; hence, a minority under consideration also spoke a minority language natively. To collect primary research material, the leadership of separatist parties and organizations

Table 11.1. Muslim Minority Languages and Ethnonational Mobilization

State	State majority: Non-Muslim	State majority: Muslim	Vernacular(s)	Vernacular print culture	Vernacular language mobilization
Iraq		Kurds	Kurdish (Sorani/ Kurmanji)	Yes	Yes
China	Uyghur		Uyghur	Yes	Yes
Pakistan		Sindhis	Sindhi	Yes	Yes
India	Kashmiri		Kashmiri	No	No
Indonesia		Acehnese	Acehnese	No	No
Philippines	Moro		Maguindanaon, Tausug, etc.	No	No

were contacted personally and interviewed specifically regarding the raison d'être of their operation, whether nationalist, Islamist, both or neither. Moreover, following a broad range of literature from the study of nations and nationalism, a specific litmus test was the separatists' view of education language policy: if ethnonationalist, then language of instruction politics is typically of paramount importance to separatists; if Islamist, then mother tongues mean little in contrast to study of the Quran.

Following fieldwork in eight countries and interviews with dozens of separatists, the results are rather straightforward. Three of the cases—the Kurds in Iraq, Uyghurs in China, and Sindhis in Pakistan—are in no uncertain terms secular ethnonational struggles for self-determination. The other three cases— the Kashmiris in India, Acehnese in Indonesia, and Moros in the Philippines— are distinct in that Islamist politics are at least present and sometimes prominent. What explains the variation? In the three cases of ethnolinguistic nationalism, all maintain a robust vernacular print culture. In the three cases where Islamism is evident, none maintain a vernacular print culture (see Table 11.1).

In the case of the Acehnese, their print culture is maintained in the official language of the state, that is, Bahasa Indonesia. This is remarkable insofar as the founder of the Aceh Sumatra National Liberation Front, Hasan di Tiro, cited Bahasa Indonesia as an instrument of Javanese imperialism. Nonetheless, after a peace agreement was struck in 2005, the new leaders of Aceh showed little to no interest in promoting their mother tongue. At the same time, elements of Islamic fundamentalism, including but not limited to the local implementation of sharia laws, spread across the province. In Kashmir, a postpartition attempt to foster an Urdu print culture failed; the print culture language of Kashmir is now English (though a low level of literacy renders even this print culture most fragile), a development that is increasingly common in modernizing and multiethnic regions where the penetration of state institutions is shallow (Rudby and Saraceni 2006). Meanwhile, Islamist elements mobilized domestically in earnest in the late 1980s and led to a bloody insurgency. In Mindanao, the Moro population is divided among thirteen distinct ethnolinguistic groups: there is no native Moro lingua franca. Instead, a print culture is maintained not in the official language of the Philippines, that is, Filipino, which is viewed as an instrument of domination by a Catholic state, but rather in English. Also in Mindanao, a movement that began as a leftist separatist insurgency ultimately fractured along ethnolinguistic lines: the two main political organizations, the Moro National Liberation Front and the Moro Islamic Liberation Front, are dominated by two of the largest ethnicities, the Tausug and the Maguindanaon, respectively. The MILF in particular later showed clear influence of Islamist politics.

As the cases in this study were drawn from across the Muslim world, from the Middle East to Southeast Asia, it is not unreasonable to suggest that this variation indicates a general phenomenon in the Muslim world whereby vernacular ethnolinguistic nationalism is essentially incompatible with Islamism.

However, at this point it is important to distinguish what is or is not meant by Islamism in the context of *religious nationalism*. The latter, a term elevated particularly by the work of Mark Juergensmeyer (1993, 1995, 2008), indicates a phenomenon whereby nationalism and religion become fused. In this case—which is not limited to Muslims but also evident among Christians, Jews, and Hindus—an *ethnonationalist* conflict morphs into an *ethnoreligious* conflict (Fox 2002, 2004). In the Muslim world this phenomenon is particularly evident in the Arab world. This book does not challenge this phenomenon—indeed, in the cases of Kashmir and post-tsunami Aceh there is evidence presented here in support of religious nationalism. However, it is important to recognize that religious nationalism is distinct from transnational Islamic fundamentalism, a phenomenon that is sometimes couched in another term from Juergensmeyer (2003), *cosmic war*, wherein there is no country, only a cosmos of good and evil forces waging an eternal fight for righteousness. In the context of Islam, this is conventionally called transnational jihad, and is perhaps best illustrated by the phenomenon of foreign fighters who travel overseas to join a fight for Islam that has little or nothing to do with the country of their birth.[1]

Put another way, people are sometimes called upon to lay down their lives for "God and country," though in the age of fundamentalist jihad it would be more precise to say "God *or* country." Whereas soldiers may do their duty as patriots, they need not adhere to a specific faith to perform their duty, even if it calls for the ultimate sacrifice. Indeed, to die for one's country is conventionally honorable. To die for one's country is to selflessly sacrifice for the good of something far greater than oneself. In the case of nation-states, soldiers may commit their life not only to their country, but also to their people, their *nation*, an entity that is perceived to endure for all time and in this way confers a kind of immortality to the dead soldiers. In the case of religious fundamentalism, however, immortality is not a metaphor but a perceived fact, and the sacrifice is neither to the nation nor the state but to the supreme being. In this way a religious fundamentalist is willing to die for the divine, to expire as a martyr, even though God is a deity without a country. Of course, faith and flag often merge, a phenomenon familiar since at least the time of Henry VIII's dismissal of the Catholic Church and the establishment of the Anglican Church, and by extension the Church of England. The same could be said of the Greek Orthodox Church in Greece: it is a nation-state with an officially sanctioned religion.

This is entirely distinct, however, from religious fundamentalism, in which case the state is either a legitimate theocracy or an illegitimate oppressor of true believers. In the case of Islam, a universal faith that welcomes all comers regardless of nationality or citizenship, religious fundamentalism explicitly excludes the state as a divisive barrier to the unification of the global ummah. Consider the words of Sayyid Qutb (1906–66), the intellectual father of modern Islamic fundamentalism, on the matter: "A Muslim has no country except that part of the earth where the Sharia of God is established and human relationships are based on the foundation of relationship with God; a Muslim has no nationality except his belief, which makes him a member of the Muslim community in Dar-ul-Islam" (Qutb 1993, 103). In the years since his execution, Qutb's vision has come to pass in the phenomenon of transnational Islamic fundamentalism. Osama bin Laden was not a nationalist, and his followers were not patriots. A cosmic war against infidels is waged by believers rather than citizens or nationals.

And what of the converse? Can Muslims fight and die for their country, their nation, or both? Absolutely. There is nothing exceptional about Muslims that prevents them from adhering to nationalism. In 1971, Bengalis fought and died for their own nation-state: in the years since, the same can be said, for example, of Albanians in Kosovo and Kurds in Iraq. They did not die, however, for sharia. Indeed, Islam is a mystical distraction from a nationalist struggle for a secure, secular, and independent nation-state.

This relationship, between nationalism and Islamic fundamentalism, is the focus of this book. In short, I argue there is an *inverse* relationship between ethnolinguistic nationalism and Islamic fundamentalism. This is a simple statement and easy to understand: the greater the attachment Muslims feels to their nation, the weaker their attachment to a cosmic Islamic fundamentalism; conversely, the greater the universal zeal of Islamic fundamentalists, the weaker their attachment to their specific nation.

Arguably, this phenomenon is also linked to the relative strength or weakness of democracy in a Muslim society: the idea that religion is the sole source of political legitimacy is in direct opposition to the idea that popular sovereignty is the sole source of political legitimacy. Given that popular sovereignty, rule of the people, is the foundation of democracy, and that democracy—good and bad, beautiful and ugly—is the most common regime type worldwide, the ethos of Islamic fundamentalism challenges the most conventional political doctrine on the planet. Of course, the contentious relationship between religion and nation is far older than Islamic fundamentalism (Pape 2005). In the context of Christianity, this is illustrated historically, from the medieval to the modern, by the dissolution of absolute papal authority among a range of polities that ultimately yielded ethnolinguistically distinct nation-states. Over time, nationalism grew stronger and the Church grew weaker: their separate claims to political legitimacy were essentially incompatible.

In the context of Islam, this pattern is less clear as there was (and is) no parallel institution as robust as the Holy See, but there are, of course, more than a few examples of modern Muslim nation-states, including but not limited to de facto secular states like Turkey, Bangladesh, and Indonesia. However, there are also a wide range of fundamentalist Islamic mobilizations that explicitly reject appeals to an ethnonational identity in favor of an idealized global ummah to be governed by a literal interpretation of the Quran. Examples of these mobilizations include, but are not limited to, the Taliban (Afghanistan), Lashkar-e-Taiba (Pakistan), al-Shabaab (Somalia), and Abu Sayyaf

(Philippines). This book argues the dependent variable that determines the political trajectory of any given Muslim population is whether or not there is a sufficient ethnonational alternative (such as Turk or Bangla) that limits political mobilization to a *specific* ethnolinguistic population, eschewing calls to a *universal* struggle. In the examples given above, the alternatives would be Pashto, Punjabi, Somali, and Moro, respectively.

This book also argues that the preferred litmus test for *ethnonational* mobilization is *language*, particularly as the anchor of a *print culture*, which defines both the extent and the limits of a given community. Whereas print culture is the strongest cultural bond of any given language community, it is described against alternate scenarios, specifically *speech culture* and *scribal culture*. Where ethnic identity and language cohesion is weak—especially in places where there is no common *printed* version of the people's mother tongue(s), such as Aceh, Kashmir, or Mindanao—there is more evidence of Islamist politics. On the other hand, a strong, distinct ethnonational identity and its concomitant print language—such as Uyghur in Xinjiang or Kurdish in Kurdistan—trumps appeals to a universal Islamist identity.

Therefore, when considering peoples and states at risk of (or actively) mobilizing in support of religious fundamentalism, this book further argues the most effective way to prevent the spread of Islamic extremism is to promote ethnolinguistic nationalism as a kind of inoculation against fundamentalism. It is acknowledged that this, in turn, can create many other very serious problems. For example, the application of this idea as policy would mean active *state* support of autonomy and/or separatist movements in places like Xinjiang, Mindanao, Chechnya, and Kashmir. This action could easily lead to a backlash by the state's broader and dominant population (Han Chinese, Filipino Catholics, Russians, Pandits, and/or other Hindus, respectively). Hence, it may be argued that the promotion of nationalism over Islamism supplants one intractable problem with another. However, the former offers the peerless advantage of *negotiation*—over symbols, schools, representation, regional autonomy, etc. (Ross 2007, 2009)—while the latter offers precious little room for compromise. This is demonstrated spectacularly in the case of contemporary Afghanistan, where the utility of negotiating with the fundamentalist Taliban may be little more than wishful thinking: "The Taliban insurgency is best defined as an insurgency wrapped in the narrative of jihad. History suggests that secular insurgents negotiate, jihadists do not . . . such individuals believe they are following the mandates of a higher calling. Indeed, history suggests that few, if any, jihads have ever ended with a negotiated settlement via reconciliation" (Goodson and Johnson 2011, 582). Because Afghanistan—an erstwhile nation-state wracked by Islamic fundamentalism—immediately suggests itself for examination, it is considered here in detail.

Afghanistan

The idea that raising literacy in Afghanistan will lower the level of violence is not new. Many programs focus on literacy indirectly by opening schools to provide public education, especially for girls and women. This would include the program detailed in Greg Mortenson's (2007) famous—or, following accusations of fabrication (Krakauer 2011), notorious—*Three Cups of Tea*. This seems to be a very good idea if for no other reason than Afghanistan is (1) one of the poorest countries in the world, (2) one of the least developed countries in the world, and (3) one of the least literate countries in the world. There is an inference that literacy is a necessary condition for development, which it is. In this discussion, however, there is little attention paid to the relevance of the following question: *which* language is taught to the illiterate? Generally, it is assumed that one learns to read and write the language one already speaks and understands. This is sensible, which is why teaching in local languages may contribute to the achievement of Millennium Development Goals (SIL International 2008). Yet this is not always the case. Most notably, the only High Culture language of education, commerce, and social mobility in the Arab world is Modern Standard Arabic (MSA), which is the mother tongue of nobody. The Arab world is also the *region* with the lowest level of literacy in the world. The fact that literacy is impeded when first taught to read and write in what is essentially a foreign language is generally not addressed, since the idea of teaching students to read and write vernacular Arabic is met with derision. Why? Because the status of MSA is very high while the status of any vernacular Arabic is very low, if not vulgar.

Separately, even when the language of instruction is also a mother tongue, another impediment to literacy in the vernacular is the lack of a standard script. Though more than six thousand languages are spoken worldwide, only some one hundred scripts are in use. Because some of these languages are spoken by just a few hundred people, many languages may not need a script of their own to aid in development. Nonetheless, in order to lift the life chances of large numbers of people, and to develop a distinct High Culture, SIL International estimates "hundreds of languages still need a writing system, with one-third needing a non-Roman or complex script" (2008, 15).

In Afghanistan, the language of public affairs is Dari. It is "the lingua franca, the language resorted to when speakers of different languages need to conduct business or otherwise communicate."[2] It is also the exclusive language of instruction for any education beyond primary school. It is a member of the Persian/Farsi language continuum, which extends from Iran to Tajikistan, and includes Hazara, Chahar Aimak, and Kizilbash: all are members of the overarching Indo-European language family.

Dari is not, however, the mother tongue of the largest ethnic group in Afghanistan, which is Pashto. In tandem with Dari, Pashto is one of the two official languages of the country, and it is taught both as a language of instruction for Pashtun children and (sometimes) as a subject for non-Pashtuns. In any country with more than one official language, the relationship between or among the multiple languages is never simple, but in Afghanistan the relationship is clearly hierarchical: "Pashto speakers are frequently bilingual in Dari, but Dari speakers rarely learn more than a few words of Pashto."[3] However, speakers of Dari, as a lingua franca, are multiethnic, and the language community includes not only Tajiks, but also the Hazara and (as the name implies) the Farsiwan. It is therefore already a force for unification among a diverse population (see Table 11.2).

Pashto does not lack a literary tradition. Most famously, Khushhal Khan Khatak, a seventeenth-century Afghan leader, is considered the founder of Pashto literature—primarily poetry—and the progenitor of a distinct scribal culture. However, Pashto literature has survived only as a specialized subject for academic researchers and aesthetes. As for Dari, which also claims a literary tradition emphasizing poetry, its dominance as the vernacular of social mobility does not mean it maintains a robust print culture: it does not. In comparison with Persian, which not only claims a literary history at least twelve hundred years old but also persists in Iran as a contemporary national language sustained by print capitalism (i.e., a print market driven by supply and demand), Dari is "mostly a spoken language." The impressions of a Dari-speaking U.S. Army officer in Kabul illustrates this point: "When compared to Persian Farsi, there are very few Dari dictionaries available for sale. Anecdotally, Dari and Persian Farsi are 99% the same in the written form, but are noticeably different when spoken. (I once incorrectly conjugated a verb and was accused of sounding like I was from Iran.) The relationship between Per-

Table 11.2. Afghanistan Ethnolinguistic Demographics: Population 31,822,848 (July 2014 Estimates)

Afghanistan: Ethnic groups	Language group	%	Afghanistan: Languages spoken	%
Pashtun	Persian	42	Pashto	35
Tajik	Persian	27	Dari (Persian)	50
Hazara	Persian	9	Turkic	11
Uzbek	Turkic	9	Other	4
Aimak	Persian	4		
Turkmen	Turkic	3		
Baloch	Persian	2		
Other	N/A	4		
Total		100		100

Source: U.S. Central Intelligence Agency. https://www.cia.gov/library/publications/the-world-factbook/geos/af.html

Note: Literacy statistics include persons over the age of fourteen who can read and write, but do not specify the language of literacy.

sian Farsi and Dari is roughly equivalent to that between French and [colloquial] Canadian French. Another telling description of Dari (which may offend some cultural sensitivities, but which I believe to be accurate) is that Dari is 'Street Persian'" (Stevens 2010, 1). What is the relative level of literacy between Dari and Pashto? It is safe to assume that literacy is lower in a region where the language of instruction beyond primary school is a foreign language, while literacy is higher in a region where the language of instruction is also the mother tongue of the students. The exact ratio is not known as such statistics are not possible to compile while the state is fighting an insurgency, that is, the Taliban. In fact, the actual literacy rate—in any language—is also unknown, and for the same reasons. Nonetheless, estimates are available for literacy writ large (see Table 11.3).

Regarding the language of literacy, the estimates available from the Central Intelligence Agency are confusing, in that the proportions of ethnic groups do not match the proportion of language speakers. However, if we assume people are counted as members of a language category if they can speak the language, then bilinguals will count in more than one category. Therefore, the language most often acquired will account for a greater share than it would otherwise. Given that Pashto speakers learn Dari but not the other way around, this helps explain why the Pashtun account for the largest ethnic group in

Table 11.3. Literacy and Population in Afghanistan

	Literacy: 2013 estimates (%)	Population: 2012 estimates (%)
Men	39	50.7
Women	13	49.3
Total	27	100.0

Sources: For literacy: World Health Organization 2013, http://www.who.int/countryfocus/cooperation_strategy /ccsbrief_afg_en.pdf . For population: World Bank 2012. http://data.worldbank.org/indicator/SP.POP.TOTL.FE.ZS Note: Literacy statistics include persons over the age of fourteen who can read and write, but do not specify the language of literacy.

the country at 42 percent, but only 35 percent of the country speaks *only* Pashto.

In this scenario, what would be required to raise the status and utility of Pashto literacy? In regard to status, Pashto is already an official state language, but in terms of social mobility it is a distant second to Dari. In regard to utility, speaking Pashto is essential in the southern half of the country, but as an undeveloped agriculture region, literacy is very low. In a constructivist view, such as that of Anderson, one route to an imagined community linked by a print language is (1) teaching the language in schools and (2) providing materials to read in that language. In the case of medieval to Renaissance Europe, the first vernacular best seller was a translated Bible, thereafter followed by humanist literature. However, in Afghanistan this is something of a nonstarter as translating the Quran remains, for doctrinal reasons, sinful. Certainly, in addition to the rich heritage of poetry, there are newer alternatives, such as newspapers and magazines, that may (eventually) find a ready readership. Nonetheless, a more direct incentive, however, would be the promotion of Pashto as a language of state institutions, at both the center and the periphery, in this case meaning the south of Afghanistan.

A continuing impediment is the Taliban, which maintains a critical link to the Pashtun community. As a continuing presence in Afghanistan, the Taliban remain strongest in areas where the majority population is also Pashtun. As for the Taliban's position on literacy vis-à-vis fundamentalist

Islam (and for Islamic fundamentalists everything must be measured vis-à-vis Islam), there is no greater illustration than this: they did (and do) burn books, shutter schools, and poison students. The short-term defeat of the Taliban is a question of strategy and tactics in a kinetic engagement, that is, force, but the long-term defeat of fundamentalist Islam in Afghanistan will require a viable alternative to fundamentalism, which in this case means a distinct ethnolinguistic identity that may develop into an ethnonational identity.

Given the importance of state institutions to maintain and promote education, which in turn requires literacy (optimally in the vernacular language), is there a "Pashtunistan" that could provide such a service? Yes and no. On the one hand, it could be argued that Afghanistan itself is already a Pashtunistan since the Pashtun dominate the state (and have since 1754) as well as the current regime. On the other hand, it could be argued that the concept of Pashtunistan is itself antithetical to the raison d'être of a nominally united *and* multiethnic Afghanistan. That being said, the spatial distribution of Pashtuns is fairly consistent across the southern part of the country; the same could be said for the north and its ethnicities, including the Hazara, Tajik, Turkmen, and Uzbek. Does this mean ethnofederalism is a viable solution to this deeply divided state (Hale 2004)? If so, how could a place like Afghanistan transition from a centralized state—with a district-based system that eschews ethnolinguistic identification—to, most likely, a federal state that explicitly recognizes a connection between the ethnolinguistic characteristics of a population and their own regional government?

Ironically, one model is offered by India, a state with a long and complicated history vis-à-vis Afghanistan, particularly as a proxy in its perennial conflict with Pakistan. At the time of partition in 1947, India was a mishmash of provinces and princely states (including the largest, Kashmir). While the first constitution of India was drafted in 1949 and enacted in 1950, the state inherited the tangle of prepartition internal borders. This was remedied in 1956 by the States Reorganization Act, which redefined the borders of India's constituent federal territories along the lines of ethnolinguistic communities. From an initial list of major states (Madras, Andhra, Hyderabad, Mysore, Bombay, and Travancore-Cochin) successive decades have witnessed the emergence of many other distinct communities claiming the same right to territorial and administrative autonomy. The current total is twenty-eight, the majority of which have clear ethnolinguistic borders, such a Tamil speakers in Tamil Nadu or Manipuri speakers in Manipur, and so forth.

Accomplishing the same kind of constitutional engineering in Afghanistan is obviously problematic, but not impossible. In twentieth-century Afghanistan, ethnicity mattered little in comparison with ideology as a source of instability, up to and including regime change following the Soviet occupation in the 1980s and the broad conflict of the 1990s (Barfield 2011). Following the ouster of the Taliban, ethnicity emerged as a much more potent force with a significant probability of zero-sum entrenchment. Indeed, following the ouster of the Taliban, voting correlates directly with ethnic parties (Johnson 2006). At this point we may ask, what is to be done? In contemporary terms, the idea of explicitly considering the institutional restructuring of Afghanistan along the lines of India's redistricting in 1956 appears to invite chaos. This is perhaps the case, though without such a consideration chaos may emerge nonetheless. In this view, "the best way to avoid such conflict—and, thus, to create a more stable Afghanistan—is to address these interests before conflict arises, not after it starts" (Barfield 2011, 65).

As the Pashtun are the largest and most volatile population of Afghanistan, addressing their interests is a necessary condition for beginning the process. However, as argued above, the best way to continue this process—which has the advantage of both supporting long-term interregional stability and weakening the appeal of Islamism—is the promotion of a Pashtun identity cemented by the creation and exchange of materials written by and printed for Pashtuns. It remains extraordinarily difficult to imagine a community of united "Afghans," but it is a far more realistic proposition to imagine a united and stable "Pashtunistan."

Conclusion

In addition to falsifying the theoretical proposition that Muslim societies are exceptionally resistant to nationalism, this book also helps answer the most pressing question in contemporary international politics: what can be done to counter the persistent emergence of Islamic fundamentalism?[4] The short answer is this: *promote* nationalism. The relative strength or weakness of an ethnolinguistic national identity strengthens or weakens the legitimacy of political institutions, which is necessary to maintain a healthy democracy. A crisis of legitimacy invites challenges from competing identities and/or ideologies. In the case of Muslim societies, a national identity may find itself challenged by a pan-national Islamic identity; in the case of most Arab countries, the nebulous character of Arab national identity means the legitimacy of most Arab states is always in question, and there remains little consensus on "what it means to be Egyptian, Moroccan, Algerian, Bahraini, or Iraqi" (Brumberg 2005, 98). This affords easy access to Islamist entrepreneurs who offer a consistent and comforting Muslim identity sine qua non.

There is a critical lesson here: to fight Islamic fundamentalism there is little point in promoting liberal democracy without first deciding who is and is not a member of the demos, that is, the *nation*. In short, (1) there is an inverse relationship between a vernacular ethnolinguistic identity and an Islamist identity; (2) the relative strength of an ethnolinguistic identity corresponds with the relative strength of a print culture; (3) if the goal is to weaken Islamism, then the alternative is to strengthen nationalism; and (4) the best way to strengthen nationalism *and* democracy is to promote literacy in the vernacular. Populations without their own written language are less responsive to ethnonational appeals and are more likely to tolerate the presence of Islamist elements. This is the case in Aceh, Kashmir, and Mindanao. This is not the case in Xinjiang, Sindh, or Kurdistan, where a strong ethnonational identity protects a population from the potential injuries of an Islamist encounter. This suggests that Islamism is not a stronger ideological force in cases of communal conflict, but rather functions as a kind of opportunistic infection. It infects citizens who are not immunized by an ethnonational bond. Hence, the prescribed treatment for Islamic fundamentalism is, in fact, nationalism.

Chapter 1

1. Credit for its coinage goes to communists active in the heyday of the American labor movement. In 1929, in New York City, the *Daily Worker* reported that the Communist International was acutely aware of "American exceptionalism" and this affected "the whole tactical line of the C.I. as applied to America." The *Oxford English Dictionary* cites a January 29 article by "Brouder & Zack" (vol. 3, no. 2).

2. After 9/11, the pervasive use of "clash of civilizations" rhetoric in the media to explain the attacks amplified the argument that all Muslims are united and equally dangerous.

3. The legal conventions of jus soli and jus sanguinus, respectively.

4. In this case, the purported threat is hordes of Latino Catholic immigrants who are neither assimilating into the general Anglophone population nor especially drawn to the staunch liberal doctrine that Huntington famously labeled the *American Creed*.

5. Unfortunately, political science fieldwork in Xinjiang, especially focusing on Uyghur separatists, is an invitation to deportation (for the interviewer) and detention (for the interviewee). For this reason I interviewed Uyghur expatriates and refugees in the United States (Washington, D.C.) and in Germany (Munich and Frankfurt), where there are sizable Uyghur communities. That being said, I have privately traveled in Xinjiang three times, including time spent in Urumqi, Kashgar, Khotan, and Ruoqiang. Some of my travel observations inform the case chapter.

6. CIA World Factbook 2012, https://www.cia.gov/library/publications/the-world-factbook /geos/xx.html.

7. See the Minorities at Risk Project (2005), Center for International Development and Conflict Management, www.cidcm.umd.edu/mar

Chapter 2

1. This spelling of the name of the holy book of Islam is adopted from John L. Esposito (2003). Alternate spellings include Koran, Kor'an, and Qur'an.

2. *Saints of the Atlas*, though not published until 1969, was his anthropology doctoral thesis and was written before *Thought and Change* (1964), which articulates a theory of nationalism in chapter 7 that rests on his Moroccan field experience and his knowledge of French anthropologists and sociologists.

3. Mark 16:17–18.

4. Acts 2:7–11.

5. Acts 10:46 and 19:6; 2 Corinthians 1:12–14.

6. Sanskrit also maintains sacred status among Hindus as the language of the Vedas, though very, very few people—most all of them are academics, spiritualists, or pretenders thereof— can actually hold a conversation in spoken Sanskrit. The language of the Native American Dakota people has also been studied as a sacred language.

7. In an interview by Wolfgang G. Schwanitz, "Europa Wird Am Ende Des Jahrhunderts Islamisch Sein," *Die Welt*, July 28, 2004.

8. In 2006, Dick Cheney remarked at a meeting of the World Affairs Council in Philadelphia, held in honor of Bernard Lewis, that the "wisdom" of the professor "is sought daily by policymakers, diplomats, fellow academics, and the news media." And, we may infer, by the former vice president of the United States. Dick Cheney, "Vice President's Remarks at the World Affairs Council of Philadelphia Luncheon Honoring Professor Bernard Lewis" (Washington, D.C.: Office of the Vice President, White House, 2006).

9. Any doubt about the sharp and sustained resistance of Catholicism to secularism was dispelled by Pope Benedict XVI's 2006 speech in Bavaria, a lecture that was widely rebuked because of its pejorative characterization of Islam as unreasonable and prone to violence, but was actually a treatise against the secularization of European society.

Chapter 3

1. This is not to say that a necessary condition for status as a language is an entire state. A nongovernmental organization based in Ireland, the European Bureau of Lesser-Used Languages, lobbies for linguistic diversity in the European Union and represents such regionals as Frisian (Netherlands), Friulian (Italy), and Sorbian (Germany).

2. For nonspecialists, an excellent overview of linguistics in relation to questions of nationalism from Ferguson forward is Millar (2005).

3. The original funding proposal is available online at http://www.let.rug.nl/gooskens/pdf /research%20proposal.pdf.

4. Heinz Kloss (1967) is credited with first clearly distinguishing between corpus planning and status planning.

5. This paper was first presented at a conference I organized, Nationalism and Language, convened at the London School of Economics and Political Science, March 28, 2003. Following its publication in *Nations and Nationalism* (Fishman 2004) it was expanded as a book (Fishman 2006).

6. An aside: at a 2009 conference in Kazakhstan I argued that Afghanistan and Pakistan are hobbled by very low literacy rates, and are also less stable and less democratic than their more literate Central Asian neighbors. An ethnic Russian academic in the audience lambasted me for supporting what he called a typical "Western" chauvinism, i.e., literacy as a necessary condition of democracy.

7. As objective evidence of its claimed influence, it may be noted that this article was awarded the 2008 Gregory M. Luebbert Prize for Best Article in Comparative Politics Published in 2006 or 2007 by the American Political Science Association.

8. It bears noting, however, that the view of nationalism spreading simply by the dissemination of an *idea* is at the heart of an early and important work on the subject by Kedourie ([1960] 1993).

9. Note, however, that the first book printed in Finnish was a Christian mass, the Missale Aboense (1488). At that time, the printing press had yet to arrive in Finland, so it was actually printed in Lübeck, Germany. The first book printed in Finnish in Finland was a grammar primer, called ABCkiria or the ABC Book. Unsurprisingly, it was written by a clergyman, Mikael Agricola, who thereafter wrote the first Finnish translation of the Christian Bible (1548). Therefore, it is Agricola who is widely considered the father of the Finnish language.

10. The Chinese had already explored the possibilities of moveable wood type, which allowed for a cheaper cost per unit of production, but the results were considered aesthetically inferior to lithography (Reed 2004).

11. This volume, originally published in French in 1958, was published in English translation in 1976, seven years before the first edition of *Imagined Communities*: we must all stand on the shoulders of giants. Hence, Eisenstein's general admonition that the revolution was "unacknowledged" is not entirely accurate since it had been acknowledged explicitly decades earlier, though not in English.

12. In Quebec, for example, the notorious Office de la langue française created an uproar in Montreal when it ruled that signage displaying the word "bagel"—emblematic of the city's long-established Jewish population—should be amended to *baguel* as the form closer to French phonetics (http://www.oqlf.gouv.qc.ca/ressources/bibliotheque/officialisation/terminologique/fiches/1299013.html).

Chapter 4

1. An earlier draft of this chapter appeared as "Arab Dinationalism" in *Levantine Review* 2, no. 1 (2013): 27–53.

2. On this point, Gelvin (1998, 287) is an important exception. Recounting events in post-Ottoman Syria, the historian showed "the presumption that there existed a singular and undifferentiated 'Arab nationalism' and 'Arab nationalist movement' is not borne out by the evidence."

3. The original is "prophete du nationalisme integral arabe des annees 1930 et guide spirituel de Michel Aflak, ideologue-en-chef et fondateur du fameux parti Baas." My translation.

4. It may be noted that the Palestinians in the Occupied Territories number about 3.5 million, or less than 0.3 percent of the Muslim world.

5. CIA World Factbook 2006, https://www.cia.gov/library/publications/the-world-factbook/geos/ag.html.

6. See "Table 4: Population by National and/or Ethnic Group, Sex, Urban/Rural Residence and Percentage: Each Census, 1985–2002" (first release: September 1, 2005; current version: June 30, 2006) in United Nations, "Demographic Yearbook Special Census Topics," unstats.un.org/unsd/demographic/products/dyb/DYBcensus/V2_Table4.pdf.

7. Encyclopaedia Britannica, *Britannica Book of the Year* (Chicago: Encyclopaedia Britannica, 2006).

8. Ibid., 503.

9. "Algeria," in ibid.

10. Judeo-Arabic languages are noted in this chapter as varieties of "Arabic" because they are classified genetically under the branch Afro-Asiatic/Semitic/Central/South/Arabic. They are not, however, included among the thirty languages incorporated into the macrolanguage Arabic (ARA). Instead, they are aggregated under a separate macrolanguage code, Judeo-Arabic (JRB).

11. During the academic year 1988–89, I was a student at Fudan University in Shanghai studying the state language of China, Mandarin Chinese. As I learned immediately on arrival, however, this was of relatively little use in daily affairs: Shanghainese and Mandarin are as different as chalk and cheese. Even Shanghainese people who knew Mandarin well nonetheless spoke with a very distinct and difficult accent.

12. Alternate transliterations from Arabic include 'amiya and 'amiyya. The language may also be called by the name of the people who speak it, such as *Masri*, meaning "Egyptian."

13. Rather exceptionally, the Egyptian *ammiyya* of Cairo is written if the context is informal, such as in advertising, cartoon captions, song lyrics, etc.

14. A third example is Tamil.

15. The qualifier "American" may be in deference to Oxford's prolific professor of Arabic, Clive Holes.

16. To this list I would certainly add the panoply of peoples in the nineteenth-century Balkans and Caucasus, as well as the Kurds.

17. Tremblay's first play, *Les Belles-Sœurs* (1965), introduced a broader public to the spoken language of Québec, named *joual* after the vernacular pronunciation of the French word *cheval* (horse). The celebration of Tremblay's work heightened the sense of Québécois national identity that bloomed in the Quiet Revolution (Révolution Tranquille) of the 1960s.

18. For a thorough examination of ethno-*linguistic* identity in Iran, see Meskoob 1992; for a review discussion, see also Farokh 2001.

19. In the summer of 2002, my tutor in MSA at the British Council in Cairo, Hatem El-Sayed, looked forward each day to the evening news—and its promise of linguistic gaffes—as a form of entertainment.

20. Marc Lynch, personal communication, September 2, 2006, at APSA annual meeting in Philadelphia.

21. I know this from firsthand experience. When still in college, I spent a summer working outside Toronto, packing meat alongside immigrants from Jamaica and migrants from Newfoundland. When they had trouble understanding each other, which was constantly, both groups would complain with the same interjection: "Speak English!"

22. The original text reads, "engouements desquels s'étaient imprégnés Sati' al-Housri, Michel Aflak et tous leurs compagnons de route arabisants." My translation.

23. Personal communication, October 30, 2006.

Chapter 5

1. Another common expression describing the Kurds' view of their modern history is that they "have no friends but the mountains."

2. http://www.kurdishacademy.org.

3. Sami Shorish, interview by the author, Erbil, Iraq, October 12, 2005. As a result of the KDP/PUK administrative merger, there is now one KRG minister of culture and youths; at the time of writing (2013) he is Dr. Kawa Mahmood Shakir of the Communist Party.

4. Fatah Zakhoy, PUK minister of culture, interview by the author, Sulaimaniya, Iraq, October 17, 2005.

5. https://www.cia.gov/library/publications/the-world-factbook/geos/iz.html.

6. http://www.krg.org/p/p.aspx?l=12&s=020000&r=304&p=214.

7. http://new.krg.us/faqs/general-information/.

8. Shorish interview.

9. Kurmanji is also known as Badinani, an allusion to the Badinan area where this vernacular is prevalent.

10. Shawnm Abdulkadir Muheadin, PUK minister of education, Sulaimaniya, interview by the author, Sulaimaniya, Iraq, October 16, 2005.

11. Abdul-Aziz Tayyib, KRG minister of education (KDP), interview by the author, Erbil, Iraq, October 12, 2005. Again, as a result of the KDP/PUK administration merger, the former post of minister of education has evolved into a pair of posts, one for higher education and scientific research, currently (2013) Dr. Ali Saeed (PUK), and a separate minister of (primary and secondary) education, Dr. Asmat Muhammed Khalid (KDP).

12. Muheadin interview.

13. Zakhoy interview.

14. Shorish interview.

15. Zakhoy interview.

16. Stafford Clarry, interview by the author, Erbil, Iraq, October 12, 2005.

17. Falah Mustafa Bakhir, interview by the author, Erbil, Iraq, October 13, 2005.

18. Zakhoy interview.

19. http://www.stanford.edu/group/mappingmilitants/cgi-bin/groups/view/11.

Chapter 6

1. The phrase "go west, young man" was popularized in a *New York Tribune* editorial by Horace Greeley on July 11, 1865 (two months after the end of the Civil War).

2. The Chinese translation of Uyghur is 维吾尔, pronounced *wei-wu-er*.

3. 新疆 维吾尔 自治区.

4. 少数民族.

5. The settlements are more generally known as *bingtuan* (兵团) meaning "corps," from the last two characters of the full Chinese name for the XPCC: 新疆生产建设兵团.

6. There are thirteen official nationalities recognized as resident in Xinjiang: Han, Uyghur, Kazak, Mongol, Kirgiz, Tajik, Uzbek, Tatar, Hui, Man, Xibo, Daur, and Russian.

7. Xinjiang Uygur Autonomous Region Bureau of Statistics, 2011—Sixth Xinjiang Census (2010): summary available in English from *China Daily*, http://www.chinadaily.com.cn/dfpd/xj/2011-05/06/content_12460967.htm.

8. The exact figure from 1997 is 72.5 percent.

9. This was certainly the case when I was a foreign exchange student in Shanghai 1988–89. Public service directives on television regularly showed hapless visitors to Beijing fumbling around the city because they could not speak Mandarin. In 2001, on a bus trip from Qinghai into Tibet, I was pulled off with three other foreign travelers to be interrogated at a police station. While two Japanese were unmolested, a third tourist—a florist from Hong Kong—was openly ridiculed because he could speak only Cantonese (and limited English). Because his hobby was photography, he carried a good deal of gear; the spiteful officers accused him of being a journalist and deported him. By speaking Mandarin and—much more important—adopting a tone of fawning deference, I managed to talk my way through security and arrived in Lhasa the next day.

10. Though the term "Han" is now applied reflexively as a term that includes anyone "Chinese," the concept of a unified Chinese ethnicity is relatively new, coaxed into consciousness by the first leader of postimperial China, Sun Yat-sen, in 1911.

11. My own experiences illustrate this attitude as well. In 1997, while flying out of Urumqi, I spoke with a young Han woman, in her early twenties, who was born and raised in Urumqi. I asked how well she could understand Uyghur. She replied that she could not speak or understand a single word, not even "thank you." To put this in context, it is hard to imagine a native of San Diego never learning the word "gracias."

12. Asgar Can, interview by the author, Munich, September 26, 2005.

13. Like "paper tiger" or "Capitalist roader" during the Cultural Revolution, "splittists" is an example of the difficulty of translating the particular and peculiar tone of Chinese political rhetoric.

14. Two people were reportedly executed immediately after the rally.

15. Dolqun Isa, interview by the author, Munich, September 26, 2005.

16. The host nations included Bermuda, Palau, Switzerland, and El Salvador.

17. Isa interview.

18. Erkin Alptekin, interview by the author, Frankfurt, September 27, 2005.

19. Ibid.

20. Ibid.

21. Abduljelil Qarkash, interview by the author, Munich, September 26, 2005.

22. Note that while Omer Kanat is the UAA general secretary, the UAA president is Alim Seytoff.

23. Omer Kanat, interview by the author, Washington, D.C., August 17, 2005.

Chapter 7

1. The country was not self-styled as the *Islamic* Republic of Pakistan until it settled on a first constitution in 1956.

2. Sahar Imdad, interview by the author, Hyderabad, Pakistan, November 8, 2005. Interestingly, as a Sindhi academic, she considers the role of Sindhi poetry in the nationalist movement as akin to that of "Irish romantic nationalism" in the modern history of Ireland.

3. This point, however, requires a caveat. It would be misleading to characterize the Mohajirs generally as usurpers of ethnic Sindhis, displacing them broadly across high-status jobs; due

to the post-Partition exodus of Hindus, Parsis, and even Jews, a fair number of these posts were suddenly left vacant, allowing the Mohajirs to fill the vacuum created.

4. The language has also benefited from the satellite broadcast of Sindhi programming. Since the 1970s there has been a daily broadcast of about thirty minutes worth of Sindhi-language television on the domestic channel PTV, but most Sindhis now watch satellite television channels broadcast from Dubai. The most popular is KTN, followed by Sindh TV; both feature news and entertainment programming in Sindhi.

5. Mumtaz Ali Bhutto, interview by the author, Hyderabad, Pakistan, November 13, 2005.

6. Ibid.

7. Muhammad Qasim Bughio, interview by the author, Hyderabad, Pakistan, November 8, 2005.

8. Mazahar Ulhaq Siddiqi, interview by the author, Hyderabad, Pakistan, November 8, 2005.

9. Sajjad Ali Shah, interview by the author, Karachi, Pakistan, November 10, 2005.

10. Annual Status of Education Report: ASER-Pakistan 2012, http://aserpakistan.org/docu ment/aser/2012/reports/national/National2012.pdf.

11. Qadir Magsi, interview by the author, Hyderabad, Pakistan, November 7, 2005.

12. Ibrahim Joyo, interview by the author, Hyderabad, Pakistan, November 8, 2005.

13. Bashir Qureshi, interview by the author, Hyderabad, Pakistan, November 12, 2005.

14. In 1970, 1977, 1988, 1993, and 2008, respectively.

15. Mazhar al Haq, interview by the author, Karachi, Pakistan, November 10, 2005.

16. Joyo interview.

17. Magsi interview.

18. Rasul Bux Palijo, interview by the author, Hyderabad, Pakistan, November 7, 2005.

19. Though the Jeay Sindh spawned a number of successive parties, a current (2013) claimant to its legacy is the Sindh United Party (SUP), led by G. M. Syed's grandson, Syed Jalal Mahmood Shah. It is, however, one among many others claiming to speak for the people of Sindh. A stronger claim can actually be made by the JSQM, which continues to call for an independent Sindhu Desh, while the SUP does not.

20. In 1997, the Mohajir Qaumi Movement, or Migrant National Movement, changed its name to the Muttahida Qaumi Movement, or United National Movement. This was due in part to the MQM's efforts to evolve into a political force not limited to provincial politics.

21. Following the most recent provincial elections in 2008, the PPP came in first by securing 91 out of 166 seats; the MQM came in second with 51 seats.

22. His name is withheld for reasons of personal security.

23. Nasreen Jalil, interview by the author, Karachi, Pakistan, November 14, 2005. The resolution was ultimately passed by the provincial assembly in 2010 with the following language: "This Assembly resolves that the Government of Sindh ensure the implementation of the Sindh (Teaching, Promotion and Use of Sindhi Language) Act, 1972 and the Sindh (Teaching, Promotion and Use of Sindhi Language) (Amendment) Act, 1990 in the entire Province of Sindh." http:// www.pas.gov.pk/index.php/mediacenter/ntf/en/19/247.

24. Syed Shafqat Ali Shah, interview by the author, Karachi, Pakistan, November 10, 2005.

25. Bhutto interview.

26. Joyo interview.

27. Palijo interview. Despite this sentiment, however, it must be remembered that Palijo is a proautonomy Sindhi nationalist, but not a separatist.

28. Ironically, perhaps the best example of such a system is found in the one state most dreaded by Pakistan: India.

Chapter 8

1. Abdul Gani Bhat, interview by the author, Srinagar, India, November 23, 2005.

2. G. M. Shah, interview by the author, Srinagar, India, November 23, 2005.

3. G. R. Badana, interview by the author, Srinagar India, November 23, 2005.

4. Taskeena Fazil, interview by the author, Srinagar, India, November 22, 2005.

5. Statistics India 2011. This is in contrast to the literacy rate for all India, which stands at 73 percent.

6. Rafiq Maqbool, interview by the author, Srinagar, India, November, 2005.

7. Ibid.

8. Shabir Ahmad Shah, interview by the author, Srinagar, India, November 26, 2005.

9. The conventional translation of "Hurriyat" is "freedom."

10. Mirwaiz Umar Farooq, interview by the author, Srinagar, India, November 26, 2005.

11. Ibid.

12. Ibid.

13. Ibid.

14. Syed Ali Shah Geelani, interview by the author, Srinagar, India, November 26, 2005.

15. Mehbooba Mufti of the People's Democratic Party had this to say about Geelani: "You can call him extremist; you can call him fundamentalist, but he is consistent." Interview by the author, Srinagar, India, November 26, 2005.

16. Geelani interview.

17. Ibid.

Chapter 9

1. That being said, most citizens can communicate to some extent in the official state language, Indonesian; more on this below.

2. Alternate spellings for "Aceh" include "Atjeh," a version used by the Dutch in their colonial administration, and more recently "Acheh." Similarly, "Acehnese" may also appear as "Achehnese" (as preferred by the United Nations Office of the High Commissioner for Human Rights), "Achinese" (an antiquated British spelling), or, following the Dutch style, "Atjehnese."

3. From the 2010 census.

4. Note, however, that adat *precedes* the advent of Islam in Aceh.

5. In addition to ideology, Beureueh was also motivated by local political protest after Aceh lost its provincial status.

6. The Acehnese were not alone in the fight: while fought in Aceh, the rebellion actually started in West Java and included supporters from across the country.

7. He is also, famously, the grandson of Cik di Tiro, an Indonesian national hero (officially designated thus in 1973, i.e., before GAM) who led the Acehnese fight against the Dutch.

8. However, it should be noted that there might be a question of tailoring this declaration to foreign ears. Some later publications targeting the Acehnese audience do invoke Islamic idioms.

9. The Kolakops Jaring Merah, or Military Operations Implementation Command Red Net, became known as DOM, an Indonesian acronym for *daerah operasi militer* or Military Operations Area.

10. Note, however, that unlike Gellner's model, the promotion of the official language does not intend to eliminate local languages, which are used effectively in early years of elementary school.

11. Note, however, that there are at least ten dialects of spoken Acehnese, including Pasè, Peusangan, Matang, Pidië, Buëng, Banda, Daya, Meulabôh, Seunagan, and Tunong.

12. As a result of this history, and problematically for Acehnese nationalists, it is difficult to argue that Indonesian was imposed as a High Language on the Acehnese as the Acehnese themselves had already adopted a separate and entirely similar High Language—Malay—to serve as their own High Culture language.

13. The form of Acehnese written in the Arabic script is called Jawoë (Acehnese) or Jawi (Malay).

14. Mawardi Hasan, personal communication, March 21, 2011.

15. Malik Mahmud, interview by the author, Norsborg, Sweden, September 16, 2005.

16. Bakhtiar Abdullah, interview by the author, Banda Aceh, Indonesia, December 18, 2005.

17. Irwandi Yusuf, interview by the author, Banda Aceh, Indonesia, December 18, 2005.

18. Mark Durie, personal communication, March 12, 2011.

19. Aceh is administratively divided among eighteen regencies (*kabupaten*) and five autonomous cities (*kota*).

20. Note, however, that while Samsuddin cites Zaini Abdullah's support for sharia, there is no evidence Abdullah actually supported the ban on tight clothing.

21. Zaini Abdullah, interview by the author, Norsborg, Sweden, September 16, 2005.

22. Mahmud interview.

23. It is important to note here, however, that the assembly elected prior to the 2009 elections—which lacked representation from the Aceh Party—drafted this bylaw. It is possible the outgoing assembly was attempting to propel sharia as far as possible before the power shifted to more secular politicians. Note also that despite the fact the unsigned bylaw expired, the draft qanun remains on the fringes of the legislature's to-do list. Hence, the bylaw may return, though probably in a weakened form. I am indebted to Edward Aspinall for this point.

Chapter 10

1. As is so often the case, the separatists argue this figure is significantly higher.

2. Note that in this chapter the term *Mindanao*, unless specified otherwise, refers to both the island of Mindanao and the islands of the Sulu Archipelago. This follows common practice in both the Philippines and the academic literature.

3. This is despite the fact that the Spanish established a fort in Zamboanga in 1635.

4. Figures are from the 2000 census.

5. In the United States, an example of this social phenomenon is the gay rights group Queer Nation (1990–95).

6. There are now twenty-four provinces in Mindanao divided among six regions, one of which is the ARMM.

7. According to the 2000 census, there are 2,410,845 people in the ARMM, of whom 2,182,245 are Muslim.

8. Note, however, that this agreement did not include representatives from a number of other active militant groups, including the Bangsamoro Islamic Freedom Fighters (BIFF), an Islamist MILF splinter faction founded in 2010. Yet this has not seriously hampered progress toward a final settlement. In 2013, the MILF and Manila reached a wealth-sharing agreement whereby the Bangsamoro government will keep three-quarters of tax revenue, three-quarters of natural resource revenue (especially from minerals), and half of all energy revenue, including that derived from oil, natural gas, and uranium.

9. It had also been labeled "Pilipino" in 1959.

10. The other ten groups consist of the Sama, Sangil, Iranun, Kalagan, Kalibugan, Yakan, Jama Mapun, Palawani, Molibog, and Badjao.

11. That being said, in some areas there was a tradition of a vernacular script culture (as in Aceh using an Arabic script) that preserved some of the oral histories that had been traditional for many centuries, though this was employed by a small number of literate elites.

12. This disinterest in language policy (aside from the imposition of Filipino) includes the sacred language of the Quran: "the presence or absence of Arabic instruction in public schools had never been one of the top concerns of Muslim Filipinos regarding public schools" (Milligan 2005b, 102).

13. Abraham Iribani, interview by the author, Manila, December 2, 2005.

14. Ibid.

15. Hadja Bainon G. Karon, interview by the author, Cotabato, Philippines, December 2, 2005.

16. Note, however, that Islamic consciousness ascended previously in the 1950s in response to the arrival of Christian immigrants. It was also bolstered in the 1970s by the explosion of Islamic schools "in response to the desire of many Muslim Filipinos to emphasize their Islamic cultural identity" (Milligan 2001, 439).

17. Iribani interview.

18. The name Abu Sayyaf literally translates as "Bearer of the Sword."

19. Emphasis added.

20. This is not to say the Maranao have not pursued their own interests. In 1955, Manila established Mindanao State University in Marawi City. This area, in the province of Lanao del Sur, is predominantly Maranao. Hence, "Maranao Muslims gradually came to dominate the administrative structure and non-teaching staff" so "the university became a major source of patronage employment and thus an important component in local politics." Manila's policy goal for the institution was to integrate Muslims, but the multiethnic reality of the region proved Tip O'Neill's maxim that all politics is local: instead of furthering the goal of integrating Moros or

Muslims into the state, the Maranao assimilated Mindanao State University into the "Maranao political culture" (Milligan 2005a, 77).

21. Iribani interview.

22. Eid Kabalu, interview by the author, Cotabato, Philippines, December 8, 2005.

23. Benny Bacani, interview by the author, Washington, D.C., July 25, 2005.

24. Father William Kreutz, interview by the author, Zamboanga, Philippines, December 2, 2005.

Chapter 11

1. This was evidenced, for example, by the abundance of Arabs who fought alongside the Taliban in Afghanistan.

2. Center for Applied Linguistics, www.cal.org.

3. Ibid.

4. *Why* this is the most pressing question in international politics depends on one's perspective regarding the relative importance of (1) state stability and (2) human rights. This book explicitly assumes both are important and preferable to the alternatives of state instability and the systemic violation of human rights. These are claims both instrumental and ethical, but at this point in the development of our planet's politics, both claims are virtually axiomatic. Objections to either claim may be valid, but such a debate is far beyond the scope and scale of this book.

BIBLIOGRAPHY

Abdelal, Rawi, Yoshiko M. Herrera, Alastair Iain Johnston, and Rose McDermott. 2006. "Identity as a Variable." *Perspectives on Politics* 4 (4): 695–711.

Aberbach, David. 2008. *Jewish Cultural Nationalism: Origins and Influences, Routledge Jewish Studies Series.* London: Routledge.

Abinales, Patricio N. 2000. *Making Mindanao: Cotabato and Davao in the Formation of the Philippine Nation-State.* Quezon City, Philippines: Ateneo de Manila University Press.

Abuza, Zachary. 2003. *Militant Islam in Southeast Asia: Crucible of Terror.* Boulder, Colo.: Lynne Rienner.

———. 2005. "The Moro Islamic Liberation Front at 20: State of the Revolution." *Studies in Conflict & Terrorism* 28 (6): 453–79.

Ajami, Fouad. 1998. *The Dream Palace of the Arabs: A Generation's Odyssey.* 1st ed. New York: Pantheon Books.

Alesina, Alberto, and Enrico Spolaore. 2003. *The Size of Nations.* Cambridge, Mass.: MIT Press.

Al Jazeera. 2012. Interview with Massoud Barzani. Al Jazeera English, July 29, http://www.aljazeera.com/indepth/features/2012/07/201272991311907942.html.

Al-Khalesi, Yasin M. 2006. *Modern Iraqi Arabic.* Washington, D.C.: Georgetown University Press.

Amara, Tarek. 2011. "Tunisian Leader Bows to Unrest, Sets Departure Date." Reuters, January 13.

Amnesty International. 2004. *People's Republic of China: Uighurs Fleeing Persecution as China Wages Its "War on Terror."* London: Amnesty International.

———. 2013. *India: Arbitrary and Unlawful Detentions in Jammu and Kashmir Must End.* London: Amnesty International.

Anderson, Benedict R. 1983. *Imagined Communities: Reflections on the Origins and Spread of Nationalism.* London: Verso.

———. 1999. "Indonesian Nationalism Today and in the Future." *Indonesia Journal* (67): 1–12.

Antonius, George. 1938. *The Arab Awakening.* London: Hamish Hamilton.

Armbrust, Walter. 2002. "The Rise and Fall of Nationalism in the Egyptian Cinema." In *Social Constructions of Nationalism in the Middle East,* edited by Fatma Müge Göçek, 15–59. Albany: State University of New York Press.

Aspinall, Edward. 2005. *The Helsinki Agreement: A More Promising Basis for Peace in Aceh?* Policy Studies. Washington, D.C.: East-West Center Washington.

———. 2006. "Violence and Identity Formation in Aceh Under Indonesian Rûle." In *Verandah of Violence: The Background to the Aceh Problem*, edited by Anthony Reid, 149–76. Seattle: University of Washington Press.

———. 2007. "From Islamism to Nationalism in Aceh, Indonesia." *Nations and Nationalism* 13 (2): 245–64.

———. 2009. *Islam and Nation: Separatist Rebellion in Aceh, Indonesia, Studies in Asian Security.* Stanford, Calif.: Stanford University Press.

Aspinall, Edward, and Mark T. Berger. 2001. "The Break-up of Indonesia? Nationalisms After Decolonisation and the Limits of the Nation-State in Post–Cold War Southeast Asia." *Third World Quarterly—Journal of Emerging Areas* 22 (6): 1003–24.

Aspinall, Edward, and Harold A. Crouch. 2003. *The Aceh Peace Process: Why It Failed.* Washington, D.C.: East-West Center Washington.

Associated Press. 2009. "Two Face Death over Quran Translation: 4 More Jailed over Pocket-Size Book Deemed a Mistranslation of God's Word." February 6.

Ayres, Alyssa. 2003. "The Politics of Language Policy in Pakistan." In *Fighting Words: Language Policy and Ethnic Relations in Asia*, edited by Michael E. Brown and Sumit Ganguly, 51–80. Cambridge, Mass.: MIT Press.

———. 2009. *Speaking Like a State.* New York: Cambridge University Press.

Aytürk, İlker 2004. "Turkish Linguists Against the West: The Origins of Linguistic Nationalism in Atatürk's Turkey." *Middle Eastern Studies* 40 (6): 1–25.

Aziz, Mahir A. 2011. *The Kurds of Iraq: Ethnonationalism and National Identity in Iraqi Kurdistan.* New York: I. B. Tauris.

Barasa, Simiyu. 2008. "Kenya's War of Words." *New York Times*, February 12, 21.

Barfield, Thomas. 2011. "Afghanistan's Ethnic Puzzle." *Foreign Affairs* 90 (5): 54–65.

Barter, Shane Joshua. 2004. "Holy War or Open Door? The Role of Islam in the Aceh Conflict." Paper read at the 12th Annual CANCAPS Conference, Quebec City, December 3–5.

———. 2012. "Ulama, the State, & War: Community Islamic Leaders in the Aceh Conflict." *Contemporary Islam* 5 (1): 19–36.

Basri, Hasan. 2010a. "Applying Islamic Law (Syari'at) in Aceh: A Perspective from Within." In *Aceh: History, Politics and Culture*, edited by Arndt Graf, Susanne Schroter, and Edwin Wieringa, 265–86. Singapore: Institute of Southeast Asian Studies.

———. 2010b. "Islam in Aceh: Institutions, Scholarly Traditions, and Relations Between Ulama and Umara." In *Aceh: History, Politics and Culture*, edited by Arndt Graf, Susanne Schroter, and Edwin Wieringa, 180–200. Singapore: Institute of Southeast Asian Studies.

Bayat, Asef. 2013. *Post-Islamism: The Changing Faces of Political Islam.* Oxford: Oxford University Press.

Beckett, Gulbahar H., and Gerard A. Postiglione. 2011. *China's Assimilationist Language Policy: The Impact on Indigenous/Minority Literacy and Social Harmony.* London: Routledge.

Behera, Navnita Chadha. 2006. *Demystifying Kashmir.* Washington, D.C.: Brookings Institution.

Bell-Fialkoff, Andrew. 1993. "A Brief-History of Ethnic Cleansing." *Foreign Affairs* 72 (3): 110–21.

Bellér-Hann, Ildikó. 1991. "Script Changes in Xinjiang." In *Cultural Change and Continuity in Central Asia*, edited by Shirin Akiner, 71–83. London: Kegan Paul.

———. 2002. "Temperamental Neighbors: Uighur-Han Relations in Xinjiang, Northwest China." In *Imagined Differences: Hatred and the Construction of Identity*, edited by Gunther Schlee, 57–81. New York: Palgrave.

Belnap, R. Kirk, and Niloofar Haeri, eds. 1997. *Structuralist Studies in Arabic Linguistics: Charles A. Ferguson's Papers, 1954–1994*. Studies in Semitic Languages and Linguistics, 24. Leiden: Brill.

Bengio, Ofra. 2012. *The Kurds of Iraq: Building a State Within a State*. Boulder, Colo.: Lynne Rienner.

Berger, Joseph. 2005. "An English Talmud for Daily Readers and Debaters." *New York Times*, February 10, 1.

Bergman, Elizabeth M. 2002. *Spoken Sudanese Arabic: Grammar, Dialogues, and Glossary*. Springfield, Va.: Dunwoody Press.

———. 2005. *Spoken Algerian Arabic*. Springfield, Va.: Dunwoody Press.

Berman, Harold Joseph. 1983. *Law and Revolution: The Formation of the Western Legal Tradition*. Cambridge, Mass.: Harvard University Press.

Berman, Sheri. 2003. "Islamism, Revolution, and Civil Society." *Perspectives on Politics* 1 (2): 257–72.

Bertrand, Jacques. 2003. "Language Policy and the Promotion of National Identity in Indonesia." In *Fighting Words: Language Policy and Ethnic Relations in Asia*, edited by Michael E. Brown and Sumit Ganguly, 263–90. Cambridge, Mass.: MIT Press.

Blau, Joyce. 2006. "Refinement and Oppression of Kurdish Language." In *The Kurds: Nationalism and Politics*, edited by Faleh A. Jabar and Dawod Hosham, 103–12. London: Saqi.

Bose, Sumantra. 2003. *Kashmir: Roots of Conflict, Paths to Peace*. Cambridge, Mass.: Harvard University Press.

———. 2007. *Contested Lands: Israel-Palestine, Kashmir, Bosnia, Cyprus, and Sri Lanka*. Cambridge, Mass.: Harvard University Press.

Boureau, Alain, and Roger Chartier. 1989. *The Culture of Print: Power and the Uses of Print in Early Modern Europe*. Cambridge: Polity.

Bovingdon, Gardner. 2002. "The Not-So-Silent Majority: Uyghur Resistance to Han Rule in Xinjiang." *Modern China* 28 (1): 39–78.

———. 2010. *The Uyghurs: Strangers in Their Own Land*. New York: Columbia University Press.

Brady, Henry E., and David Collier. 2004. *Rethinking Social Inquiry: Diverse Tools, Shared Standards*. Lanham, Md.: Rowman & Littlefield.

Brady, Henry E., David Collier, and Jason Seawright. 2006. "Toward a Pluralistic Vision of Methodology." *Political Analysis* 14: 353–68.

Bratcher, Robert G. 1993. "Translation, English Language." In *The Oxford Companion to the Bible*, edited by Bruce M. Metzger and Michael D. Coogan, 758–63. New York: Oxford University Press.

Braude, Joseph. 2005. Language Barrier. *New Republic*, February 22, http://www.tnr.com/doc.mhtml?pt=Z5fd4nS%2BQ2MstROyUeJGyh%3D%3D.

Breuilly, John. (1982) 1993. *Nationalism and the State*. 2nd ed. Manchester: Manchester University Press.

Bruce, Steve. 2007. *Fundamentalism*. Cambridge: Polity.

Brumberg, Daniel. 2005. "Islam Is Not the Solution (or the Problem)." *Washington Quarterly* 29 (1): 97–116.

Brynen, Rex. 2012. *Beyond the Arab Spring: Authoritarianism & Democratization in the Arab World.* Boulder, Colo.: Lynne Rienner.

Bughio, Muhammad Qasim. 2001. *Sociolinguists of Sindhi.* Munich: LINCOM Europa.

Bukhari, Shujaat. 2013. "J&K: The Classic Fight." *Rising Kashmir,* August 7.

Carlson, A. 2009. "A Flawed Perspective: The Limitations Inherent Within the Study of Chinese Nationalism." *Nations and Nationalism* 15 (1): 20–35.

Castro-Caldas, A., P. C. Miranda, I. Carmo, A. Reis, F. Leote, C. Ribeiro, and E. Ducla-Soares. 1999. "Influence of Learning to Read and Write on the Morphology of the Corpus Callosum." *European Journal of Neurology* 6 (1): 23–28.

Chalk, Peter. 2001. "Separatism and Southeast Asia: The Islamic Factor in Southern Thailand, Mindanao, and Aceh." *Studies in Conflict and Terrorism* 24 (4): 241–69.

Chalk, Peter, Angel Rabasa, William Rosenau, and Leanne Piggott. 2009. *The Evolving Terrorist Threat to Southeast Asia: A Net Assessment.* Santa Monica, Calif.: RAND.

Chandran, Suba. 2012. "Prospects for Autonomy in Jammu and Kashmir." In *Autonomy and Ethnic Conflict in South and Southeast Asia,* edited by Rajat Ganguly, 8–26. London: Routledge.

Choueiri, Youssef M. 2000. *Arab Nationalism—A History: Nation and State in the Arab World.* Oxford: Blackwell.

Chung, Chien-peng. 2002. "China's 'War on Terror': September 11 and Uighur Separatism." *Foreign Affairs* 81 (4): 8–12.

Cloud, David S., and Ian Johnson. 2004. "Friend or Foe: In Post-9/11 World, Chinese Dissidents Pose U.S. Dilemma—Uighur Nationalists Have Peaceful, Violent Wings; Deciding Who Is a Threat." *Wall Street Journal,* August 3, A1.

Cohen, Stephen P. 2004. *The Idea of Pakistan.* Washington, D.C.: Brookings Institution Press.

Collin, Richard Oliver. 2009. "Words of War: The Iraqi Tower of Babel." *International Studies Perspectives* 10: 245–64.

Connor, Walker. 1994. *Ethnonationalism: The Quest for Understanding.* Princeton, N.J.: Princeton University Press.

———. 2001. "From a Theory of Relative Economic Deprivation Towards a Theory of Relative Political Deprivation." In *Minority Nationalism and the Changing International Order,* edited by Michael Keating and John McGarry, 114–33. New York: Oxford University Press.

Cooper, Robert Leon. 1989. *Language Planning and Social Change.* New York: Cambridge University Press.

Coulmas, Florian. 2000. "The Nationalization of Writing." *Studies in the Linguistic Sciences* 30 (1): 47–59.

Coulson, Andrew. 2004. *Education and Indoctrination in the Muslim World: Is There a Problem? What Can We Do About It?* Washington, D.C.: Cato Institute.

Coury, R. M. 2005. "The Demonization of Pan-Arab Nationalism." *Race & Class* 46 (4): 1–19.

Croft, Stuart. 2012. *Securitizing Islam: Identity and the Search for Security.* New York: Cambridge University Press.

Csergő, Zsuzsa. 2007. *Talk of the Nation: Language and Conflict in Romania and Slovakia.* Ithaca, N.Y.: Cornell University Press.

Darden, Keith, and Anna Maria Grzymała-Busse. 2006. "The Great Divide: Literacy, Nationalism, and the Communist Collapse." *World Politics* 59 (1): 83–115.

Daud, Bukhari. 1997. *Writing and Reciting in Aceh: Perspectives on Language and Literature in Aceh, Department of Linguistics and Applied Linguistics.* Melbourne: University of Melbourne.

Dawisha, A. I. 2003. *Arab Nationalism in the Twentieth Century: From Triumph to Despair.* Princeton, N.J.: Princeton University Press.

Dehaene, Stanislas. 2009. *Reading in the Brain: The Science and Evolution of a Human Invention.* New York: Viking.

Deutsch, Karl Wolfgang. 1953. *Nationalism and Social Communication: An Inquiry into the Foundations of Nationality.* Cambridge, Mass.: MIT Press.

Dowley, K. M., and B. D. Silver. 2005. "Crossnational Survey Research and Subnational Pluralism." *International Journal of Public Opinion Research* 17 (2): 226–38.

Drexler, Elizabeth F. 2008. *Aceh, Indonesia: Securing the Insecure State.* Ethnography of Political Violence. Philadelphia: University of Pennsylvania Press.

Durie, Mark. 1996. "Framing the Acehnese Text: Language Choice and Discourse Structures in Aceh." *Oceanic Linguistics* 35 (1): 113–37.

Dwyer, Arienne M. 1998. "The Texture of Tongues: Languages and Power in China." *Nationalism and Ethnic Politics* 4 (1–2): 68–85.

Economist. 2005. "The World Through Their Eyes." February 24, 1.

———. 2006. "Tales from Eurabia." June 24, 11.

Eickelman, Dale F. 1998. "From Here to Modernity: Ernest Gellner on Nationalism and Islamic Fundamentalism." In *The State of the Nation: Ernest Gellner and the Theory of Nationalism,* edited by John A. Hall, 258–71. New York: Cambridge University Press.

———. 2005. "New Media in the Arab Middle East and the Emergence of Open Societies: The New Arab 'Street.'" In *Remaking Muslim Politics: Pluralism, Contestation, Democratization,* edited by Robert W. Hefner, 37–59. Princeton, N.J.: Princeton University Press.

Eisenstein, Elizabeth L. 1979. *The Printing Press as an Agent of Change: Communications and Cultural Transformations in Early Modern Europe.* 2 vols. Cambridge: Cambridge University Press.

———. 2002. "An Unacknowledged Revolution Revisited." *American Historical Review* 107 (1): 87–105.

Elshtain, Jean Bethke. 2009. "Religion and Democracy." *Journal of Democracy* 20 (2): 5–17.

Errington, James Joseph. 1998. *Shifting Languages: Interaction and Identity in Javanese Indonesia.* Cambridge: Cambridge University Press.

Esposito, John L. 2003. *The Oxford Dictionary of Islam.* New York: Oxford University Press.

Evans, Alexander. 2008. "Kashmiri Exceptionalism." In *The Valley of Kashmir: The Making and Unmaking of a Composite Culture?,* edited by Aparna Rao, 713–41. New Delhi: Manohar.

Farah, Samar. 2002. "So You'd Like to Learn Arabic. Got a Decade or So?" *Christian Science Monitor,* January 17.

Farokh, Kaveh. 2001. "Review: Iranian Nationality and the Persian Language." *International Journal of the Sociology of Language* 148: 117–24.

Fasold, Ralph W. 1984. *The Sociolinguistics of Society.* Oxford: Blackwell.

Fearon, James D., and David D. Laitin. 2003. "Ethnicity, Insurgency, and Civil War." *American Political Science Review* 97 (1): 75–90.

Febvre, Lucien, and Henri-Jean Martin. 1976. *The Coming of the Book: The Impact of Printing 1450–1800*. New ed. Foundations of History Library. London: N.L.B.

Feghali, Habaka J. 2004. *Gulf Arabic: The Dialects of Riyadh and Eastern Saudi Arabic: Grammar, Dialogues, and Lexicon*. Springfield, Va.: Dunwoody Press.

Ferguson, Charles. 1959. "Diglossia." *Word* 15: 325–40.

———. 1997. "Come Forth with a Surah Like It: Arabic as a Measure of Arab Society." In *Structuralist Studies in Arabic Linguistics: Charles A. Ferguson's Papers, 1954–1994*, edited by R. Kirk Belnap and Niloofar Haeri, 261–72. Leiden: Brill.

Ferguson, Gibson. 2006. *Language Planning and Education, Edinburgh Textbooks in Applied Linguistics*. Edinburgh: Edinburgh University Press.

Filali-Ansary, Abdou. 1999. "Muslims and Democracy." *Journal of Democracy* 10 (3): 18–32.

Firro, K. M. 2004. "Lebanese Nationalism Versus Arabism: From Bulus Nujaym to Michel Chiha." *Middle Eastern Studies* 40 (5): 1–27.

Fish, M. Steven. 2002. "Islam and Authoritarianism." *World Politics* 55 (1): 4–37.

———. 2011. *Are Muslims Distinctive? A Look at the Evidence*. New York: Oxford University Press.

Fisher, Ian. 2007. "Pope Eases Restrictions on Latin Mass." *New York Times*, July 8, http://www.nytimes.com/2007/07/08/world/08POPE.html?_r=0.

Fishman, Joshua A. 1966. *Language Loyalty in the United States: The Maintenance and Perpetuation of Non-English Mother Tongues by American Ethnic and Religious Groups, Janua Linguarum*. The Hague: Mouton.

———. 1967. "Bilingualism With and Without Diglossia." *Journal of Social Issues* 32: 29–38.

———. 1973. *Language and Nationalism: Two Integrative Essays*. Rowley, Mass.: Newbury House.

———. 2002. "Diglossia and Societal Multilingualism: Dimensions of Similarity and Difference." *International Journal of the Sociology of Language* 157: 93–100.

———. 2004. "Ethnicity and Supra-ethnicity in Corpus Planning: The Hidden Status Agenda in Corpus Planning." *Nations and Nationalism* 10 (1/2): 79–94.

———. 2006. *Do Not Leave Your Language Alone: The Hidden Status Agendas Within Corpus Planning in Language Policy*. Mahwah, N.J.: Lawrence Erlbaum.

Fishman, Joshua A., Charles Albert Ferguson, and Jyotirindra Dasgupta. 1968. *Language Problems of Developing Nations*. New York: John Wiley.

Foreman, William. 2002. "U.S. Adds Chinese Separatists to Terror List." Associated Press, August 27.

Foulcher, Keith. 1990. "The Construction of an Indonesian National Culture: Patterns of Hegemony and Resistance." In *State and Civil Society in Indonesia*, edited by Arief Budiman, 301–20. Clayton, Victoria, Australia: Centre of Southeast Asian Studies, Monash University

Fox, Jonathan. 2000. "Is Islam More Conflict Prone Than Other Religions? A Cross-Sectional Study of Ethnoreligious Conflict." *Nationalism & Ethnic Politics* 6 (2): 1–24.

———. 2002. *Ethnoreligious Conflict in the Late Twentieth Century: A General Theory*. Lanham, Md.: Lexington Books.

———. 2003. "Do Muslims Engage in More Domestic Conflict Than Other Religious Groups?" *Civil Wars* 6 (1): 27–46.

———. 2004. "The Rise of Religious Nationalism and Conflict: Ethnic Conflict and Revolutionary Wars from 1945 to 2001." *Journal of Peace Research* 41 (6): 715–31.

Frake, Charles O. 1998. "Abu Sayyaf: Displays of Violence and the Proliferation of Contested Identities Among Philippine Muslims." *American Anthropologist* 100 (1): 41–54.

Frangoudaki, Anna. 2002. "Greek Societal Bilingualism of More Than a Century." *International Journal of the Sociology of Language* 157: 101–7.

Friedman, E. 2008. "Where Is Chinese Nationalism? The Political Geography of a Moving Project." *Nations and Nationalism* 14 (4): 721–38.

Friend, Theodore. 2006. *Religion and Religiosity in the Philippines and Indonesia: Essays on State, Society, and Public Creeds.* Baltimore: Southeast Asia Studies Program, Johns Hopkins University.

Fukuyama, Francis. 1992. *The End of History and the Last Man.* New York: Free Press.

Galbraith, Peter. 2005. "Kurdistan in a Federal Iraq." In *The Future of Kurdistan in Iraq,* edited by Brendan O'Leary, John McGarry, and Khaled Salih, 268–81. Philadelphia: University of Pennsylvania Press.

Ganguly, Sumit. 1997. *The Crisis in Kashmir: Portents of War, Hopes of Peace,* Woodrow Wilson Center Series. Washington, D.C.: Woodrow Wilson Center Press.

———. 2001. *Conflict Unending: India-Pakistan Tensions Since 1947.* Washington, D.C.: Woodrow Wilson Center Press.

———. 2006. "Will Kashmir Stop India's Rise?" *Foreign Affairs* 85 (4): 45–56.

Gellner, Ernest. 1964. *Thought and Change: The Nature of Human Society.* Chicago: University of Chicago Press.

———. 1969. *Saints of the Atlas.* London: Weidenfeld & Nicolson.

———. 1981. *Muslim Society.* Cambridge: Cambridge University Press.

———. 1983. *Nations and Nationalism.* Oxford: Blackwell.

———. 1985. "Introduction." In *Islamic Dilemmas: Reformers, Nationalists and Industrialization—The Southern Shore of the Mediterranean,* edited by Ernest Gellner, 1–9. Berlin: Mouton.

———. 1992. *Postmodernism, Reason and Religion.* London: Routledge.

———. 1994. *Conditions of Liberty: Civil Society and Its Rivals.* London: Hamish Hamilton.

Gelvin, James L. 1998. *Divided Loyalties: Nationalism and Mass Politics in Syria at the Close of Empire.* Berkeley: University of California Press.

Geng, Shimin. 1984. "On the Fusion of Nationalities in the Tarim Basin and the Formation of the Modern Uighur Nationality." *Central Asian Survey* 3 (4): 1–14.

George, T. J. S. 1980. *Revolt in Mindanao: The Rise of Islam in Philippine Politics.* Kuala Lumpur: Oxford University Press.

Gladney, Dru C. 2002. "Xinjiang: China's Future West Bank?" *Current History* 101 (656): 267–70.

Göçek, Fatma Müge. 2002. "The Decline of the Ottoman Empire and the Emergence of Greek, Armenian, Turkish, and Arab Nationalisms." In *Social Constructions of Nationalism in the Middle East,* edited by Fatma Müge Göçek, 15–59. Albany: State University of New York Press.

Gonzalez, Andrew. 2006. "The Language Planning Situation in the Philippines." In *Language Planning and Policy in the Pacific: Fiji, the Philippines and Vanuatu*, edited by Richard B. Baldauf and Robert B. Kaplan, 114–53. Clevedon, UK: Multilingual Matters.

———. 2007. "Language, Nation and Development in the Philippines." In *Language, Nation and Development in Southeast Asia*, edited by Lee Hock Guan and Leo Suryadinata, 17–38. Singapore: Institute of Southeast Asian Studies.

Goodman, David S. G. 2004. *China's Campaign to "Open up the West": National, Provincial, and Local Perspectives.* The China Quarterly Special Issues. Cambridge: Cambridge University Press.

Goodson, Larry, and Thomas Johnson. 2011. "Parallels with the Past: How the Soviets Lost in Afghanistan, How the Americans Are Losing." *Orbis* 55 (4): 577–99.

Gordon, Raymond G., Jr. 2005. *Ethnologue: Languages of the World.* 15th ed. Dallas: SIL International.

Gries, P. H. 2005. "Chinese Nationalism: Challenging the State?" *Current History* 104 (683): 251–56.

Gries, P. H., Q. M. Zhang, H. M. Crowson, and H. J. Cai. 2011. "Patriotism, Nationalism and China's US Policy: Structures and Consequences of Chinese National Identity." *China Quarterly* (205): 1–17.

Gross, Max L. 2007. *A Muslim Archipelago: Islam and Politics in Southeast Asia.* Washington, D.C.: National Defense Intelligence College.

Guang, L. 2005. "Realpolitik Nationalism—International Sources of Chinese Nationalism." *Modern China* 31 (4): 487–514.

Gutierrez, Eric, and Saturnino Borras Jr. 2004. *The Moro Conflict: Landlessness and Misdirected State Policies.* Washington, D.C.: East-West Center Washington.

Haeri, Niloofar. 2000. "Form and Ideology: Arabic Sociolinguistics and Beyond." *Annual Review of Anthropology* 29: 61–87.

———. 2003. *Sacred Language, Ordinary People: Dilemmas of Culture and Politics in Egypt.* New York: Palgrave Macmillan.

Hahn, Reinhard F. 1991. *Spoken Uyghur.* Edited by Ablahat Ibrahim. Seattle: University of Washington Press.

Hale, Henry. 2004. "Divided We Stand: Institutional Sources of Ethnofederal State Survival and Collapse." *World Politics* 56: 165–93.

Hall, John A. 1993. "Nationalisms: Classified and Explained." *Daedalus* 122 (3): 1–28.

———. 1998. "Introduction." In *The State of the Nation: Ernest Gellner and the Theory of Nationalism*, edited by John A. Hall, 1–20. New York: Cambridge University Press.

———. 2014. *Ernest Gellner: An Intellectual Biography.* London: Verso.

Han, Enze. 2011. "From Domestic to International: The Politics of Ethnic Identity in Xinjiang and Inner Mongolia." *Nationalities Papers* 39 (6): 941–62.

Hangloo, Rattan Lal. 2008. "Mass Conversion in Medieval Kashmir: Academic Perceptions and People's Practice." In *The Valley of Kashmir: The Making and Unmaking of a Composite Culture?*, edited by Aparna Rao, 97–138. New Delhi: Manohar.

Harris, Albert W. 2010. "Coming to Terms with Separatist Insurgencies." *Negotiation Journal* 26 (3): 327–56.

Harris, Gardiner. 2013. "Homesick Militants Are Offered a Way Back to Kashmir." *New York Times*, September 6.

Hasan, Nurdin. 2013. "Indonesia: Aceh Removes Stoning Sentence from Sharia." *Jakarta Globe*, March 12.

Hassanpour, Amir. 1992. *Nationalism and Language in Kurdistan, 1918–1985*. San Francisco: Mellen Research University Press.

Hassoubah, Ahman Mohammad H. 1983. *Teaching Arabic as a Second Language in the Southern Philippines*. Marawi City: Mindanao State University Research Center.

Hastings, Adrian. 1997. *The Construction of Nationhood: Ethnicity, Religion and Nationalism*. Wiles Lectures, 1996 ed. Cambridge: Cambridge University Press.

Hau, Catherine S., and Victoria L. Tinio. 2003. "Language Policy and Ethnic Relations in the Philippines." In *Fighting Words: Language Policy and Ethnic Relations in Asia*, edited by Michael E. Brown and Sumit Ganguly, 319–49. Cambridge, Mass.: MIT Press.

Herrera, Yoshiko M., Devesh Kapur, and Sogomon Tarontsi. 2007. "Improving Data Quality: What Is to Be Done?" *APSA-CP* 18 (1): 25–28.

Hirschi, Caspar. 2012. *The Origins of Nationalism*. New York: Cambridge University Press.

Hobsbawm, Eric J. 1962. *The Age of Revolution, 1789–1848*. 1st ed., The World Histories of Civilization. Cleveland, Ohio: World.

——. 1990. *Nations and Nationalism Since 1780: Program, Myth, Reality*. 2nd ed. New York: Cambridge University Press.

Hogan-Brun, Gabrielle, and Stefan Wolff, eds. 2003. *Minority Languages in Europe: Frameworks, Status, Prospects*. Houndmills, UK: Palgrave Macmillan.

Holes, Clive. 1984. *Colloquial Arabic of the Gulf and Saudi Arabia*. London: Routledge Kegan Paul.

——. 1987. *Language Variation and Change in a Modernising Arab State: The Case of Bahrain, Library of Arabic Linguistics*. Monograph No. 7. London: Kegan Paul.

——. 1990. *Gulf Arabic*. Croom Helm Descriptive Grammars Series. London: Routledge.

——. 2001. *Dialect, Culture, and Society in Eastern Arabia*. Leiden: Brill.

——. 2004. *Modern Arabic: Structures, Functions, and Varieties*. Rev. ed., Georgetown Classics in Arabic Language and Linguistics. Washington, D.C.: Georgetown University Press.

Horner, Charles. 2002. "The Other Orientalism: China's Islamist Problem." *National Interest*, April 15.

Howell, Anthony, and C. Cindy Fan. 2011. "Migration and Inequality in Xinjiang: A Survey of Han and Uyghur Migrants in Urumqi." *Eurasian Geography and Economics* 52 (1): 119–39.

Huebner, Thom. 1996. *Sociolinguistic Perspectives: Papers on Language in Society, 1959–1994*. Oxford Studies in Sociolinguistics. New York: Oxford University Press.

Hughes, Christopher R. 2006. *Chinese Nationalism in the Global Era, Politics in Asia Series*. London: Routledge.

——. 2011. "Reclassifying Chinese Nationalism: The Geopolitik Turn." *Journal of Contemporary China* 20 (71): 601–20.

Human Rights Watch. 2010. *Indonesia: Local Sharia Laws Violate Rights in Aceh*. Jakarta: Human Rights Watch.

Hunter, Shireen, Huma Malik, and Center for Strategic and International Studies. 2005. *Modernization, Democracy, and Islam*. Westport, Conn.: Praeger.

Huntington, Samuel P. 1991. *The Third Wave: Democratization in the Late Twentieth Century.* The Julian J. Rothbaum Distinguished Lecture Series, vol. 4. Norman: University of Oklahoma Press.

———. 1993. "The Clash of Civilizations?" *Foreign Affairs* 72 (3): 22–28.

———. 2004. *Who Are We? The Challenges to America's National Identity.* New York: Simon & Schuster.

Huntington, Samuel P., and Fouad Ajami. 1993. *The Clash of Civilizations?* New York: Foreign Affairs.

Hutton, Christopher. 1999. *Linguistics and the Third Reich: Mother-Tongue Fascism, Race, and the Science of Language.* Routledge Studies in the History of Linguistics. London: Routledge.

Ibrahim, Saad Eddin. 1998. "Ethnic Conflict and State-Building in the Arab World." *International Social Science Journal* 50 (156): 229–42.

International Crisis Group. 2003. *Radical Islam in Iraqi Kurdistan: The Mouse That Roared?* ICG Middle East Briefing. Amman: International Crisis Group.

———. 2004. *Pakistan: Reforming the Education Sector.* Asia Report 84. Islamabad: International Crisis Group.

———. 2013. *Indonesia: Tensions over Aceh's Flag.* Asia Briefing 139. Jakarta: International Crisis Group.

Irwin, Robert. 2006. *Dangerous Knowledge: Orientalism and Its Discontents.* New York: Overlook Press.

Israeli, Raphael. 2002. *Islam in China: Religion, Ethnicity, Culture, and Politics.* Lanham, Md.: Lexington Books.

Jacobs, Andrew. 2009. "Migrants to China's West Bask in Prosperity." *New York Times*, August 7.

———. 2014. "Three Dea in Clash at Police Station in Western China, Report Says." *New York Times*, January 23.

Jamal, Amal. 2011. *Arab Minority Nationalism in Israel: The Politics of Indigeneity, Routledge Studies in Middle Eastern Politics.* London: Routledge.

Jane's Intelligence. 2013. "Abu Sayyaf Group (ASG)." In *Jane's World Insurgency and Terrorism,* http://www.ihs.com/products/janes/security/terrorism-insurgency-intelligence-centre/world.aspx.

Johnson, Thomas. 2006. "Afghanistan's Post-Taliban Transition: The State of State-Building After War." *Central Asian Survey* 25 (1–2): 1–26.

Juergensmeyer, Mark. 1993. *The New Cold War? Religious Nationalism Confronts the Secular State.* Berkeley: University of California Press.

———. 1995. "The New Religious State." *Comparative Politics* 27 (4): 379–91.

———. 2003. *Terror in the Mind of God: The Global Rise of Religious Violence.* 3rd ed., Comparative Studies in Religion and Society, vol. 13. Berkeley: University of California Press.

———. 2008. *Global Rebellion: Religious Challenges to the Secular State from Christian Militias to Al Qaeda.* Berkeley: University of California Press.

Kachru, Braj B. 2002. *The Dying Linguistic Heritage of the Kashmiris: Kashmiri Literary Culture and Language.* Urbana: University of Illinois.

Kadeer, Rebiya, and Alexandra Cavelius. 2009. *Dragon Fighter: One Woman's Epic Struggle for Peace with China*. 1st ed. Carlsbad, Calif.: Kales Press.

Kaltman, Blaine. 2007. *Under the Heel of the Dragon: Islam, Racism, Crime, and the Uighur in China*. Athens: Ohio University Press.

Kaplan, Robert D. 2007. "Arab Nationalism's Last Gasp: Saddam Hussein's Execution Likely Means the End of the Foolish Secular Arab Nationalism Movement." *Los Angeles Times*, January 7, M6.

Karl, Rebecca E. 2002. *Staging the World: Chinese Nationalism at the Turn of the Twentieth Century, Asia-Pacific*. Durham, N.C.: Duke University Press.

Karouny, Mariam. 2006. "Iraqi Kurds See Government Merger Ending Civil War." Reuters, January 10.

Kaya, Ayhan. 2012. *Islam, Migration, and Integration: The Age of Securitization*. New York: Palgrave.

Kedourie, Elie. 1992. *Democracy and Arab Political Culture*. Washington, D.C.: Washington Institute for Near East Policy.

———. (1960) 1993. *Nationalism*. 4th expanded ed. Oxford: Blackwell.

Kedourie, Sylvia. 1971. *Arab Nationalism and a Wider World*. New York: American Academic Association for Peace in the Middle East.

Keister, Jennifer M. 2012. *A Diplomatic Milestone for Mindanao?* Peace Brief. Washington: U.S. Institute of Peace.

Kepel, George. 1994. *The Revenge of God: The Resurgence of Islam, Christianity and Judaism in the Modern World*. University Park: Pennsylvania State University Press.

Khan, Adeel. 2005. *Politics of Identity: Ethnic Nationalism and the State in Pakistan*. Thousand Oaks, Calif.: Sage.

Khan, Mohammad Ishaq. 2005. *Kashmir's Transition to Islam: The Role of Muslim Rishis*. 4th ed. Srinigar, Kashmir: Gulshan Books.

Khan, Riz. 2005. "Why I'm Joining Al Jazeera." *Wall Street Journal*, June 13, A12.

Kingsbury, Damien. 2006. *Peace in Aceh: A Personal Account of the Helsinki Peace Process*. Jakarta: PT Equinox.

———. 2007. "The Free Aceh Movement: Islam and Democratisation." *Journal of Contemporary Asia* 37 (2): 166–89.

———. 2010. "The Aceh Peace Process." In *Aceh: History, Politics and Culture*, edited by Arndt Graf, Susanne Schroter, and Edwin Wieringa, 135–54. Singapore: Institute of Southeast Asian Studies.

Kloss, Heinz. 1967. "Abstand Languages and Ausbau Languages." *Anthropological Linguistics* 9 (7): 29–41.

Krakauer, Jon. 2011. *Three Cups of Deceit*. New York: Anchor.

Kramer, Martin S. 2006. "Is Sharansky Right? Does Everyone Want to Be Free?" George Mason University. Available from http://www.hnn.us/articles/13658.html.

Kroeger, Alix. 2007. "Afghan Koran Distributor Arrested." BBC.

Kurniawait, Dewi. 2010. "West Aceh District Chief Says Shariah Law Needed or There Will Be Hell to Pay." *Jakarta Globe*, August 18.

Kymlicka, Will. 1995. *Multicultural Citizenship: A Liberal Theory of Minority Rights*. Oxford: Clarendon.

——. 2001. *Politics in the Vernacular: Nationalism, Multiculturalism, and Citizenship*. Oxford: Oxford University Press.

Kymlicka, Will, and Alan Patten, eds. 2003. *Language Rights and Political Theory*. Oxford: Oxford University Press.

Labov, William. 1966. *The Social Stratification of English in New York City*. Washington, D.C.: Center for Applied Linguistics.

——. 1972. *Language in the Inner City: Studies in the Black English Vernacular*. Philadelphia: University of Pennsylvania Press.

Labov, William, Sharon Ash, and Charles Boberg. 2006. *The Atlas of North American English: Phonetics, Phonology, and Sound Change*. Berlin: Mouton de Gruyter.

Laitin, David D. 1992. *Language Repertoires and State Construction in Africa*. Edited by Peter Lange, Cambridge Studies in Comparative Politics. New York: Cambridge University Press.

——. 1993. "The Game Theory of Language Regimes." *International Political Science Review* 14 (3): 227–39.

——. 1998. *Identity in Formation: The Russian-Speaking Populations in the Near Abroad*. Ithaca, N.Y.: Cornell University Press.

——. 2000. "Language Conflict and Violence: The Straw That Strengthens the Camel's Back." *Archives Européennes de Sociologie* 41 (1): 97–137.

——. 2001. "National Identities in the Emerging European State." In *Minority Nationalism and the Changing International Order*, edited by Michael Keating and John McGarry, 84–113. New York: Oxford University Press.

Laitin, David D., and Daniel N. Posner. 2001. "The Implications of Constructivism for Constructing Ethnic Fractionalization Indices." *APSA-CP* 12 (1): 13–17.

Laitin, David D., and Rob Reich. 2003. "A Liberal Democratic Approach to Language Justice." In *Language Rights and Political Theory*, edited by Will Kymlicka and Alan Patten, 80–104. Oxford: Oxford University Press.

Lakoff, Sanford. 2004. "The Reality of Muslim Exceptionalism." *Journal of Democracy* 14 (4): 133–39.

Lapidus, Ira Marvin. 2002. *A History of Islamic Societies*. 2nd ed. Cambridge: Cambridge University Press.

Lawrence, Bruce B. 1998. *Shattering the Myth: Islam Beyond Violence*. Princeton Studies in Muslim Politics. Princeton, N.J.: Princeton University Press.

Lee, Don. 2006. "Double Opportunity in China's Far West." *Los Angeles Times*, August 28, A1.

Leezenberg, Michiel. 2006. "Political Islam Among the Kurds." In *The Kurds: Nationalism and Politics*, edited by Faleh A. Jabar and Dawod Hosham, 203–27. London: Saqi.

Levy, David M. 1997. "Adam Smith's Rational Choice Linguistics." *Economic Inquiry* 35 (3): 672–78.

Lewis, Bernard. 1990. The Roots of Muslim Rage. *Atlantic Monthly*, September, 47–60.

——. 1998. *The Multiple Identities of the Middle East*. London: Weidenfeld & Nicolson.

——. 2003. *The Crisis of Islam: Holy War and Unholy Terror*. New York: Modern Library.

Lewis, Paul M. 2009. *Ethnologue: Languages of the World*. 16th ed. Dallas: SIL International.

Liddicoat, Anthony. 2007. *Language Planning and Policy: Issues in Language Planning and Literacy, Language Planning and Policy*. Clevedon, UK: Multilingual Matters.

Lieven, Anatol. 2011. *Pakistan: A Hard Country*. 1st ed. New York: PublicAffairs.

Liow, Joseph Chinyong. 2006. *Muslim Resistance in Southern Thailand and Southern Philippines: Religion, Ideology, and Politics*. Washington, D.C.: East-West Center Washington.

Lipset, Seymour Martin. 1959. "Some Social Requisites of Democracy: Economic Development and Political Legitimacy." *American Political Science Review* 53 (1): 69–105.

Lockman, Zachary. 2004. *Contending Visions of the Middle East: The History and Politics of Orientalism*. The Contemporary Middle East. Cambridge: Cambridge University Press.

Lynch, Marc. 2006. *Voices of the New Arab Public: Iraq, Al-Jazeera, and Middle East Politics Today*. New York: Columbia University Press.

———. 2012. *The Arab Uprising: The Unfinished Revolutions of the New Middle East*. 1st ed. New York: PublicAffairs.

Maamouri, Mohamed. 1998. "Language Education and Human Development: Arabic Diglossia and Its Impact on the Quality of Education in the Arab Region." Paper read at the Mediterranean Development Forum, Marrakech, Morocco.

Mabry, Tristan James. 1998. "Modernization, Nationalism and Islam: An Examination of Ernest Gellner's Writings on Muslim Society with Reference to Indonesia and Malaysia." *Ethnic and Racial Studies* 21 (1): 64–88.

———. 2003. "*Review of* Language Rights and Political Theory, Will Kymlicka and Alan Patten, Eds. (Oxford and New York: Oxford University Press, 2003)." *Studies in Ethnicity and Nationalism* 3 (2): 60–62.

———. 2011. "Language and Conflict." *International Political Science Review* 31 (2): 189–207.

Mackey, W. F. 1993. "Introduction." In *Diglossia: A Comprehensive Bibliography, 1960–1990*, edited by Mauro Fernández, xiii–xx. Amsterdam: J. Benjamins.

Madan, T. N. 2008. "Kashmir, Kashmiris, Kashmiriyat." In *The Valley of Kashmir: The Making and Unmaking of a Composite Culture?*, edited by Aparna Rao, 1–36. New Delhi: Manohar.

Mandaville, Peter. 2013. "Islam and Exceptionalism in American Political Discourse." *PS: Political Science & Politics* 46 (2): 235–39.

Marks, Kathy. 2010. "In Aceh Indonesia, Islamic Police Take to the Streets." *Christian Science Monitor*, February 19.

Matthews, Peter H. 1997. *The Concise Oxford Dictionary of Linguistics*. Oxford: Oxford University Press.

May, Ronald J. 2012. "History, Demography and Factionalism: Obstacles to Conflict Resolution through Autonomy in the Southern Philippines." In *Autonomy and Armed Separatism in South and Southeast Asia*, edited by Michelle Ann Miller, 278–95. Singapore: Institute for Southeast Asia Studies.

May, Stephen. 2001. *Language and Minority Rights: Ethnicity, Nationalism and the Politics of Language*. Edited by Christopher N. Candlin, Language in Social Life Series. Harlow: Pearson.

———. 2003. "Misconceiving Minority Language Rights: Implications for Liberal Political Theory." In *Language Rights and Political Theory*, edited by Will Kymlicka and Alan Patten, 123–52. Oxford: Oxford University Press.

Mazraani, Nathalie. 1997. *Aspects of Language Variation in Arabic Political Speech-Making.* Richmond, UK: Curzon Press.

McDowall, David. 2004. *A Modern History of the Kurds.* 3rd rev. and updated ed. New York: I.B. Tauris.

McGibbon, Rodd. 2004. *Secessionist Challenges in Aceh and Papua: Is Special Autonomy the Solution?* Washington, D.C.: East-West Center Washington.

———. 2006. "Local Leadership and the Aceh Conflict." In *Verandah of Violence: The Background to the Aceh Problem,* edited by Anthony Reid, 315–59. Seattle: University of Washington Press.

McKenna, Thomas M. 1998. *Muslim Ruler and Rebels: Everyday Politics and Armed Separatism in the Southern Philippines.* Edited by Barbara D. Metcalf, Comparative Studies on Muslim Societies. Berkeley: University of California Press.

McKiernan, Kevin. 2006. *The Kurds: A People in Search of Their Homeland.* 1st ed. New York: St. Martin's Press.

McNally, Peter F. 1987. *The Advent of Printing: Historians of Science Respond to Elizabeth Eisenstein's "the Printing Press as an Agent of Change."* Montreal: McGill University Graduate School of Library and Information Studies.

Means, Gordon Paul. 2009. *Political Islam in Southeast Asia.* Boulder, Colo.: Lynne Rienner.

Mellor, Noha. 2005. *The Making of Arab News.* Lanham, Md.: Rowman & Littlefield.

Mercado, Eliseo. 2007. "The Effect of 9/11 on Mindanao Muslims and the Mindanao Peace Process." In *Asian Islam in the 21st Century,* edited by John L. Esposito, John Obert Voll, and Bakar Osman, 229–44. New York: Oxford University Press.

Merry, Michael S., and Jeffrey Ayala Milligan. 2010. "Citizenship as Attachment and Obligation." In *Citizenship, Identity, and Education in Muslim Communities,* edited by Michael S. Merry and Jeffrey Ayala Milligan, 1–20. London: Palgrave Macmillan.

Meskoob, Shahrokh, and John R. Perry. 1992. *Iranian Nationality and the Persian Language.* Washington, D.C.: Mage Publishers.

Mietzner, Marcus. 2012. "Ending the War in Aceh: Leadership, Patronage and Autonomy in Yudhoyono's Indonesia." In *Autonomy and Ethnic Conflict in South and Southeast Asia,* edited by Rajat Ganguly, 88–113. London: Routledge.

Millar, Robert McColl. 2005. *Language, Nation, and Power.* Basingstoke: Palgrave Macmillan.

Miller, Catherine. 2007. *Arabic in the City: Issues in Dialect Contact and Language Variation.* New York: Routledge.

Miller, Michelle Ann. 2006. "What's Special About Special Autonomy in Aceh?" In *Verandah of Violence: The Background to the Aceh Problem,* edited by Anthony Reid, 292–314. Seattle: University of Washington Press.

———. 2012. "Self-Governances as a Framework for Conflict Resolution in Aceh." In *Autonomy and Armed Separatism in South and Southeast Asia,* edited by Michelle Ann Miller, 3–15. Singapore: Institute for Southeast Asia Studies.

Milligan, Jeffrey Ayala. 2001. "Religious Identity, Political Autonomy and National Integrity: Implications for Educational Policy from Muslim-Christian Conflict in the Southern Philippines." *Islam and Christian-Muslim Relations* 12 (4): 435–48.

———. 2004. "Democratization or Neocolonialism? The Education of Muslims under US Military Occupation, 1903–20." *History of Education* 33 (4): 451–67.

———. 2005a. "Faith in School: Educational Policy Responses to Ethno-Religious Conflict in the Southern Philippines, 1935–1985." *Journal of Southeast Asian Studies* 36 (1): 67–86.

———. 2005b. *Islamic Identity, Postcoloniality, and Educational Policy: Schooling and Ethno-Religious Conflict in the Southern Philippines.* New York: Palgrave Macmillan.

Millward, James A. 2004. *Violent Separatism in Xinjiang: A Critical Assessment.* Washington, D.C.: East-West Center Washington.

———. 2006. *Eurasian Crossroads: A History of Xinjiang.* New York: Columbia University Press.

Milner, Henry. 2002. *Civic Literacy: How Informed Citizens Make Democracy Work.* Civil Society. Hanover, N.H.: University Press of New England.

Mohammad, Mohammad A. 2000. *Word Order, Agreement, and Pronominalization in Standard and Palestinian Arabic, Amsterdam Studies in the Theory and History of Linguistic Science.* Amsterdam: J. Benjamins.

Mohsin, Amena. 2003. "Language, Identity, and the State in Bangladesh." In *Fighting Words: Language Policy and Ethnic Relations in Asia*, edited by Michael E. Brown and Sumit Ganguly, 81–104. Cambridge, Mass.: MIT Press.

Monroe, Kristen R. 2005. *Perestroika! The Raucous Rebellion in Political Science.* New Haven, Conn.: Yale University Press.

Morcos, Gamila, and Edmund A. Aunger. 1989. *Bilinguisme Et Enseignement Du Français.* Montréal: Editions du Méridien.

Mortenson, Greg. 2007. *Three Cups of Tea: One Man's Mission to Promote Peace One School at a Time.* New York: Penguin.

Munshi, Sadaf. 2006. "Kashmiri." In *Encyclopedia of Language and Linguistics*, edited by Keith Brown. Oxford: Elsevier.

Myhill, John. 2004. *Language in Jewish Society: Towards a New Understanding.* 1st ed. Clevedon, UK: Multilingual Matters.

———. 2006. *Language, Religion and National Identity in Europe and the Middle East: A Historical Study.* Discourse Approaches to Politics, Society, and Culture, vol. 21. Philadelphia: J. Benjamins.

Nafi, Basheer M. 1998. *Arabism, Islamism and the Palestine Question, 1908–1941: A Political History.* London: Ithaca Press.

Nairn, Tom. 1981. *The Break-up of Britain: Crisis and Neonationalism.* 2nd expanded ed. London: NLB.

Nasr, Vali. 2001. "The Negotiable State: Borders and Power-Struggles in Pakistan." In *Right-Sizing the State: The Politics of Moving Borders*, edited by Brendan O'Leary, Ian S. Lustick, and Thomas Callaghy, 168–200. Oxford: Oxford University Press.

Natali, Denise. 2001. "Manufacturing Identity and Managing Kurds in Iraq." In *Right-Sizing the State: The Politics of Moving Borders*, edited by Brendan O'Leary, Ian S. Lustick, and Thomas Callaghy, 253–88. Oxford: Oxford University Press.

National Bureau of Statistics of China. 2002. *China Statistical Yearbook 2002.* Vol. 21. Beijing: China Statistics Press.

Newby, L. J. 1999. "The Chinese Literary Conquest of Xinjiang." *Modern China* 25 (4): 451–74.

Nodia, Ghia. 1994. "Nationalism and Democracy." In *Nationalism, Ethnic Conflict and Democracy*, edited by Larry Diamond and M. F. Plattner, 3–22. London: Johns Hopkins University Press.

Nussbaum, Martha C. 2012. *The New Religious Intolerance: Overcoming the Politics of Fear in an Anxious Age*. Cambridge, Mass.: Belknap.

O'Leary, Brendan. 1998. "Ernest Gellner's Diagnoses of Nationalism." In *The State of the Nation: Ernest Gellner and the Theory of Nationalism*, edited by John A. Hall, 40–88. New York: Cambridge University Press.

———. 2001. "Introduction." In *Right-Sizing the State: The Politics of Moving Borders*, edited by Brendan O'Leary, Ian S. Lustick, and Thomas Callaghy, 1–14. Oxford: Oxford University Press.

———. 2005. "Power-Sharing, Pluralist Federation, and Federacy." In *The Future of Kurdistan in Iraq*, edited by Brendan O'Leary, John McGarry, and Khaled Salih, 47–91. Philadelphia: University of Pennsylvania Press.

———. 2006. "Liberalism, Multiculturalism, Danish Cartoons, Islamist Fraud, and the Rights of the Ungodly." *International Migration* 44 (5): 22–33.

O'Leary, Brendan, and Khaled Salih. 2005. "Introduction." In *The Future of Kurdistan in Iraq*, edited by Brendan O'Leary, John McGarry, and Khaled Salih, 3–43. Philadelphia: University of Pennsylvania Press.

O'Malley, John W. 2008. *What Happened at Vatican II*. Cambridge, Mass.: Harvard University Press.

Ong, Walter. (1982) 2002. *Orality and Literacy: The Technologizing of the Word*. 2nd ed. New York: Routledge.

O'Reilly, Camille. 2003. "When a Language Is 'Just Symbolic': Reconsidering the Significance of Language to the Politics of Identity." In *Minority Languages in Europe: Frameworks, Status, Prospects*, edited by Gabrielle Hogan-Brun and Stefan Wolff, 16–36. Houndmills, UK: Palgrave Macmillan.

Orwell, George. 1949. *Nineteen Eighty-Four*. London: Secker and Warburg.

Orwell, George, and Bruce Rogers. 1947. *Politics and the English Language: An Essay*. New York: Typophiles.

O'Shea, Maria. 2006. "Tying Down the Territory: Conceptions and Misconceptions of Early Kurdish History." In *The Kurds: Nationalism and Politics*, edited by Faleh A. Jabar and Dawod Hosham, 113–29. London: Saqi.

Padden, Brian. 2011. "In Aceh, Enforced Sharia Law Has Outsized Impact." *Voice of America*, October 3.

Pape, Robert Anthony. 2005. *Dying to Win: The Strategic Logic of Suicide Terrorism*. 1st ed. New York: Random House.

Pathoni, Ahmad. 2012. "Aceh to Ban Sales of Tight Clothing." *Jakarta Globe*, June 7.

Paul, T. V., and William Hogg. 2005. "South Asia's Embedded Conflict: Understanding the India-Pakistan Rivalry." In *The India-Pakistan Conflict: An Enduring Rivalry*, edited by T. V. Paul, 251–66. Cambridge: Cambridge University Press.

Pearce, Sussana. 2005. "Religious Rage: A Quantitative Analysis of the Intensity of Religious Conflicts." *Terrorism and Political Violence* 17 (3): 333–52.

Perlez, Jane. 2005. "Separatists: Military-Rebel Tensions Complicate Relief in Aceh." *New York Times*, January 8.

Phillipson, Robert. 1999. "Political Science." In *Handbook of Language and Ethnic Identity*, edited by Joshua A. Fishman, 94–108. New York: Oxford University Press.

Pipes, Daniel. 1996. "Muslim Exceptionalism." Paper read at the 92nd annual meeting of the American Political Science Association, San Francisco, August 30.

Pogge, Thomas W. 2003. "Accommodation Rights for Hispanics in the United States." In *Language Rights and Political Theory*, edited by Will Kymlicka and Alan Patten, 105–22. Oxford: Oxford University Press.

Posner, Daniel N. 2004. "Measuring Ethnic Fractionalization in Africa." *American Journal of Political Science* 48 (4): 849–63.

———. 2005. *Institutions and Ethnic Politics in Africa*. Political Economy of Institutions and Decisions. New York: Cambridge University Press.

Pratyush, R. 2007. "J&K, Northeastern States Ahead in English-Medium Education." *India Daily*, January 30.

Prusher, Ilene R. 2002. "Language Also Shifts for Afghans." *Christian Science Monitor*, January 11.

Pryor, Frederic L. 2007. "Are Muslim Countries Less Democratic." *Middle East Quarterly* 14 (4): 53–58.

Quimpo, Nathan Gilbert. 2012. "Mindanao, Southern Philippines: The Pitfalls of Working for Peace in a Time of Political Decay." In *Autonomy and Ethnic Conflict in South and Southeast Asia*, edited by Rajat Ganguly, 114–37. London: Routledge.

Qutb, Sayyid. 1993. *Milestones*. Ann Arbor: University of Michigan.

Rahman, Tariq. 1995. "Language and Politics in a Pakistan Province: The Sindhi Language Movement." *Asian Survey* 35 (11): 1005–16.

———. 1996a. "Language Policy in Pakistan." *Ethnic Studies Report* 14 (1): 73–98.

———. 1996b. *Language and Politics in Pakistan*. Karachi: Oxford University Press.

———. 1997. "Language and Ethnicity in Pakistan." *Asian Survey* 37 (9): 833–39.

———. 1999. *Language, Education and Culture*. Oxford: Oxford University Press.

———. 2002. *Language, Ideology and Power: Language Learning Among the Muslims of Pakistan and North India*. Karachi: Oxford University Press.

———. 2004. "Denizens of Alien Worlds: A Survey of Students and Teachers at Pakistan's Urdu and English Language-Medium Schools, and Madrassas." *Contemporary South Asia* 13 (3): 307–26.

Rappa, Antonio L., and Lionel Wee. 2006. *Language Policy and Modernity in Southeast Asia: Malaysia, the Philippines, Singapore, and Thailand*. 1st ed. New York: Springer.

Rashid, Toufiq. 2009. "Valley Divide Impacts Kashmiri, Pandit Youth Switch to Devanagari." *Indian Express*, June 8.

Redfield, Robert. 1962. *Papers*. Chicago: University of Chicago Press.

Reed, Christopher A. 2004. *Gutenberg in Shanghai: Chinese Print Capitalism, 1876–1937*. Honolulu: University of Hawaii Press.

Reed, J. Todd, and Diana Raschke. 2010. *The ETIM: China's Islamic Militants and the Global Terrorist Threat.* PSI Guides to Terrorists, Insurgents, and Armed Groups. Santa Barbara, Calif.: Praeger.

Reid, Anthony. 2004. "War, Peace and the Burden of History in Aceh." *Asian Ethnicity* 5 (3): 301–14.

———. 2005. *An Indonesian Frontier: Acehnese and Other Histories of Sumatra.* Singapore: Singapore University Press.

———. 2006. "Introduction." In *Verandah of Violence: The Background to the Aceh Problem,* edited by Anthony Reid, 1–21. Seattle: University of Washington Press.

Reilly, Benjamin. 2001. *Democracy in Divided Societies: Electoral Engineering for Conflict Management.* Theories of Institutional Design. New York: Cambridge University Press.

Renan, Ernest. (1882) 1996. "What Is a Nation?" In *Nationalism in Europe, 1815 to the Present,* edited by Stuart Woolf, 48–60. London: Routledge.

Ressa, Maria A. 2003. *Seeds of Terror: An Eyewitness Account of Al-Qaeda's Newest Center of Operations in Southeast Asia.* New York: Free Press.

Rodriguez, Cindy. 2006. "From Businessman to Community Activist." *Morning Edition* (NPR).

Roger, Antoine. 2000. "Expliquer Le Nationalisme: Les Contradictions D'ernest Gellner." *Archives Européennes de Sociologie* 16 (2): 189–224.

Romano, David. 2007. *An Outline of Kurdish Islamist Groups in Iraq.* Occasional Paper. Washington, D.C.: Jamestown Foundation.

Rood, Steven. 2005. *Forging Sustainable Peace in Mindanao: The Role of Civil Society.* Washington, D.C.: East-West Center Washington.

———. 2012. "Interlocking Autonomy: Manila and Muslim Mindanao." In *Autonomy and Armed Separatism in South and Southeast Asia,* edited by Michelle Ann Miller, 256–77. Singapore: Institute for Southeast Asia Studies.

Ross, Marc Howard. 2007. *Cultural Contestation in Ethnic Conflict.* Cambridge Studies in Comparative Politics. New York: Cambridge University Press.

———. 2009. *Culture and Belonging in Divided Societies: Contestation and Symbolic Landscapes.* Philadelphia: University of Pennsylvania Press.

Ross, Michael L. 2003. "Resources and Rebellion in Aceh, Indonesia." Paper read at the Yale–World Bank Project The Economics of Political Violence, Los Angeles, June 5.

Routray, Bibhu Orasad. 2012. "Autonomy and Armed Separatism in Jammu and Kashmir." In *Autonomy and Armed Separatism in South and Southeast Asia,* edited by Michelle Ann Miller, 177–95. Singapore: Institute for Southeast Asia Studies.

Rubin, Michael. 2001. "The Islamist Threat from Iraqi Kurdistan." *Middle East Intelligence Bulletin* 3 (12), http://www.meforum.org/meib/articles/0112_ir1.htm.

Rudby, Rani, and Mario Saraceni. 2006. *English in the World: Global Rules, Global Roles.* London: Continuum.

Rudelson, Justin Jon Ben-Adam. 1998. *Oasis Identities: Uyghur Nationalism Along China's Silk Road.* New York: Columbia University Press.

———. 1999. "China." In *Islam Outside the Arab World,* edited by David Westerlund and Ingvar Svanberg, 190–211. Richmond, UK: Curzon Press.

Rugh, William A. 2004. *Arab Mass Media: Newspapers, Radio, and Television in Arab Politics.* Westport, Conn.: Praeger.

Rustow, Dankwart. 1970. "Transitions to Democracy." *Comparative Politics* 2: 337–63.

Ruzza, Carlo. 2000. "Language and Nationalism in Italy: Language as a Weak Marker of Identity." In *Language and Nationalism in Europe*, edited by Stephen Barbour and Cathie Carmichael, 168–82. Oxford: Oxford University Press.

Safran, William. 2004. "Introduction: The Political Aspects of Language." *Nationalism and Ethnic Politics* 10 (1): 1–14.

———. 2005. "Language and Nation-Building in Israel: Hebrew and Its Rivals." *Nations and Nationalism* 11 (1): 43–63.

Sageman, Marc. 2008. *Leaderless Jihad: Terror Networks in the Twenty-First Century*. Philadelphia: University of Pennsylvania Press.

Sagolj, Damir. 2012. "Living with Sharia Law: Crime and Punishment in Indonesia's Aceh." Reuters, December 20.

Said, Edward W. 1978. *Orientalism*. New York: Pantheon Books.

———. 2004. "Eloquent, Elegant Arabic." *Le Monde Diplomatique*, August.

Saideman, Stephen M. 2005. "At the Heart of the Conflict: Irredentism and Kashmir." In *The India-Pakistan Conflict: An Enduring Rivalry*, edited by T. V. Paul, 202–24. Cambridge: Cambridge University Press.

Salame, Ghassan. 1994. *Democracy Without Democrats? The Renewal of Politics in the Muslim World*. London: I.B. Tauris.

Salameh, Franck. 2006a. "Middlebury's Arabic Morass." *Middle East Quarterly* 13 (3): 39–46.

———. 2006b. "Vous Êtes Arabes Puisque Je Vous Le Dis!" *Journal d'étude des relations internationales au Moyen-Orient* 1 (1): 52–57.

———. 2010. *Language, Memory, and Identity in the Middle East: The Case for Lebanon*. Lanham, Md.: Lexington Books.

Saragih, Bagus, and Hotli Simanjuntak. 2013. "Aceh City to Ban Women from Straddling Motorbikes." *Jakarta Post*, January 3.

Schildkraut, Deborah Jill. 2001. "Official-English and the States: Influences on Declaring English the Official Language in the United States." *Political Research Quarterly* 54 (2): 445–57.

———. 2005. *Press One for English: Language Policy, Public Opinion, and American Identity*. Princeton, N.J.: Princeton University Press.

Schmid, Carol L. 2001. *The Politics of Language: Conflict, Identity and Cultural Pluralism in Comparative Perspective*. Oxford: Oxford University Press.

Schmidt, Ronald. 2000. *Language Policy and Identity Politics in the United States, Mapping Racisms*. Philadelphia: Temple University Press.

Schneider, Norbert. 2002. *The Art of the Portrait: Masterpieces of European Portrait Painting 1420–1670*. Los Angeles: Taschen.

Schram, Sanford, and Brian Caterino. 2006. *Making Political Science Matter: Debating Knowledge, Research, and Method*. New York: New York University Press.

Schroter, Susanne. 2010. "Acehnese Culture(s): Plurality and Homogeneity." In *Aceh: History, Politics and Culture*, edited by Arndt Graf, Susanne Schroter, and Edwin Wieringa, 157–79. Singapore: Institute of Southeast Asian Studies.

Schulze, Kirsten E. 2003. "The Struggle for an Independent Aceh: The Ideology, Capacity, and Strategy of GAM." *Studies in Conflict and Terrorism* 26 (4): 241–71.

Schumann, Christoph. 2010. *Nationalism and Liberal Thought in the Arab East: Ideology and Practice.* SOAS/Routledge Studies on the Middle East. London: Routledge.

Shapiro, Ian. 2005. *The Flight from Reality in the Human Sciences.* Princeton, N.J.: Princeton University Press.

Shiraishi, Saya. 1983. "Eyeglasses: Some Remarks on Acehnese School Books." *Indonesia* 36: 66–86.

Siddiqi, Farhan Hanif. 2012. *The Politics of Ethnicity in Pakistan: The Baloch, Sindhi and Mohajir Ethnic Movements, Routledge Contemporary South Asia Series.* New York: Routledge.

SIL International. 2008. *Why Languages Matter: Meeting Millennium Development Goals Through Local Languages.* Dallas: SIL International.

Smith, Adam, and J. C. Bryce. 1985. *Lectures on Rhetoric and Belles Lettres.* Indianapolis: Liberty Classics.

Smith, Anthony D. 1986. *The Ethnic Origins of Nations.* Oxford: Basil Blackwell.

———. 1991. *National Identity.* London: Penguin.

———. 1998. *Nationalism and Modernism: A Critical Survey of Recent Theories of Nations and Nationalism.* London: Routledge.

Smith, Craig S. 2001. "China, in Harsh Crackdown, Executes Muslim Separatists." *New York Times*, December 16.

Smolicz, Jerzy J., and Illuminado Nical. 1997. "Exporting the European Idea of a National Language: Some Educational Implications of the Use of English and Indigenous Languages in the Philippines." *International Review of Education* 43 (5–6): 507–25.

Soysa, Indra de, and Ragnhild Nordås. 2007. "Islam's Bloody Innards? Religion and Political Terror, 1980–2000." *International Studies Quarterly* 51 (4): 927–43.

Stansfield, Gareth R. V. 2005. "Governing Kurdistan: The Strengths of Division." In *The Future of Kurdistan in Iraq*, edited by Brendan O'Leary, John McGarry, and Khaled Salih, 195–218. Philadelphia: University of Pennsylvania Press.

Steele, Liza, and Raymond Kuo. 2007. "Terrorism in Xinjiang?" *Ethnopolitics* 6 (1): 1–19.

Stepan, Alfred. 1998. "Modern Multinational Democracies: Transcending a Gellnerian Oxymoron." In *The State of the Nation: Ernest Gellner and the Theory of Nationalism*, edited by John A. Hall, 219–39. New York: Cambridge University Press.

Stepan, Alfred, and Graeme B. Robertson. 2004. "Arab, Not Muslim, Exceptionalism." *Journal of Democracy* 15 (4): 140–46.

Stevens, Sean. 2010. "Khastan Tawanestan!—'We Can, We Will!': Shaping the Battlefield in Afghanistan in Dari and Pashto—Not English." *Small Wars Journal*, http://smallwarsjournal.com/jrnl/art/khastan-tawanestan-we-can-we-will.

Strindberg, Anders, and Mats Warn. 2011. *Islamism.* Cambridge: Polity.

Suleiman, Yasir. 2003. *The Arabic Language and National Identity: A Study in Ideology.* Washington, D.C.: Georgetown University Press.

———. 2004. *A War of Words: Language and Conflict in the Middle East.* Cambridge Middle East Studies 19. New York: Cambridge University Press.

Suleiman, Yasir, and Ibrahim Muhawi. 2006. *Literature and Nation in the Middle East.* Edinburgh: Edinburgh University Press.

Sundhaussen, Ulf. 1989. "Indonesia: Past and Present Encounters with Democracy." In *Democracy in Developing Countries: Asia*, edited by Larry Diamond, Juan J. Linz, and Seymour Martin Lipset, 423–74. Boulder, Colo.: Lynne Rienner.

Szporluk, Roman. 1998. "Thoughts About Change: Ernest Gellner and the History of Nationalism." In *The State of the Nation: Ernest Gellner and the Theory of Nationalism*, edited by John A. Hall, 23–39. New York: Cambridge University Press.

Taheri, Amir. 2003. "Iraq's Identity Crisis: The Future of Pan-Arabism." *National Review*, June 6.

Tamadonfar, Mehran. 2002. "Islamism in Contemporary Arab Politics: Lessons in Authoritarianism and Democratization." In *Religion and Politics in Comparative Perspective: The One, the Few, and the Many*, edited by Ted G. Jelen and Clyde Wilcox, 141–68. Cambridge: Cambridge University Press.

Tan, Andrew. 2000. "Armed Muslim Separatist Rebellion in Southeast Asia: Persistence, Prospects and Implications." *Studies in Conflict & Terrorism* 23 (4): 267–88.

Thaib, Lukman. 2000. "Aceh's Case: Possible Solution to a Festering Conflict." *Journal of Muslim Minority Affairs* 20 (1): 105–10.

Thalang, Chanintira Na. 2009. "The Fluidity of Nationalistic and Ethnic Aspirations in Aceh." *Nations and Nationalism* 15 (2): 319–39.

Tigno, Jorge V. 2006. "Migration and Violent Conflict in Mindanao." *Population Review* 45 (1): 23–47.

Toft, Monica Duffy. 2003. *The Geography of Ethnic Violence: Identity, Interests, and the Indivisibility of Territory*. Princeton, N.J.: Princeton University Press.

Torres, Wilfredo Magno. 2007. "Introduction." In *Rido: Clan Feuding and Conflict Management in Mindanao*, edited by Wilfredo Magno Torres, 11–35. Makati City, Philippines: Asia Foundation.

Tremblay, Reeta Chowdhari. 1997. "Nation, Identity and the Intervening Role of the State: A Study of the Secessionist Movement in Kashmir." *Pacific Affairs* 69 (4): 471–97.

———. 2005. "Institutional Causes of the India-Pakistan Rivalry." In *The India-Pakistan Conflict: An Enduring Rivalry*, edited by T. V. Paul, 225–48. Cambridge: Cambridge University Press.

———.2009. "Kashmir's Secessionist Movement Resurfaces: Ethnic Identity, Community Competition, and the State." *Asian Survey* 49 (6): 924–50.

Tupas, T. Ruanni F. 2007. "Go Back to Class: The Medium of Instruction Debate in the Philippines." In *Language, Nation and Development in Southeast Asia*, edited by Lee Hock Guan and Leo Suryadinata, 17–38. Singapore: Institute of Southeast Asian Studies.

Uddin, Sufia M. 2006. *Constructing Bangladesh: Religion, Ethnicity, and Language in an Islamic Nation*. Chapel Hill: University of North Carolina Press.

UNI. 2008. "Kashmiri Made Compulsory Subject in Schools." November 1.

United Nations Development Program, Regional Bureau for Arab States. 2006. *The Arab Human Development Report 2005*. New York: United Nations.

Varshney, Ashutosh. 2002. *Ethnic Conflict and Civic Life: Hindus and Muslims in India*. New Haven, Conn.: Yale University Press.

Vellema, Sietze, Saturnino Borras Jr., and Francisco Lara Jr. 2011. "The Agrarian Roots of Contemporary Violent Conflict in Mindanao, Southern Philippines." *Journal of Agrarian Change* 11 (3): 298–320.

Volpi, Frédéric. 2011. *Political Islam: A Critical Reader.* New York: Routledge.

Wang, David. 1998. "Han Migration and Social Changes in Xinjiang." *Issues and Studies: A Journal of Chinese Studies and International Affairs* 34 (7): 33–61.

Waquet, Françoise. 2001. *Latin; or, The Empire of a Sign.* Translated by John Howe. London: Verso.

Warikoo, K. 1996. "Language and Politics in Jammu and Kashmir: Issues and Perspectives." In *Jammu. Kashmir & Ladakh: Linguistic Predicament,* edited by K. Warikoo and P. N. Pushp. Delhi: Himalayan Research and Cultural Foundation.

Warner, Carolyn M., and Manfred W. Wenner. 2006. "Religion and the Political Organization of Muslims in Europe." *Perspectives on Politics* 4 (3): 457–79.

Watenpaugh, Keith David. 2006. *Being Modern in the Middle East: Revolution, Nationalism, Colonialism, and the Arab Middle Class.* Princeton, N.J.: Princeton University Press.

Weber, Eugen Joseph. 1976. *Peasants into Frenchmen: The Modernization of Rural France, 1870–1914.* Stanford, Calif.: Stanford University Press.

Whaley, Floyd. 2014. "Peace Deal to End Insurgency Came After Philippine Leader's Ultimatum to Rebels." *New York Times,* January 26.

Wilkins, Richard J., and Pekka Isotalus. 2009. "Finnish Speech Culture." In *Speech Culture in Finland,* edited by Richard J. Wilkins and Pekka Isotalus, 1–16. Lanham, Md.: University Press of America.

Wingfield-Hayes, Rupert. 2002. *Language Blow for China's Muslims.* Urumqi, China: BBC.

Wirsing, Robert. 2004. "The Autonomy Puzzle: Territorial Solutions to the Kashmir Crisis." In *Democracy and Ethnic Conflict: Advancing Peace in Deeply Divided Societies,* edited by Adrian Guelke, 80–102. New York: Palgrave Macmillan.

Wogan, Peter. 2001. "Imagined Communities Reconsidered: Is Print-Capitalism What We Think It Is?" *Anthropological Theory* 1 (4): 403–18.

Wolf, Eric R. 1967. "Understanding Civilizations: A Review Article." *Comparative Studies in Society and History* 9 (4): 446–65.

Wolff, Stefan. 2003. *Disputed Territories: The Transnational Dynamics of Ethnic Conflict Settlement, Studies in Ethnopolitics.* New York: Berghahn Books.

Wu, G. G. 2008. "From Post-imperial to Late Communist Nationalism: Historical Change in Chinese Nationalism from May Fourth to the 1990s." *Third World Quarterly* 29 (3): 467–82.

Yahuda, Michael. 2000. "The Changing Faces of Chinese Nationalism: The Dimensions of Statehood." In *Asian Nationalism,* edited by Michael Leifer, 21–37. New York: Routledge.

Yusuf, Moeed, and Adil Najam. 2009. "Kashmir: Ripe for Resolution?" *Third World Quarterly* 30 (8): 1503–28.

Zhao, Suisheng. 2004. *A Nation-State by Construction: Dynamics of Modern Chinese Nationalism.* Stanford, Calif.: Stanford University Press.

Zheng, Yong-Nian. 1999. *Discovering Chinese Nationalism in China: Modernization, Identity, and International Relations.* Cambridge Asia-Pacific Studies. New York: Cambridge University Press.

Zubaida, Sami. 1995. "Is There a Muslim Society? Ernest Gellner's Sociology of Islam." *Economy and Society* 24 (2): 151–88.

———. 1998. "Muslim Societies: Unity or Diversity?" *International Institute for the Study of Islam in the Modern World Newsletter* 1 (1): 1.

———. 2004. "Islam and Nationalism: Continuities and Contradictions." *Nations and Nationalism* 10 (4): 407–20.

Zutshi, Chitralekha. 2004. *Languages of Belonging: Islam, Regional Identity, and the Making of Kashmir.* New York: Oxford University Press.

———. 2012. "Whither Kashmir Studies? A Review." *Modern Asian Studies* 46 (4): 1033–48.

ACKNOWLEDGMENTS

In the course of pursuing an answer to a fundamental question—what is the relationship between nationalism and Islam?—I traveled to ten countries and interviewed over a hundred people. All of them contributed in some way to this book and to each I extend my heartfelt thanks. In addition, sections of this manuscript emerged over time in the form of conference papers and journal articles, which benefited tremendously from the valuable feedback of discussants and reviewers.

I am especially grateful to friends who helped me on the road. For their hospitality while I was traveling through London I thank Alessandra Grignaschi and Richard Reilly; similarly in Hong Kong I was welcomed warmly by Caleb Goddard and his family. In Karachi, I was graciously hosted by the family of my former student, Nada Ali Anwar, including her parents, Itrat and Shabnam, and their entire extended household. Equally valuable was guidance on how to maneuver in some very troubled parts of the world. In this regard, I was helped enormously by the careful directions of Bakhtiar Abdullah, Erkin Alptekin, Benny Bacani, Sumantra Bose, Munawar Halepota, Eugene Martin, Scott Peterson, and Khaled Salih.

As a project grounded in the literature on nationalism and ethnic conflict, I am most grateful to the inestimable Brendan O'Leary for his review of the entire book, as well as Marc Howard Ross for his expertise in the politics of identity. Moreover, given the wide range of case studies contained herein, I frequently depended on the expertise of country and area specialists, who read specific chapters and provided essential commentary, including but not limited to Edward Aspinall, Shane Barter, Mark Durie, Thomas Johnson, Jeffrey Ayala Milligan, Franck Salameh, Farhan Hanif Siddiqi, and Robert Vitalis. I also depended on help from students, including my Georgetown research assistant, Min J. Kim.

I am sincerely grateful to the peerless Erica Ginsburg for bringing the project to completion at the University of Pennsylvania Press. I am also grateful to Bill Finan for his essential assistance in the early development of the manuscript and to Joseph Dahm for his excellent work editing the copy.

An essential acknowledgement: this volume, which took more than a few years to evolve, would have never been completed without the unconditional support and encouragement of my wife and partner in all things, Holly Ashbrook Temple, and it is to her that I dedicate this book.

Finally, a disclaimer: the opinions expressed in this book are mine alone and do not necessarily reflect the views of the Naval Postgraduate School, the Department of the Navy, or any part of the U.S. government.